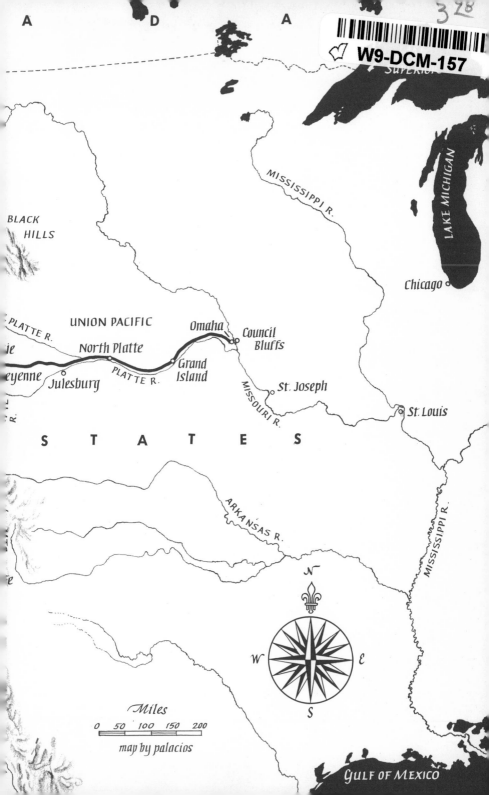

THE GREAT IRON TRAIL

OTHER BOOKS BY ROBERT WEST HOWARD

Rodeo: Last Frontier of the Old West (with Oren Arnold)

Hoofbeats of Destiny: The Story of The Pony Express (with **Agnes** Wright Spring, Frank C. Robertson and Roy E. Coy)

This Is the South (editor and co-author)

The Bench Mark (editor and co-author)

This Is the West (editor and co-author)

The Real Book About Farms

Educational Planning By Communities (with **Dr.** Paul Essert)

Two Billion Acre Farm

THE
GREAT
IRON TRAIL

The Story of the First Trans-
Continental Railroad

ROBERT WEST HOWARD

G. P. PUTNAM'S SONS   NEW YORK

TO

those Valiant Dreamers and Doers
who, by linking the Union with its
Pacific sisters, achieved more than
Northwest Passage.

TABLE OF CONTENTS

The Far Pacific Shore

All hail, thou western world! by heaven designed
Th' example bright to renovate mankind.
Soon shall thy sons across the mainland roam
And claim, on far Pacific shores, their home;
Their rule, religion, manners, art convey
And spread their freedom to the Asian sea.
    —Timothy Dwight, "Greenfield Hill" (1794)

CHAPTER 1

PREDESTINATION, 1836

Intimates are predestined . . . Henry Brooks Adams.

During 1836, the American passion for individual freedom and home rule exploded across the Far West. Texas declared its independence from Mexico on March 2, tortured through the massacres of the Alamo and Goliad, defeated Santa Anna at San Jacinto in April, and inaugurated General Samuel Houston as first president of the Texas Republic in October.

That same summer the ranchers and herdsmen of Taos, New Mexico, organized a revolt that swept on to a massacre of Mexican officials in Santa Fe and the inauguration of a full-blooded Indian as governor of an autonomous State of New Mexico. During November another ranchers' revolt drove Mexican officials out of Monterey and San Francisco and proclaimed "the Free and Sovereign State of Alta California."

Far to the north, between April and September of 1836, the Reverend Marcus Whitman and a group of Congregational missionaries drove the first wagon train across the Rocky Mountains' South Pass, then walked northwest through the Snake and Columbia river valleys to establish the Oregon Trail.

The governments of the New Mexico and Alta California

11

revolutions survived only a few months. But their meaningful-
ness was as clear to Boston and New York shipmasters and
New Orleans cotton factors as it was to the fur dealers, Santa
Fe traders and frontier farmers hoping for the renomination of
Thomas Hart Benton for a fourth term as United States Sena-
tor from Missouri.

In 1818, as the boyish editor of the St. Louis *Enquirer,*
Benton had written a series of editorials about "The Passage
to India." The rivers emptying into the "big and muddy Missouri," he forecast then, would become "what the Euphrates,
the Oxus, the Phasis and the Cyrus were to the ancient
Romans: lines of communication with Eastern Asia, and channels for that rich commerce which, for 40 centuries, has created so much wealth and power wherever it has flowed."

Glibly, Benton adapted the ancient Norse and British dream
of Northwest Passage to the Mississippi-Missouri river system.
He advocated a series of canal locks up the Missouri to the
Great Falls of "the Montana." Westward, a portage road could
be built across the Rockies to the valley of the Snake. This, he
envisioned, assured "the road to India" and a throughway for
trade between Europe and the Orient. St. Louis would, of
course, become its eastern portal and remain the "Queen City
of the West."

Benton's editorials, like his speeches in the Senate, presumed
that the United States would somehow annex the Far West
territories of Mexico. This vision of a Union of American
States extending across the midriff of the continent—3,200
miles from the Atlantic to the Pacific—elicited an "Amen"
from Maine to Georgia. Nantucket's whalers were already
commonplace sights from the Siberian Coast to the Indian
Ocean. New England missionaries in Hawaii and the other
Sandwich Islands routinely shipped converts back to Connecticut for schooling in Christian ethics. That summer of
1836, the brig *Pilgrim* was one of the score of New England
ships trading for hides and furs along the California Coast.
(One of the *Pilgrim's* deck hands was a Harvard student

named Richard Henry Dana. He spent off-duty hours scribbling details about the brutal life of the American sailor. The book he planned would be titled *Two Years Before the Mast*.) Ships out of Salem, Newburyport and Boston had been on the Canton run for two years. Their owners were financing a Washington lobby to persuade Congress to send a commissioner to Peking and open negotiations for an "open-ports" treaty with the Che'ing emperor. Down south, cattlemen from the Tennessee highlands and cotton planters from the coastal plains ferried the Mississippi to pioneer new territories into states. The fierce "Mountain Men" out of St. Louis and Mackinac had pushed their search for beaver, mink and otter pelts southwest to Tucson's Presidio, due west to San Francisco's Presidio, and northwest to Oregon's Astoria.

Thus most Americans believed that this vision of a transcontinental United States—the great New Greece of the Western world—was right and natural. Yet disaster might follow unless roads were built and systems of intercommunication established between the Atlantic and the Pacific. Senator Benton's daring proposals for a canal-and-portage Northwest Passage between St. Louis and Oregon would achieve more than a "trade route to India"; the peace and harmony of that future "United States of North America" would depend on some type of throughway across the Rockies and the Great American Desert.

Amos Eaton, John Stevens, John B. Jervis and other professional engineers endorsed the theory. But they were beginning to realize that this Westward destiny of the United States seemed to operate on a strange new system of timetabling. A code had shaped, invention by invention, for four decades. Unlike the hour-and-minute timetables of the stagecoaches, canalboats, packets and mail carriers, the United States' surge West was being scheduled by a timetable of new machines.

The Yankee tinkerer, Eli Whitney, first demonstrated this in 1793 when his invention of the "cotton (en)gin' " enabled a speedy processing of short-staple "upland" cotton, so sent thousands of planters into the virgin deltalands of Alabama, Mississippi and Kentucky. Again, in 1797, Whitney shaped another timetable tool of Western destiny by inventing a rifle with interchangeable parts. The succeeding development of the machine tool and the assembly line influenced both commercial and military ventures west across Ohio, Indiana and Illinois.

Young Robert Fulton levered the frontier on to the fall lines of the Mississippi, Red, Arkansas and Missouri rivers in 1807 when his steamboat *Clermont* successfully chuffed up the Hudson from New York to Albany in thirty-two hours.

After 1815, civil engineers in Maryland, Pennsylvania and Ohio created a fourth machine digit in the timetable by constructing the crushed-stone tollway of the National Road over the Alleghanies to the Ohio and Indiana prairies. Promptly the wagon builders of Pennsylvania adapted their great-wheeled, boat-bodied Conestoga wagons for use as freight carriers on this "pike." By 1830, Missourians were using them, under the nickname of "prairie schooners," to haul goods on the Santa Fe Trail.

In 1825, New Yorkers made new farms and trade centers possible as far west as Wisconsin and the Lake Superior borderlands of the Sioux by dredging the Erie Canal up their Mohawk River Valley and creating a shipping route between the Hudson and the Great Lakes.

In 1834, Cyrus McCormick and Obed Hussey invented reaping machines that permitted the rapid harvesting of grain and opened the prairies west from Indiana to the potential of the world's largest and richest wheat belt.

Concurrently, scores of machine tinkerers searched for two other machines that could enable McCormick-Hussey reapers to swirl on across all the West. The first would be a plow sturdy enough to rip through the prairies' tough shield of grass and weed roots. The second must be a windmill, or similar pump, that could tap the water known to exist 50 to 300 feet below the prairies. A sod-buster plow and a deep-level water pump would enable Americans to transform the Great Desert to a 2,000-mile vista of rich farms and trade centers.

Eaton, Jervis, Stevens and a growing corps of professional engineers were convinced that the creation and perpetuation of a transcontinental United States would come via this technologic timetable of new machines. This would enable the economic development, quick communication, high living standards, and the enrichment of individual freedoms essential to a strong union of states and territories. And right now, they suspected, the greatest of all machines for Western destiny and the coherencies of true union might be about to appear.

Currently it was little more than a toy—an expensive, dangerous toy that spread fire and terror along its right of way, was constantly capable of blowing its crew and passengers to kingdom come, and could haul only insignificant cargoes on costly and unreliable roadbeds. But the first models of Whitney's cotton gin had been little more than parlor toys, as were the steamboats that numerous young men had tried out on the Delaware and Hudson rivers in the 1790's. In 1836, there were only 100 miles of railroad and not more than 10 steam locomotives in the United States. West Point Foundry, opposite the United States Military Academy in the mid-Hudson Valley, was our only manufacturer of steam locomotives. In 1834, upon delivery of a second locomotive to the ambitious South Carolina Railroad, the West Point Foundry's engineers had advised the use of a barrier car, loaded with cotton bales, between the engine and the passenger coaches. "The barrier car," they explained bluntly, "will afford greater protection to the passengers when the locomotive explodes."

Yet Henry Farnam, as chief engineer of Connecticut's Farmington–New Haven Canal, was trying to secure options and cash for construction of a New York–New Haven–Boston Railroad, while John B. Jervis, as chief engineer of the Mohawk & Hudson Railroad, promoted plans for a line that would parallel the Erie Canal to Buffalo, then clang on along the shores of the Great Lakes to the Mississippi Valley. Robert

Mills, the architect commissioned to design both the Washington and the Bunker Hill monuments, was as obsessed about the Western destiny of the railroad as Thomas Hart Benton was about the canal-and-portage road to Oregon. Via letters and speeches Mills urged Congressional backing for a railroad from the Mississippi Valley over the Rockies to the Pacific.

Opposite Troy, New York, in 1609, Henry Hudson had concluded that the majestic river he was exploring did not afford a navigable channel to the South Sea and the Indies; he veered the *Half Moon* south to report his discoveries to the Dutch East India Company. But the legend persisted. During the next 175 years scores of Dutch, English and French explorers clambered the bluffs at the Hudson-Mohawk junction to search for the "waterway to the Pacific" so persistently reported by trappers and traders.

Only two generations before, Yankee immigrants had founded Troy as a Hudson River ferrying place for their new short-cut wagon road to the eastern terminal of Mohawk River bateaux at Schenectady. Now, since 1817, the old dream of Northwest Passage had glimmered again. DeWitt Clinton, Stephen Van Rensselaer and Gouverneur Morris lobbied a bill through New York's Legislature for construction of a $7,000,-000 Lake Erie Barge Canal along the Mohawk's natural water-level route through the Alleghany escarpment. In seven years, pick-and-shovel gangs, powder-stained blasting crews, 10,000 "bogtrotters" imported from Ireland and 5,000 horse-and-mule teams, gouged the "big ditch"—40 feet wide and 4 feet deep—across the 350 miles of New York State to the shore of Lake Erie at Buffalo. It earned the construction costs within two years.

In 1836 more than 15,000 barges cleared the east terminal locks of Watervliet, opposite Troy. A standard canal packet, sloshing three miles an hour behind a tow team of Spanish mules or shaggy Schoharie mares, carried thirty tons of freight and passengers. Utica—Syracuse—Rochester—Buffalo—Detroit were booming cities. Cleveland, as the Lake Erie terminal for Cuyahoga Valley–Erie Canal trade, received its city charter in 1836. That fall the first shipment of Illinois wheat was barged through Watervliet from the bog-ridden port of Chicago at the foot of Lake Michigan.

The Mohawk-Hudson junction became an experimental laboratory for the new railroad. One year after the Erie Canal opened, a group of Schenectady and Albany merchants obtained a charter for construction of the Mohawk & Hudson Railroad across the sixteen miles of limestone bluff and sand plain between the two cities. The road operated its first train, with Chief Engineer John B. Jervis as engineman, in August, 1831. Three years later Troy began construction of its own railroad—the Rensselaer & Saratoga—to operate daily freight and passenger service from the Hudson's ferry terminal northwest across the Adirondack foothills to the hotels clustered beside the mineral-water springs of Ballston Spa. Now, like chuffing young dragons from this Mohawk-Hudson seedbed, railroads were surveying in every direction: east across the Berkshires toward New England; south down the Hudson Valley to New York City; north along the Champlain Canal to Canada; and most importantly, west on the Mohawk's water-level route toward that wonderland of prairie, high plains and mountains that raised a 2,000-mile barrier against the ancient dream of Northwest Passage.

No hillside in the United States offered as clear a perspective of Western destiny as the ridge that lifted the Greek Revival home of Rensselaer Polytechnic Institute above the Troy skyline. What with the clangs, hisses and grunts from the new stove factories and iron foundries, the endless thumps, curses and mule whinnies from the barge terminal, the musky odors of beaver pelts, wheat, cheese, ginseng and all the earthy treasures of the Michigan and Wisconsin Northwest wafted upstream from the Albany piers, the Institute's students literally heard, breathed, and touched it every hour.

Thus Stephen Van Rensselaer organized his Institute with keen regard for both causal awareness and western Destiny when he purchased the Vanderheyden mansion and offered the distinguished scientist, Amos Eaton, a lifetime post as senior professor if he would develop the United States' first curriculum for a professional degree in Civil Engineering.

As upperclassmen, the first civil engineering candidates were entitled to use the rocking chairs and benches on the mansion's front porch. Each morning and late afternoon a three-ton locomotive clanked the Rensselaer & Saratoga's train of two or three box wagons and a stagecoach over the track through the Vanderheydens' former bull pasture. These trains averaged a speed of ten miles per hour, including stops to refuel at woodyards; stops to shoo cattle and pigs off the right of way; stops to enable the engineman and fireman to sprint back to the coach with leather buckets of water and douse passengers whose top hats or capes had been ignited by the carbon chunks spewed out of the smokestack.

Senior Professor Eaton avowed, as vehemently as did John B. Jervis, that the railroad was the wave of the future. He varied his lectures about it with field trips to the Mohawk & Hudson and Rensselaer & Saratoga enginehouses and teeth-jarring excursions over the routes. Several civil engineering students were assigned, on Saturdays and during summer recess, to assist the survey crews on the routes for the Schenectady & Troy, Troy & Albany, Utica & Schenectady railroads. So they were as familiar as Jervis and Eaton themselves with the railroad's shortcomings and the multitude of inventions necessary before it could become a tool comparable to Whitney's cotton-gin, Fulton's steamboat, the Conestoga covered wagon, the Erie Canal and the McCormick-Hussey reapers.

Currently, railroad trains ran on a giddy contraption of stone blocks, planks and L-shaped strips of iron. The stone blocks, spaced every three to five feet, supported the wood planks at a wavy level one foot above the ground. The

L-shaped strips of iron were bolted atop the planks, with the high side of the L forming the outer edges of the track. The locomotive, box wagons and stagecoaches—linked by iron bars —ran in this perilous trough, veered from derailing only by the brittle flange of the L-irons. A stone or stick washed or dropped inside the L-angle of the rail could fulcrum the locomotive wheels over the flange, usually capsizing the entire train and sometimes exploding the boiler. The same sequence of catastrophe could be achieved by speeding the engine around a curve.

A host of other shortcomings made the railroad a helpless infant in this boisterous surge toward transcontinental union. Its trains could travel only by daylight; they could not grope through the night like horses, mules or boats. And although trains wandered willy-nilly along streets and across public highways, the only means of warning pedestrians and vehicles of their approach was a tin megaphone, or brass trumpet, carried by the conductor. Worst of all, the laws of matter explored by Professor Eaton and other scientists indicated that a railroad must be built on level—or almost level—terrain; a locomotive could not push up grades that were steeper than one or two degrees from the horizontal.

Nevertheless, the locomotive was the fastest vehicle yet invented by man. Fulton's steamboat averaged only 4¾ miles an hour on its upstream runs between New York City and Albany. An ox team averaged 2 miles an hour, a canalboat 3 miles an hour, a stagecoach 6 to 8 miles an hour. Theoretically a railroad train could travel 150 miles during a summer's day, hence offered the wonderous potential of a shad-roe breakfast in Albany and a late dinner of planked whitefish and salt potatoes at a Syracuse inn. The Mohawk throughway would present no insurmountable problems to the railroad. A few tunnels could assure a tablesmooth gradient along the shores of the Great Lakes. The limitless horizons and gentle swells of the Western prairie, Professor Eaton lectured, were fashioned as though the good Lord intended them for railroads. But farther West. . . .

"Intimates," the Boston aristocrat, Henry Brooks Adams, would point out a generation later, "are predestined." The allegation had so much circumstantial evidence at the Mohawk-Hudson junction during 1836 that it would have been judged a "miracle" or "witchcraft" in the seventeenth and eighteenth centuries and is still presumed, during the last half of the twentieth, to be a form of electronics probably related to extra-sensory perception.

Some of the Institute students, daydreaming about the Troy-Erie Canal that year, saw a small, tousle-haired boy similarly musing on the steps of St. Paul's rectory and a bull-necked adolescent hawking newspapers alongside the Rensselaer & Saratoga Railroad's station. They could also make out the bleary bull's-head symbol painted over the doorway of Josiah Stanford's former tavern on the Watervliet shore.

The ten-year-old boy huddled on the steps of St. Paul's was Theodore Dehone Judah. He had been born on March 4, 1826, in Bridgeport, Connecticut. In 1833, his father, the Reverend Henry R. Judah was assigned to the pastorate of St. Paul's in Troy. He had transformed the move into a thrilling adventure by engaging accommodation for his family on the overnight packet from Bridgeport to Manhattan's East River. He then toured them up Broadway to Greenwich Village and bustled them off to the Albany steamer for the majestic 24-hour cruise past the Palisades, the highlands and the Catskills.

The three years at the Mohawk-Hudson junction had been an idyll. Father Judah possessed a keen awareness of the New West, applied his scholarship to its potentials, and during afternoon strolls and bedtime chats transformed the grubby canalboats, the clanking locomotives, and the dissonance of tow mules, stove factory and iron foundry into a gallant American saga. Snuggled in Father Judah's lap, Ted had drifted between dreams of becoming an explorer . . . or a railroad engineer . . . or a minister who would preach sermons as wise as Father's.

But now Father was gone. Just gone. He could not bring himself to use that other word for it. Hunched on the rectory steps those afternoons, Ted Judah endured the helplessness that only a child can know in trying to accept the lonely reality of death.

Three blocks away, those same afternoons, fourteen-year-old Charles Crocker hawked newspapers. Big-nosed, squat "Bull" Crocker was a native of Troy and as pugnacious as any mule skinner. His father Ike had operated a saloon on the waterfront for several years, but had recently decided that the Indiana frontier offered greater opportunities for a man who yearned to get back to farming. After Ike and his elder sons floated off up the Erie to locate a homestead somewhere southeast of Chicago, Bull became the man of the family. The eagerness of his foghorn bellows and the readiness of his fists established him among the peddlers at the Hudson River ferry and the Rensselaer & Saratoga terminal.

Sidney Dillon, a dapper, mustached foreman for the railroad, was one of Bull Crocker's customers. Born at Northampton, Long Island, in 1812, Dillon became intrigued by newspaper stories about the railroads. At nineteen he signed on as a barge-tow crewman in order to get to Albany. John Jervis hired him as an errand boy for the Mohawk & Hudson's engineers, then promoted him to apprentice. A veteran railroader at twenty-two, Dillon moved over to the Rensselaer & Saratoga as a construction foreman. He was considering another move—either to the proposed Schenectady & Troy or to the Schenectady & Utica—provided he could wangle a post as at least an assistant superintendent of construction.

The bleary sign of the Bull's Head Tavern near the ferry dock on the Hudson's Watervliet shore was a victim of the railroad. Josiah Stanford sired seven sons and one daughter there during his decade as the Bull's Head's owner-manager. His fourth son Leland was born there on March 9, 1824, exactly one month after Jedediah Strong Smith discovered the South Pass across the Rocky Mountains. When Leland was six, construction of the Mohawk & Hudson across the Albany-Schenectady plateau seeded a bold plan in the innkeeper's mind. The Elm Grove Hotel operated as a halfway house for wagonmen and stagecoaches on the Albany–Schenectady Pike. The property included a 300-acre forest that, propitiously, extended to the Mohawk & Hudson right of way. The elm, pine, birch, beech and maple on that acreage would provide a ten-year supply of fuel for the locomotives. And it was an ideal spot for a refueling station, with the long grades of the river bluffs at each end of the railroad.

Josiah sold his idea to Jervis and borrowed enough cash to purchase the Elm Grove Hotel. He put his sons to work as timberjacks and sawyers on the 300 acres. When their energies surpassed the locomotives' needs the boys peddled firewood in Albany. In 1836, any Albanian had the privilege of observing twelve-year-old Leland Stanford as he drove a wagonload of logs and kindling along the streets of Rose Hill. He was pudgy, with a long jaw, deep-set eyes and jug ears, and had learned to mask emotion with the popeyed stare of a startled owl. He rarely spoke except to answer questions, and gave these such ponderous consideration that most customers concluded he was "touched."

Creaking along Lark, Swan, Dove and Hawk Streets, the Stanford wagon may have passed, at one time or other, four—and perhaps eight—other youngsters who would play critical roles in the railroad's Northwest Passage.

John and Mary Meenagh Sheridan brought their little family via the filth of a three-master's steerage from County Cavan, Ireland, to Albany sometime in 1830. It is generally accepted that on March 6, 1831, Philip Henry Sheridan was born in one of the goatyard tenements on the northeast slope of Rose Hill.

By the summer of 1836, little Phil could cope admirably with any freckle-nose on the hillside. As an Irisher with a fey love for horses and mules, he assumed the right to pat any horse that clumped down the alley. It was equally proper that he occasionally whoop—in excellent imitation of a banshee—along the hill to State Street or Washington Avenue where the freight vans and carriages paced by. Possibly he stood on a corner when the Gansevoort's landau passed, and his eyes met those of the Gansevoort's seventeen-year-old grandson, Herman Melville. Herman was living with his grandparents that year. His father had taken another flyer on the New York Stock Exchange, and couldn't support his family. Promptly, then, it would have been logical for little Phil to dart to the gutter, grab a fistful of pebbles, and pelt them at the coach wheels. But Phil Sheridan was ignored in "Moby Dick," and Herman Melville never enlisted in the United States Cavalry.

Up State Street, too, John A. Dix hurried home to his invalid wife each afternoon. As New York's Secretary of State and General Superintendent of Schools, Lawyer Dix was creating a national reputation as a statesman and capable executive. But that summer of 1836 he was more concerned about the state of Mrs. Dix's health and debating the advisability of seeking a year's leave of absence in order to take her abroad.

Henry Harte was equally worried. Son of a New York merchant, Henry had brought his bride, Elizabeth Rebecca Ostrander, to Albany in 1834 or 1835, and opened a School For Literary and Artistic Instruction. He announced his availability, too, as a lecturer and as a translator of Latin, Greek, Hebrew and French. However, all the literary or artistic instruction the Albanians wanted was available at Albany Academy, Madame Emma Willard's School and Van Rensselaer Polytechnic Institute. And now there was a baby, born on August 25, 1836, and baptized Francis Brett Harte.

A professional interest in that baby's crying might have been felt by one young medical student strolling past the Harte home. Thomas Clark Durant of Hinsdale, Massachusetts, was a sixteen-year-old freshman at Albany Medical College. He was lean and had black eyes, a sprouting mustache, a quick mind and a pit viper's temper.

For part of a day, the previous spring, William Tecumseh Sherman, too, had wandered Albany's streets. He was waiting for the steamboat to West Point. "Cump" Sherman was born in Lancaster, Ohio, on February 8, 1820. His father died in 1829, and Cump went to live with Thomas Ewing, an attorney and family friend. In the spring of 1836, Ewing negotiated the boy's appointment to the United States Military Academy. So that May, thin, red-headed Cump slung his carpetbags aboard a Columbus-Toledo stage, transferred to a Lake Erie schooner for Buffalo, then traveled at mule pace on a passenger barge to Albany.

Collis Potter Huntington would not have indulged in such extravagant modes of transportation, even if he could have afforded them. Son of a village tinker, Collis was born at Harwinton, Connecticut, on October 22, 1821. His father revered Ben Franklin's observations about thrift. Collis had arrogant eyes, narrow lips, ears set tight against his skull, and a disposition as tart as a green cranberry. He left Harwinton in 1835 to hire out as a farmhand. A year later he walked off the farm with $84 in savings, and headed for the grocery store his brother had opened in the Catskill village of Oneonta. He reached Oneonta with the $84 intact, plus a dollar or two picked up along the way. That summer of 1836, Collis went to Oneonta from Connecticut, via Albany, and became a grocery clerk.

Another day that summer, the wagon of Richard Montague teetered down the Berkshire Trail to the Troy ferry landing. Richard and Content Montague were finally succumbing to New West fever. Their farm at Keene, New Hampshire, had brought barely enough to pay for provisions on the two months' drive to the prairie homesteads around Rockford, Illinois. Their route through Troy took them past St. Paul's rectory. Six-year-old Samuel Skerry Montague rode, in the pioneer tradition, on the wagon's tailboard.

Was Ted Judah on the rectory porch when the Montague wagon passed? Did Ted and Sam size one another up with typical small-boy belligerence? In view of the timetable for Northwest Passage being readied at the Mohawk-Hudson junction that summer and fall, the questions are an appropriate prelude to Ted Judah's decision, reached in Sacramento, California, on February 12, 1862, to hire Samuel Skerry Montague as his assistant engineer.

By late fall the massive developments in the United States' Western destiny dimmed the usual excitements of the Presidential election campaign. Texas voted in favor of its new republic's annexation by the United States. Arkansas, as the Union's newest state, pushed civil government and homesteading four hundred miles west of the middle Mississippi Valley. The prairie port of Chicago, urged on by promises of subsidies from the Illinois Legislature and the War Department, began construction of the Illinois & Michigan Canal that would connect Lake Michigan with the Mississippi—another new horizon of water transportation between the Atlantic seaboard, the falls of the Yellowstone, and the Mississippi's Falls of St. Anthony at St. Paul in the northwest wilderness of the new Wisconsin Territory.

The students at Rensselaer Polytechnic scuffed the scarlet-and-gold leaf carpet on their front lawn. This term, Professor Eaton was quoting from Washington Irving's new book, *Astoria,* and urging it as essential reading for every junior and senior. Glory! Could a railroad ever be built to Astoria and that misty Beulahland of the Pacific's shore? Would gunpowder blast the ledges and tunnels that would permit a locomotive to hiss over and through the Rocky Mountains on a 1 or 2 per cent grade? How could fuel wood and water be secured for crossing the thousand-mile deserts described by the explorers? Could a system be devised that would permit railroad trains to travel at night? And what about the Indians and —equally savage—cyclones and blizzards of that "Great American Desert"? Perhaps. . . .

Theodore Dehone Judah, Charles Crocker, Sidney Dillon, Leland Stanford, Philip Henry Sheridan, John A. Dix, Francis Brett Harte, Thomas Clark Durant, William Tecumseh Sherman, Collis Potter Huntington, Samuel Skerry Montague. This was the roll call of Western destiny at the Mohawk-Hudson junction that year. Here each encountered the challenge of the railroad for the first time and unconsciously began his role in the railroad's achievement of Northwest Passage. This was Predestination, 1836.

CHAPTER 2

THE HIGHER IRONS

*Handle your tools without mittens, remember, the
cat in gloves catches no mice. . . .* Benjamin Franklin
in *Poor Richard's Almanack.*

During the spring semester in 1837, Professor Eaton and his
assistants delivered a series of lectures about the significance
of the higher irons, swivel trucks, headlights and steam whistles
planned for the Schenectady & Troy Railroad. Since John B.
Jervis was the inventor of the swivel truck, and the West Point
Foundry was installing these along with radical flanged wheels
on its new locomotives, a field trip was organized for the
upperclassmen in Civil Engineering.

The new T-shaped "higher irons" they saw on the testing
tracks were, they agreed, about as awesome an invention as the
locomotive itself. The T-rail system of track adherence had
been invented in 1831 by Robert Livingston Stevens, eldest
son of the great engineer-inventor John Stevens. The idea
seized young Stevens during a voyage to England to purchase
locomotives and rails for the family's Camden & West Amboy
Railroad in New Jersey. The awkward L-shaped rails with
board and stone-block supports would—he reasoned—forever
doom the railroad as a costly engineer's toy of little economic

27

value. But the whole prospect of the railroad might be changed if some method could be devised that would permit heavier locomotives and higher speeds. He begged a few blocks of hardwood from the ship's carpenter and began whittling. Before Land's End was sighted he had the model for a rail that was actually a broad-based T. Such a rail, he reasoned, could be spiked into thick wood beams that would be partially buried, horizontally, in the earth of the railroad bed. This structure should not heave up out of the ground during winter freeze-ups, the way the stone blocks did.

But a flat-top rail also called for a new design in the wheels of railroad cars. Simple enough. Stevens moved the precarious L-rail's flange over to the inside rim of the car's wheel. There it would act as a guide to bevel the wheel safely around curves at speeds of—oh, possibly even twenty miles an hour.

The British ironmongers roared protests but finally cast the "utterly insane" T-rails, O-headed spikes and flanged wheels. The invention's only defect on the Camden & Amboy right of way back in New Jersey was that the locomotive shivered and squealed like a Halloween witch whenever it rolled into a curve. Then Isaac Dripps, Camden & Amboy's master mechanic, built an iron V-shaped shield mounted on two small wheels. He substituted this device for the large fore wheels of the locomotive. Huzza! It ended the pressure squeals and shivers on curves. Moreover, the V-shaped shield proved to be a safety plow; it butted tree limbs, stones and livestock away from the wheels, and prevented derails. Only a few townships had passed laws against the ancient prerogative of "free range" for cattle, so Dripps' invention won the nickname of "cow-catcher."

The Stevens-Dripps inventions were adopted for the Mo-hawk & Hudson by John Jervis—and improved. Jervis designed a four-wheel fore truck that attached to the locomotive's front end by a swivel. This enabled the boiler to act as a counter-balance on curves and heralded locomotives that might weigh as much as 25 or 30 tons and achieve speeds of 35 or 40 miles an hour.

Such speeds, explained the Mohawk & Hudson foremen, demanded new safety devices. Two of these would be tried out on the Schenectady & Troy, together with the Jervis swivel truck, the Dripps cowcatcher, and the T-iron rail. First, a massive bull's-eye lantern was being designed for attachment to the front of the locomotives' boilers, a foot or two above the cowcatcher. This was an adaptation of the thick-lensed hand lamp carried by ship watches and town criers. By using a series of tin and mercury-glass reflectors behind the foot-high lens, a beam of light could be focused 50 to 100 feet down the track. Obviously this locomotive "head" light offered the prospect of railroad travel after dark; at slower speeds, of course. The second innovation on these locomotives would be an adaptation of that law of matter that enabled any boy to pucker up and whistle. Air under pressure seeks prompt escape and shrills resentment if the only escape is through a small hole. The same law holds with steam. By incorporating a small dome with valves atop a locomotive boiler, and attaching a cord from the top valve back to the engineman's seat, a locomotive could be induced to produce an infinite number of shrieks. These would be decidedly superior to the conductor's megaphone, or bugle, as a safety measure to frighten cattle, horses and pigs off the right of way, and to warn pedestrians and teams at the turnpike crossings.

On the Rensselaer Institute's porch, after field trips to West Point Foundry and the local railroad shops, the seniors and juniors declaimed their new wisdom to freshmen and sophomores and even to a few of the "children" in the Classical Course. One of the "Classical kids" permitted to eavesdrop was Theodore Dehone Judah. The records show that he enrolled during 1837. The average age of the Classical (or College-Preparatory) Course pupils was fifteen. Ted was eleven and a half that fall. But, the teachers had decided, he was precocious, if moody. The lectures of Senior Professor Eaton and the porch seminars of the Civil Engineering candidates between fall 1837 and summer 1839 shaped Ted Judah's life goals.

Through the same months the railroad grew from an inventor's toy to a machine of promise. Congress recognized this in July, 1838, when it ruled that all the railroads in the United States could be used as postal routes. New England began to acknowledge it when engineers completed the New Haven & Hartford Railroad, started construction on a Boston–New Haven Line, and began surveys for a score of "higher irons" in Maine, the Connecticut River Valley and the Berkshires. The Reverend Samuel Parker (just back from Oregon) recognized it when he told reporters at the Erie Barge Terminal about Reverend Marcus Whitman's new mission post on the Columbia River and assured them that a transcontinental railroad to Oregon could be built via the South Pass–Snake River route. He was saying just that, he continued, in the book he was writing, *The Tour Beyond The Rocky Mountains,* and would act as guide to any expedition of engineers who wished to examine the route and measure its gradients.

These railroad excitements had influenced Ted Judah to study Mechanics, Composition, Geometry and the other subjects of the Classical Course. Now he had reached a decision. The Institute's tuition fees were really beyond his mother's means. When the spring term of 1839 ended, three months after his thirteenth birthday, he went to work on the Schenectady & Troy Railroad as a surveyor's assistant. The two years at Rensselaer Polytechnic were his only formal education for his Jason role in the railroad's tedious search for Northwest Passage.

The lures of Western destiny had already moved Phil Sheridan, Charles Crocker and Brett Harte out over the Erie Canal. John Sheridan took his family to Somerset, Ohio, where fine money could be earned building new canals and turnpikes.

Charles Crocker escorted his mother and sisters to the new family cabin in Marshall County, Indiana, and joined his father and brothers in the brutal job of burning and "stumping" woodland into crop fields and pasture. Henry Harte barged his wife and son up the Mohawk Valley in search of a community that would show appreciation for a School of Literature and Art.

Leland Stanford followed, too, when his father enrolled him in the Methodist Seminary at Cazenovia, New York. Cazenovia's cluster of saltbox and Greek Revival homes was typical of the villages created in western upstate New York by the post-Revolution Yankees and the commercial influences of the Erie Canal. Its largest tavern specialized in lodging, grog and thick steaks for the cowboys who drove herds of steers over the Great Western Turnpike to Albany and New York City markets. Ten miles east, bordering Peterboro Swamp, the 1,000-acre estate of Gerrit Smith was divided into 50-acre plots for the Negro slaves being smuggled out of the South via hay wagons and peddlers' carts. (Smith and his fellow Abolitionists identified the technique as "our Underground Railroad.")

Nine miles west on the turnpike the village of Pompey was bucolically New England, with a village green, a Christopher Wren church steeple, a fieldstone general store and big-chimneyed Early Northern Colonial homes. By 1860 one United States Senator, two State governors, three Supreme Court justices, five big-city mayors, one major general and two industrial titans (one of them the grandfather of Winston Churchill) would give Pompey the right to refer to itself as the "Birthplace of Giants." But in 1841 its most distinguished local boys were Horatio and Silas Seymour, sons of a teetotaling Episcopalian farm family. Horatio Seymour, after a commendable term as military secretary to Governor William L. Marcy, had just been elected mayor of Utica, with excellent prospects of one day becoming New York's governor. Younger brother Silas found engineering a more intriguing livelihood than politics, and was winning a reputation in New York City as a civil engineer and an authority on the construction and maintenance of railroads.

Another Pompeyan, twenty-three-year-old William George Fargo, had left the village only a few months before to become a messenger for the Albany firm of Pomeroy & Company. It was a new, hence uncertain, form of employment. He delivered parcels and letters entrusted to the Pomeroy Company at the railroad and Erie Canal stops between Albany and Buffalo. That summer Bill Fargo made the acquaintance of a former Albany shoemaker named Henry Wells; in 1844 they formed their own parcel-delivery service and titled it Wells, Fargo & Company.

West across the lovely hills another 40 miles, the Montezuma Swamp lies at the north end of Cayuga, largest of the Finger Lakes. Montezuma's 20 miles of ooze and malarial fogs were the despair of the Erie Canal's engineers; Irish shovelmen earned the nickname of "bogtrotters" by mucking the barge channel through it. Again, engineering problems centered on Montezuma when the New York Legislature approved plans for an Erie Canal channel that could handle 50-ton barges. Samuel Benedict Reed reported for duty at Montezuma as a junior engineer on the channel enlargement. He was twenty-three years old, a native of Arlington, Vermont, and had several years' experience as a surveys and engineering assistant on New England railroad projects. Sam Reed worked in the swamp through 1841, came down with malaria, shook it off and went on West to join the engineering staff of the Detroit & Pontiac Railroad.

Geneva, the headwaters port of Lake Seneca, is 25 miles southwest of the Montezuma Swamp. Robert Casement, his wife Ann and five children, emigrated to Geneva in 1828 from Ramsey, Isle of Man. Like most Manx, Robert was an instinctive boatman and builder. (An ancestor had built the great water wheel at Loxey; a Casement had designed and built the mercantile piers at Southampton, England.) John Stephen Casement was born in Geneva on January 19, 1829. Daniel

Casement was born there three years later. By 1841 there were ten children in Robert Casement's household. Some of them were big enough to put in a 12-hour day on a farm. Robert began asking questions about Michigan. Were those home-steading lands over there as good as the newspaper writers made out?

Cazenovia, Pompey and Geneva were still abuzz about the Latter-day Saints. On September 22, 1827, on a hilltop just north of the Rochester Pike and twenty miles northwest of Geneva, a twenty-two-year-old farmer named Joseph Smith claimed to have dug up a chest containing gold plates that had been "revealed to him by the angel Moroni." In 1830 Smith published *The Book of Mormon,* attesting it to be a faithful translation of the script engraved on these gold plates by the prophet Mormon at the dictation of the angel Moroni. Within a year *The Book of Mormon* and the Church of Latter-day Saints that Smith and his counselors formed to perpetuate its teachings had thousands of converts. The glacial mound where the plates had been revealed was formally named the Hill of Cumorah. Religious bias set off fist fights, gun battles and home burnings and forced the Latter-day Saints—most people called them Mormons—onto the trails West.

By 1841 the Saints were settled on a hilly peninsula jutting out into the Mississippi River toward the new Territory of Iowa. Joseph Smith named the new town Nauvoo, and inter-preted it as meaning, "the City Beautiful." It was reputed to have 15,000 residents, hence excelled both Galena and Chi-cago as the largest city in Illinois.

Another "upstater" was not only becoming a powerful figure in Mormonism, but seemed likely to send thousands of converts to the City Beautiful from the British Isles. Brigham Young was an excellent carpenter and the owner of a chair factory at Mendon—a few miles west of the Hill of Cumorah—when *The Book of Mormon* persuaded him out of Methodism. In 1835 he was elected to the Latter-day Saints' ruling presidium, the Council of Twelve. During the last year or two he had preached stirring sermons throughout Wales, Scotland and the English Midlands, urging farmers, miners and tradesmen to accept the revelations of *The Book* and join the Saints in the Promised Land of the American West. Rumor had it that Brigham Young's future in Mormonism was as assured as Horatio Seymour's was in Democratic politics.

So the tide rolled on. Cazenovia, Pompey, Geneva and the little Hill of Cumorah had all been the New West a generation before. But by 1842 there were 3,300,000 settlers west of New York State. Even Leland Stanford, daydreaming over his stolid Methodist textbooks, planned a future as a lawyer in Chicago or Milwaukee, or one of the new cities on the frontier. Obviously steamboats, canalboats and Conestoga wagons could not handle the transportation and bulk distribution needs of three million . . . five million . . . ten million people pushing relentlessly toward the Rockies and the Great Desert. The railroad's swivel trucks, higher irons, headlights and steam whistles had been invented just in time.

CHAPTER **3**

THE DESERT DREAMERS

The Plains were snowy white with salt. The grass that grew in small spots on the plains was laden with salt which had formed itself on the stalks and blades in lumps, from the size of a pea to that of a hen's egg. This was the kind we procured, it being very white, strong and pure. . . . John Bidwell's journal entry en route to Promontory Pass (August 24, 1841).

In 1841 the Pacific Coast was two months and several thousand miles farther from the trade and population centers of the United States than were Bombay, India, or Shanghai, China. Geographic distance is, after all, a mathematician's deceit. The 2,000 statute miles of high plain, mountain ranges and deserts that separated the Mississippi Valley and the Alta California Presidio of San Francisco were considered as impossible—for normal trade and communication purposes—as the North Pole route to the Russian Tsar's palaces in St. Petersburg. Hence the trade route from Boston, New York and Philadelphia to Oregon and Alta California began with a 7,000-mile sail down the Gulf Stream, and across the Sargasso Sea, the Amazon-stained waters of the Equator to Cape Horn. The terrors of the Straits of Magellan at this "bottom of the world" were only the halfway point. Ships beat another 7,000 miles past the treacherous coasts of Chile, Central America and Baja California. The four to six months' voyage, plus scurvy, yellow fever, malaria, dysentery, pirates, hurricanes and typhoons, was the routine for communication and trade between the Atlantic and Pacific seaboards of the North American continent.

Queen Victoria could receive messages from any port in Great Britain within two or three days, or from distant India in two months. The giant empires of Russia and China maintained corps of couriers who galloped dispatches to the most distant provinces in a week or two. But any message, delegation or Congressman journeying from Oregon or California to the United States' boggy Capital would require from four to six months for the journey. A Union sprawled on opposite sides of a 2,000-mile wilderness could collapse under such a time lag in interstate commerce and communication. Trails across the Indian strongholds of the Great American Desert must be the first step toward transcontinental union. Then, somehow, the railroad must follow.

During the winter of 1840–41, a dozen Missouri families decided to attempt the overland journey to California. They would subsequently be called the Bartleson-Bidwell party because John Bartleson was elected train captain, while John Bidwell proved to be the best organizer and kept a daily journal of the trip. Thomas Fitzpatrick agreed to guide the 45 men and 15 women and children as far west as the Hudson's Bay Company trading post at Fort Hall on the Snake River in Eastern Idaho. Fitzpatrick had been with Jedediah Smith during the discovery of South Pass in 1824. The only known northern route to California, he warned, was to do just what the Reverend Whitman and his party had done in 1836: abandon the wagons at Fort Hall; then pack-train down the Snake and on in a huge semicircle from Western Oregon to Northern California. Fitzpatrick refused to guide them beyond Fort Hall.

The wagon train left the upper Missouri Valley in May, 1841. Its members had heard stories about "rivers flowing from the Great Salt Lake down into California." At Soda Springs, 150 miles west of South Pass and 50 miles east of Fort Hall, Bartleson ordered the train south down the Bear River Valley toward the Great Salt Lake and these "rivers to California." Fitzpatrick refused to go along. After a vote, Bidwell and 30 other men and one woman and her small daughter, agreed to follow Bartleson. Only 26 stayed with Fitzpatrick on the Fort Hall Trail.

The Bear River adventurers found the valley passable for their wagons over the 100 miles to the Great Salt Lake Desert. In mid-August, camped on the meadows that would echo the bawdiness of "Sinful Corinne" 28 years later, Bartleson decided to march the train northwest across the sage plains and salt flats. It was an epochal but almost disastrous decision. The terrain forced them over a 200-mile arc around the north end of Great Salt Lake, through the natural pass in the Promontory Mountain range, then south to a second pass through the fanged black peaks of the Pilot range along the future Utah-Nevada boundary.

So between August 20 and September 15, 1841, the first wagon train crossed Utah and pioneered the route that Crocker, Stanford, Huntington, Montague, Durant, Reed and the Casements would agree upon twenty-seven years later as the final link in the Union's Pacific Railroad. With equal implications of Western destiny, the eight or ten wagons pushed on across the Nevada passes and sagebrush valleys that would be immortalized in 1860–61 by the Pony Express. Then the struggle became too great for the horses. The wagons were abandoned near Johnson Wells (thirty miles southeast of the present Wells, Nevada); the party reorganized as a pack train. On September 23, another historic moment occurred when they reached the headwaters of the Humboldt River in the Ruby Mountains (south of the present Elko), Nevada. Surveyors sent out by Theodore Judah and Sam Montague in 1862–3 would prove that the Humboldt's gorges provided a natural railroad route across Northern Nevada.

The Bartleson-Bidwell luck held. The party crawled down the awesome cliffs of the Sierras' west face, and on November 4 reached the semifeudal domain of a Swiss-American adventurer named John Augustus Sutter. The trip from Missouri had taken six months.

In 1839, after wandering from St. Louis to Santa Fe to Oregon to Hawaii to Sitka, Alaska, John Sutter had persuaded Alta California's governor to grant him a tract of 97,000 acres in the Sacramento River Valley, 100 miles northeast of San Francisco. He called the tract "New Helvetia" and offered employment to immigrants willing to work his wheat fields, herd the thousands of cattle, sheep, horses and mules he had purchased from the Franciscan Missions, and experiment with vineyards and fruit orchards on the slopes up the American and Feather rivers. The Bartleson-Bidwell party signed on as colonists in New Helvetia. John Bidwell was particularly interested in the prospects for raisins, olives and similar subtropical crops. He rode north up the Sacramento Valley to examine the soils and contours.

Thomas Fitzpatrick's contract as guide for the Bartleson-Bidwell party had ended at Fort Hall. He rode back over South Pass during the fall of 1841, then took an Upper Missouri trade boat into St. Louis. There his gossip about the Bartleson-Bidwell determination to "follow the Great Salt Lake's rivers into California" reached the West-tuned ears of Thomas Hart Benton. Senator Benton was brooding over a family problem. His daughter Jessie had recently eloped with a young Army lieutenant named John Charles Frémont. Since Frémont had taught mathematics at the United States Military Academy and proven his skills as a surveyor during an expedition up the Missouri, Benton wangled an assignment for him to map the Des Moines River Valley in the new Territory of Iowa. Now the Senator wondered whether Fitzpatrick's gossip, plus one surveyor son-in-law, might be transformed into another campaign for that "Road to India" and American conquest of the Pacific shore.

Fitzpatrick was already committed to guide a wagon train toward Oregon in the summer of 1842. Senator Benton negotiated with another Rocky Mountain veteran, Kit Carson, to guide Frémont on a five months' exploration of the Rockies. By October, 1842, Fitzpatrick, Carson and Frémont were all back in St. Louis, and replete with stories about the Far West's wonderlands. At Fort Hall, Fitzpatrick had heard the details of the Bartleson-Bidwell trip over the Great Salt Lake route to Alta California. Senator Benton was reasonably certain that some effort to conquer both New Mexico and Alta California would be made during the next few years; especially if the harangue about annexation of the Texas Republic ended favorably and the Democrats committed themselves to a platform of Territorial Expansion in the 1844 Presidential election. The more reason, then, for a survey of a wagon route to California.

As if in justification of these musings, news of another lone traveler through South Pass came down the Missouri. The Reverend Marcus Whitman was riding hard for New York, Washington and Boston to argue against a ruling by the Presbyterian-Congregationalist Missions Board that missionary work in Oregon must be curtailed. Win or lose on that score, Reverend Whitman told reporters, he would personally lead all the families and young men he could persuade back over the Oregon Trail "next summer."

John Charles Frémont, with both Thomas Fitzpatrick and Kit Carson as guides, hurried up the Missouri through the spring freshets of 1843. By fall they were taking measurements along the Humboldt River. In mid-January, 1844, Frémont ordered a march over the Sierras. The Indian guides pleaded, wept, and sang their death chants. Carson and Fitzpatrick argued against it, but Frémont held to his decision. In mid-February the starving, frostbitten column marched into Sutter's Fort on the Sacramento. In April they headed East again, spent the summer exploring the massive central Rockies in the area the New Mexicans had long called "Colorado" (red earth), then boated into St. Louis on the eve of the Presidential election. The Missouri-Snake-Columbia Canal visualized by Senator Benton in his twenty-three-year-old dream of the Passage to India was, they reported, an impossible project. But graded wagon roads to both Oregon and California were not only logical but—in view of the amazing natural resources of the New West—would be a modest investment.

Senator Benton's horizons were already roseate. During the summer of 1843 Reverend Whitman had led a column of 1,000 immigrants to Oregon. Last May 27 (three days after the painter-inventor Samuel F. B. Morse demonstrated his miraculous telegraph), the Democrats had nominated James K. Polk of Tennessee for President and drawn up a four-plank platform. One pledge promised the United States' annexation of Texas, New Mexico and California. Another preluded Polk's campaign slogan of "Fifty-four forty or fight" by demanding a Pacific Northwest boundary with Canada north of the Columbia River Valley. Henry Clay, the Whig candidate, was almost as fiery an expansionist as Polk. Transcontinental wagon roads would be imperative, to be trailed eventually by a Union's Pacific Railroad.

Otherwise, the Senator gossiped on, the most exciting event in the mid-Mississippi Valley had been the murders and riots upriver at the Mormon city of Nauvoo. The pattern was in historic step with all new religions. Some of the Latter-day Saints challenged Joseph Smith's decisions and began publishing a bombastic "We'll tell all" newspaper. They called it *The Expositor*. Matters got out of hand; *The Expositor*'s printing plant was burned; arson charges were filed against Joseph Smith. Joseph, his brother Hiram, and a few other Latter-day Saints leaders, voluntarily rode down to the county seat at Carthage, Illinois, and gave themselves up. But during the night of June 27, a mob of 200 men—carefully disguised by blackface make-up—rushed the jail and assassinated Joseph and Hiram Smith. Street fights broke out in Nauvoo. Someone set the white marble Temple afire. Joseph Smith's body was smuggled home, via armed wagon train, and hidden. The burly ex-carpenter, Brigham Young, won the election as Smith's successor to the Latter-day Saints' presidency; but with Smith's widow dissenting.

Now, rumor had it, the Mormons would abandon Nauvoo. Some of their wagons had been sighted in Iowa Territory, searching, doubtlessly, for that Promised Land of their prophecies. If they survived the guns of the Dissenters, the winter blizzards, the spring fevers, and the eternally warring Indians, another strange—and desperate—force might be shaping for the New West. Even the most conservative newspapers in England verified Brigham Young's claim that thousands of converts won to Mormonism in Yorkshire, Wales, Sussex and the Isle of Man, were selling their homes and most of their household goods to raise funds for the journey to the American West.

James Polk beat Henry Clay by 65 electoral votes. In January, 1845, the first realistic facts-and-statistics proposal for a Union's Pacific Railroad sent Congress into a dither of argument. Its timing, managed by Connecticut's Senator John M. Niles, brought it to committee hearings while the New England shipowners' lobby chortled over the news that Caleb Cushing, United States Commissioner to China, had negotiated a Treaty of Wanghai granting exterritorial rights and open trade to Americans in the 64 "treaty ports" along the China Sea. The originator of the proposal was a Connecticut merchant named Asa Whitney. He asked Congress to deed him a swathe of the Great Desert lands, 60 miles wide and extending northwest from the Mississippi in Iowa Territory to the Columbia River Valley. Whitney and a federal commission would develop this grant of approximately 75,000,000 acres as a homesteader and new-industries project. The cash from land sales, mineral rights, lumbering, irrigation projects and the like, would be used to finance construction of a Lake Michigan–Oregon Railroad.

"Here we stand forever," Whitney said in his petition. "We reach out one hand to all Asia and the other to all Europe, willing for all to enjoy the great blessings we possess, claiming free intercourse and exchange of commodities with all." Only the Pacific Railway, he concluded, could develop the wilderness west of the Great Lakes and simultaneously establish the United States as the dominant trader and carrier for "the spices, teas, precious woods and fabrics of Cathay."

Whitney had just returned from trading ventures in the China ports, with enough profit to support him while he researched the railway idea. Born in Groton, Connecticut, in 1797, he had apprenticed as a buyer's agent on Manhattan's East and North river wharves, then established his own firm. Bank failures during the Van Buren administration ruined him. He recuperated via the quick profits available to a shrewd trader at Nanking, Amoy and Shanghai.

Consultations with John B. Jervis, Henry Farnam, Silas Seymour and other veteran engineers, convinced Whitney that a Pacific Railway would cost not more than $65,000,000. (Twice the sum Congress was prepared to pay Mexico that year for peaceful annexation of New Mexico and Alta California.) The eastern terminal for the railroad, Whitney testified, should be the Lake Michigan port of Chicago.

The construction costs, the size of the land grant, and the presumption of Chicago as eastern terminal combined to make Thomas Hart Benton, Stephen A. Douglas, John C. Calhoun and President Polk uncomfortable allies in lobbying against Whitney's plan.

Whitney's frankness in pointing out that the 1,000 miles of gentle prairie and river valley between Chicago and the easternmost ramparts of the Rockies offered "the best" Pacific railway gradient forced Benton's opposition. The route meant that Illinois, Iowa and the valley of the Platte River would reap the railroad's benefits; Missouri would be by-passed; Chicago might in time succeed St. Louis as trade center of the West.

But Illinois' Junior Congressman, Stephen A. Douglas, bristled too. Whitney's plan, he told constituent newspapers, was too pat. The Pacific Railroad must "progress gradually from east to west, keeping up a connected chain of communication and following the tide of emigration and the settlement of the country. In addition to the India and China trade, and the vast commerce of the Pacific Ocean, which would pass over this route, you must create a further necessity for the road by subduing the wilderness, and peopling it with a hardy and industrious population who would soon have a surplus produce, without the means of getting it to market, and require, for their own consumption, immense quantities of goods and merchandize, which they could not obtain at reasonable rates, for want of proper facilities of transportation."

The South's opposition to the Whitney plan rooted back more than 300 years to that stupendous 1526–36 hegira of Álvar Núñez Cabeza de Vaca, two other Spaniards and the Negro, Estevan, from the site of Galveston, Texas, to the Spanish Presidio of Culiacán on the Gulf of California. The Spanish had clopped cavalry and cattle trails between Florida and the Mississippi Valley before 1600. Juan de Oñate pioneered a Camino Real from Chihuahua to the site of Santa Fe in 1598. His successors developed roads for their *"conducta"* of massive two-wheel carts and *vaquero* guards west to Tucson and east to New Orleans. Two months after the Continental Congress proclaimed its Declaration of Independence, Captain Juan Bautista de Anza of the Tucson Presidio brought 240 settlers safely through 900 miles of desert and trackless mountains to found the Presidio of San Francisco.

Virginia's colonists were equally intent on roads to the West. In 1669, Governor William Berkeley wrote from Williamsburg about "plans to finde out the East India Sea." James Adair, Dr. Thomas Walker, Richard Henderson, Daniel Boone, George Rogers Clark and James Robertson led the list of the South's trail blazers to the West before 1800. San Houston, Davy Crockett of Tennessee, and the Bowie Brothers—James and Rezin—of Georgia were household gods in the Texas Republic. After 1820, the blacksnake whip-crackers out of the Carolina, Georgia and Tennessee highlands rode into Texas to blend their cattle lore with that of the Mexican *vaqueros*. Southerners rafted wagons across the Mississippi from 1803 on, to settle Missouri, Arkansas and Western Louisiana. George Rogers Clark, his brother William, and Meriwether Lewis were Thomas Jefferson's neighbors at Charlottesville, Virginia. William Ashley, Kit Carson and James Bridger—like most of the Mountain Men—were native Southerners. Bent's Fort, the most famous trading post on the Santa Fe Trail, employed a suave Negro bartender who personally tended to a mint patch on the Arkansas River bank and was reputed to blend a superior mint julep. The Cherokee, Choctaw and Creek took hundreds of their Negro slaves with them over the Trail of Tears to Indian territory, and would prove their continuing allegiance to the South. All of these roots convinced the champions of slavery and States' rights that a permanent alliance existed between the Union's "Old South" and the New West. Plans for strengthening this alliance did not permit an all-North railroad to the Pacific.

Late in the summer of 1845, Senator John C. Calhoun of South Carolina received an invitation to deliver the keynote address before a commercial convention to be held in November at Memphis, Tennessee. The Texas Legislature had just accepted Congress' terms of annexation. General Zachary Taylor's army camped on the Rio Grande, with orders to move south against any show of force by Mexico. War might break out at any moment; Calhoun decided to turn down the invitation. Then a letter arrived from James Gadsden, the Charleston railroad promoter. "Now is the time," Gadsden urged, "to meet our Western friends at Memphis—to set the ball in motion which must bring The Valley to The South: and make them feel as allies of the Great Commercial and Agricultural interests— instead of the Tax gathering and Monopolizing interests of the North."

Calhoun accepted, and decided to go along with Thomas Hart Benton's theme of a Missouri–Columbia waterway to the

Pacific. The West and South, he told the convention, was a single region from Charleston and Savannah to the Rio Grande. He pledged his aid to Congressional grants for dredging the canals and building the locks and lighthouses that would convert "the Mississippi with all its great tributaries into an inland sea."

"Lying midway between the Atlantic and the Pacific Oceans," he concluded, "in less than one generation should the Union continue, and I hope it may be perpetual, you will be engaged in deliberations to extend your connection with the Pacific, as you now are with the Atlantic; and will ultimately be almost as intimately connected with the one as the other. In the end, you will command the commerce . . . of the world. . . ."

Gadsden addressed the convention, too, and in more direct answer to Asa Whitney. There must be a system of railways to connect the Southeast, the Mississippi Valley and the Pacific, he urged. The "most logical route" would be via New Orleans and Memphis into Texas, then west through El Paso del Norte to California. There were fewer mountains to cross on this Southern and Pacific route than on the tortuous Oregon Trail. The Tejas, Comanche, Navajo and Apache could be moved to the hunting grounds along the Platte, just as the Cherokee, Choctaw and Creek had been moved from the South's highlands to the new Indian Territory beyond Arkansas.

Sam Houston sent formal Texas approval of Gadsden's plan. Virginia and the Carolinas nodded agreement. Meanwhile Benton was working on a new plan that would perpetuate St. Louis as "Queen City of the West." And Stephen Douglas barked at Asa Whitney again for proposing the importation of European laborers for the task of building the Pacific Railway's roadbed.

Chicago herself was much too busy begging funds for the Illinois–Michigan Canal. Plans to build a railroad to the Mississippi River port of Galena, 175 miles west on lead-rich bluffs, had been drawn up in 1832. They were still locked in a lawyer's strongbox. Actually, Chicago's leaders held with the concept of waterway monopoly and argued that the railroads, aside from the sensory pleasures derived by crossing the countryside at 25 miles an hour, could never progress beyond the status of portage carriers between navigable waterways. No banker or attorney would look twice at a proposal to finance a railway that would compete against steamboats or barges. If and when the Federal Government decided that the Pacific Railway was critical to the national defense and public interest, let Congress handle it.

Whitney set off on a lecture tour. "The Pacific Railway," he told lyceums and club meetings in Boston, New York and Philadelphia, "must be the scientific and industrial basis for both Asiatic trade and new settlements beyond the Iowa and Missouri frontiers." Newspapers welcomed his speeches. Midwest Congressmen earned home-town headlines with statements about "the most logical and reasonable Pacific Railway route": out of Galena—out of Detroit—out of LaSalle, Illinois—out of Memphis, New Orleans—out of Fort Smith and even tiny St. Paul, Wisconsin Territory.

Texas became a state on December 29, 1845. General Zachary Taylor won the battles of Palo Alto and Rescaca de la Palma in May, 1846. The Oregon Treaty with Great Britain was signed on June 15. A packet boat hurried up the Potomac through the September mists with the news that most of the 500 Americans in Alta California—brashly organized by Captain John C. Frémont—had participated in the Sonoma Declaration of June 14 that created the Republic of California.

The prospects of the Pacific Railway concerned the 1,600 men in the Army of the West as it marched over the Santa Fe Trail. Its commander, Brigadier General Stephen W. Kearney, was under orders to occupy New Mexico, install a provisional government at Santa Fe, then proceed west to junction with a naval squadron that should be waiting at Monterey, California. Largely because of his publicized trip with Frémont, Thomas Fitzpatrick was appointed guide for this Army of the West. As chief topographical engineer of the expedition, Lieutenant William H. Emory kept a detailed journal about the land, its

peoples, its economic potentials and the possibilities for a
Pacific Railway. "The road from Santa Fe to Leavenworth," he
wrote at Santa Fe on August 6, "presents few obstacles for a
railway, and if it continues as good to the Pacific, will be one of
the routes to be considered, over which the United States will
pass immense quantities of merchandise into what may become,
in time, the rich and populous States of Sonora, Durango and
Southern California."

While Lieutenant Emory mused over his report—and it was
destined to become one of the classics of Western Americana
—600 lithe youngsters quick-paced up the Arkansas Valley,
under orders from Brigham Young and the Council of Twelve
to reinforce the Army of the West. They had not yet found the
heart to laugh or sing. Most of them, if they dared listen to
impulse, would have turned in their tracks and run blindly
back to that city of shacks in the cottonwood grove on the
upper Missouri's shore. But Brigham Young had preached to
them that, "The honor of the United States must be defended,
and its destiny under God fulfilled." The rape of Nauvoo and
the dreadful march of 11,000 Saints to these winter quarters
was one thing; the call to the nation's defense and New West
destiny was a separate, and equally demanding, crisis. The 600
made their farewells, then poled rafts 150 miles downriver to
Fort Leavenworth. Next spring, if the fevers and plundering
Missourians spared them, their parents, wives and sweethearts
would start up the Oregon Trail. To California? Or to the
mountain-rimmed "Deseret" that Joseph Smith was reputed
to have seen in a vision?

Through the summer and fall of 1846, the Mormon Battalion crossed the Pacific Railway route favored by the South.
In April, 1847, their kinfolk and fellow Saints marched west
by north over the Pacific Railway route proposed by Asa Whitney. In New England and New York other forces were focusing for the Union's Pacific Railroad that would finally be
blasted through the Black Hills and the Wasatch twenty years
later by veterans of both the Mormon Battalion and the Mormon Trail.

CHAPTER 4

THE HEADLIGHTS POINT WEST

Come, my tan-faced children,
Follow well in order, get your weapons ready,
Have you your pistols? have you your sharp-edged
axes?
. . . . "Pioneers! O Pioneers!"
    —Walt Whitman.

Thirty miles north of Boston on the white-pine and granite knolls framing the harbor, cobblestone wharves, and shipmaster mansions of Salem, the Widow Lander and her sons, Charles and Frederick, operated a dairy farm. During the Spring of 1845 the Landers decided to add "pond ice" to the provisions they peddled at the summer-cottage colonies along the North Shore of Massachusetts Bay. They bought an abandoned church, teamed it to the edge of their fresh-water pond, and began to insulate it for ice storage. That June, Frederick Lander received his degree as a civil engineer from Norwich University in Norwich, Vermont. Soon Charles and Mrs. Lander broached another idea. The ice pond was only a few hundred yards from the track of the Boston & Eastern Railroad. Would it be worthwhile to build a spur track to the icehouse, then expand the pond-ice distribution to Boston greengrocers and butchers? If Frederick agreed with the idea, would he survey and build the spur track? They had just hired one of Sylvanus Dodge's sons, from down Danvers way, to help with milking, egg candling, apple sorting and similar chores. The boy seemed bright and quite willing. He might be able to help on the survey and grading too. His parents had certainly given him unusual names: Grenville Mellen Dodge. ("Grenville" honored Sir Richard Grenville, the English naval hero who had brought the first Virginia Colonists to Roanoke. The middle name was subtler. Pure Saxon, it meant "to mingle" or "be a good mixer." "Dodge," in its original form, indicated "alacrity." The belief persisted in many New England families that a child's given names influenced his destiny.)

Grenville Dodge, at fourteen, was long legged and big shouldered. His eyes were brown and deep-set, with a stare that matched the belligerent pride of his broad lips, Grecian nose and jet-black hair. He listened stolidly the first afternoon while Frederick Lander explained the surveyor's telescope and spirit level, the hundred links of the engineer's chain, and the applications of trigonometry enabling these instruments to reveal the land contours that must be followed or changed to provide that gradient of "not more than 2 per cent" demanded by the steam locomotive.

The boy's hands possessed the deft sureness of the farm bred. Within a week his questions indicated that the family-name implication of nimbleness was appropriate. By fall, Gren Dodge could read a theodolite, plot data on a chart, tamp ties and line up T-rail. Frederick Lander loaned him textbooks on geometry and geography and began urging him to enroll in a classical school and prepare for the Civil Engineering course at Norwich.

A delightful new vista opened for Grenville's father Sylvanus during the summer of 1846. Sylvanus had wandered from job to job in towns along the North Shore since his marriage to Julia Theresa Phillips of Salem. By 1844 he was back in his father's profession of pig farmer and butcher. The Dodges were Democrats; the Salem-Beverly-Danvers area was overwhelmingly high-tariff Whig. Nonetheless, Sylvanus turned the pig feeding over to his family during the summer and early fall of 1844 in order to argue North Shore farmers and sailors into votes for James K. Polk and the Democrats' platform of New West expansion. The reward came in 1846 in the form of Sylvanus' appointment as United States Postmaster of South Danvers. He sold his butcher tools, sows and boars to finance the payments on a stock of books and stationery, then opened a bookstore, with his post-office equipment at the far end. As a dedicated Democrat and Expansionist, Dodge harangued customers to invest in Washington Irving's trilogy about "our New West": *A Tour on the Prairies, Astoria* and *The Adventures of Captain Bonneville, U.S.A.* Nathaniel Hawthorne had just moved back to Salem as surveyor of the port. His *Mosses From An Old Manse* was published in 1846. He called at the Dodge bookstore one afternoon, offered to autograph the copies of *Twice-Told Tales* and *Mosses From An Old Manse* in stock, stayed for tea, then became a frequent caller and family-friend.

The post-office fees, plus Sylvanus' discovery that he was an instinctive book salesman, enabled Grenville's enrollment at New Hampshire's Durham Academy. In September, 1848— six months after the Treaty of Guadalupe Hidalgo ceded New Mexico and Alta California to the United States, and four months after "the miracle of the gulls" saved the Mormons' first crops in Great Salt Lake Valley—he enrolled at Norwich University as a candidate for the degree in Civil Engineering.

Like a bright-eyed hawk, Enoch Train had perched for a quarter century in the mercantile aeries of Faneuil Hall market in Boston. He had specialized, initially, in financing trade ventures to Scandinavia and to Baltic Sea ports. His 1843 profits were so pleasing that the Democratic pledges for territorial expansion and low tariffs persuaded him to organize a Boston–Liverpool ship line. The few friends he exposed to the notion pointed out that the British Cunards were running a highly successful line of packets into New York. Train beamed back at them and continued negotiations with shipbuilder Donald McKay.

He persuaded McKay to move his shipyard from Newburyport to Boston and build several of his daring "clippers" for the new White Diamond Line. The newspapers that same summer detailed accounts of Asa Whitney's proposal for the Pacific Railway. Whitney's suggestion that the huge task be performed by workmen "imported from Europe" intrigued Train. He recalled it when the newspapers began to report the devastation caused in Ireland by the loss of the 1845 potato crop. Irish immigrants had dug out the most treacherous portions of the Erie Canal in 1823–5, and gone on west to build the canals of Ohio, Michigan and Illinois. History could repeat. The westbound United States was veering its enthusiasm from the canal to the railroad. Boston bankers reported more than 6,000 miles of railroads in operation and construction of at least another 1,000 miles a year for the foreseeable future. Moreover, unless Polk came a cropper in his pledges, there should be endless opportunities for Irish immigrants in the New West and in those New England factories that would supply New West pioneers.

A White Diamond clipper ship veered north off the Liverpool course in 1846 and sailed up the Irish Sea to Dublin and Belfast. The purser and captain went ashore to complete Train's negotiations for permanent agents in each port. The White Diamond Line would not only offer lower rates than the Cunards for passage to America, but was opening a Boston office that would secure a variety of jobs for Irish immigrants. And White Diamond offered a second important service in its Immigrants' Savings Plan. This subsidiary would encourage routine cash savings by all its Irish immigrant customers and would act as the agent to deliver any portion of these savings to specified relatives or friends in Ireland.

The plan worked splendidly. The White Diamond's job and

savings services enticed thousands of Irish to New England and established the tradition of "the Boston Irish."

Enoch Train debated the advisability of assigning his young kinsman, George Francis Train, to Belfast or Liverpool as an assistant agent of the White Diamond Line. It would be excellent experience for the headstrong but brilliant eighteen year old. An orphan, George had run away from his grandmother's home in Waltham two years before and hired out as a grocer's clerk. The grandmother appealed to Enoch, the boy's only uncle, and George went to work as a junior clerk in Enoch Train's offices. The visits down-harbor to help manifest cargoes, the talks with Donald McKay, and the trial-and-error development of plans for the White Diamond Line, had transformed the lad. He was fluent, although inclined to oratorical expressions, and wrote convincing business letters. He was shrewd. An assignment to Liverpool or Belfast would be an excellent way to test his wings.

That spring was a particularly happy one for Ted Judah. He was to be married. During the eight years since he had left Rensselaer Institute to work on the Schenectady & Troy, Ted had become one of the most promising young railroaders in the Northeast. Sidney Dillon, the ex-foreman of the Rensselaer & Saratoga, had helped Ted's progress through chainman and surveyor to assistant engineer. Dillon had taken his first gamble as a railroad construction contractor about 1840, and made a profit. Between 1841 and 1846 he undertook a series of railroad contracts on the lines beginning to crisscross Vermont and Massachusetts. Ted Judah worked on several of these lines during the same years.

In 1843–4 Ted had been a surveyor on the line routing up the Connecticut River Valley from Springfield, Massachusetts toward Brattleboro, Vermont. The high iron was trajected to cross the Deerfield River at Greenfield, the village founded in 1686 as eastern terminal of the Berkshire Trail. Attending services at St. James Episcopal Church in Greenfield, Ted had met John J. Pierce, senior warden of the church. Then he met the Pierce daughter Anna.

The courtship spanned three difficult years. The Pierces were a distinguished and wealthy New England family. A cousin in the New Hampshire branch was Franklin Pierce, recently resigned as United States Senator and pursuing a law practice at Concord. A Boston cousin—"S. S."—operated one of New England's finest grocery stores and was currently financing experiments to develop "vacuum-canning" processes for corn, beans and succotash so that the plagues of "scurvy" and "rot" might be avoided by ship crews on long voyages. The prospect of entrusting a Pierce daughter to an impoverished young railroader, even though he was an Episcopalian of good blood, had loomed as a crisis.

Yet the young people's devotion held while Ted moved down-river to Hartford as a location engineer on the New Haven, Hartford & Springfield. He proposed soon after his return to Greenfield as assistant to Colonel Childs, chief engineer of the Connecticut Valley Railroad, and the Pierces finally approved.

Anna's father may have played a part in the move West that opened for Ted soon after the engagement was announced.

Horatio and Silas Seymour were also devout Episcopalians. In 1846–7, Horatio Seymour was one of the Democratic leaders in the New York Legislature and a "dark-horse" potential for the party's nomination as governor. Brother Silas was prospering as a consulting engineer for the Erie Railroad's push over the Catskill Mountains toward Buffalo. Early in 1847 Ted Judah was offered a position as an associate engineer on the Niagara Gorge Railroad. Both New York's Legislature and the Erie Railroad's backers were involved in this daring project for a rail connection down the canyon of the Niagara Falls' rapids between the ship piers on Lake Erie and Lake Ontario.

Theodore Dehone Judah and Anna Ferona Pierce were married in St. James Episcopal Church, Greenfield, on May

10, 1847, and rode west to a honeymoon cottage overlooking Niagara Falls.

Thomas Clark Durant possessed the daring, the urge for analysis and the impersonal precision that could have developed him into one of the leading surgeons of the nineteenth century. He graduated *cum laude* from the Albany College of Medicine in 1840, and was held in such esteem at the dean's office that he was offered an assistant professorship. But the routine of lecturing freshmen soon bored him. One of his uncles was becoming wealthy by the sly process of sitting in the New York Grain Exchange and betting on the future markets for flour and wheat. Dr. Durant resigned from the staff of Albany College and joined his uncle's firm in 1842. He became the firm's specialist in data about the prairie-wheat funneling down the Great Lakes–Erie Canal route from Milwaukee and Chicago. This intrigued him toward stock promotions of a Lake Erie–Lake Michigan railroad.

Boat traffic across the lakes and the Mohawk–Hudson throughway was a slave of the weather. Ice began crinkling a barricade across the Mackinac Strait in November; the spring thaws rarely unlocked it before April. Consequently, freight and passenger boats could operate only seven months of the year, with the summerlong prospect of fogs, windstorms and tornadoes.

The railroad offered the prospects of travel twelve months of every year. And in view of the new inventions in freight cars, signal systems and locomotives, a railroad across Michigan's peninsula and the sand plains of northern Indiana should be able to earn a profit. The Rogers Locomotive Works at Paterson, New Jersey, was producing engines that weighed 20 tons and could rattle a train of freight and passenger cars over straightaway T-rail at 40 miles an hour. These Sandusky types had 8 wheels with 5-foot drivers and 18-inch cylinders. Headlights, cowcatchers, sandboxes, steam whistles and windowed cabs for the engineman and fireman were standard equipment. Since the Erie Railroad would be the first line to operate through trains from New York City to Lake Erie, development of a system of devices to warn enginemen about traffic conditions was imperative. One of the ideas advanced by its engineers called for a colored iron ball suspended from a pole alongside the track at each station. When a train left the station the station-master cranked the ball down until it was suspended on a level with a locomotive's smokestack. Thus, a "low ball" would mean "stop," and a "high ball" indicated "Clear track ahead." A train-dispatching technique might be developed by coordinating the "high-ball" poles and the new British semaphore lights with a station-to-station telegraph system.

A telegraph line was building across Indiana toward Chicago. The Michigan Central Railroad was starting construction West out of Kalamazoo toward the Lake Michigan shore. Boston bankers had advanced loans to build the Cleveland, Columbus & Cincinnati Railroad across Ohio. In the fall of 1846, the leading bankers and merchants of Hannibal, Missouri, held a series of meetings at the office of John Clemens, a local justice of the peace, to discuss incorporation of a railroad that would cross the state due west 200 miles to the Missouri River's port of St. Joseph. A Hannibal & St. Joseph railroad, they reasoned, would not only provide rapid transit to Fort Leavenworth, Independence, West Port and other terminal villages of the Santa Fe and Oregon Trails, but could become the eastern link for that Pacific Railway advocated by Asa Whitney. (Since Justice Clemens' son Samuel possessed a fiendish skill in plotting practical jokes, the founders of the Hannibal & St. Joseph specifically requested that their evening meetings be held at Justice Clemens' chambers in the Pilaster House, rather than in his home parlor, and thus happily avoided any contact with the future Mark Twain.)

These potent developments in western railroading, coupled with Cyrus McCormick's decision to move his reaper factory from Cincinnati to Chicago and the brash offers of free farm-and-dairy homesteads by the new State of Wisconsin, persuaded Thomas Durant to launch promotions for a Michigan–Indiana–Illinois railroad. John Jervis indicated his willingness to become chief engineer of such a project. Henry Farnam and his wealthy backer, Joseph Sheffield, expressed interest in backing a Michigan–Chicago railroad, provided plans included a lobbying operation in Illinois and Wisconsin to secure charters for rights of way on west to Iowa Territory.

During the fall of 1848, Durant contacted the directors of the Michigan-Southern Railroad that connected Detroit and Ann Arbor. He proposed that he serve as New York broker on a bonds campaign to build the Michigan-Southern west through Hillsdale to the Indiana port of South Bend, thence over the cactus and pine desert of Lake Michigan's south shore dunes to Chicago.

A few weeks after the Senate approved the Treaty of Guadalupe Hidalgo, Senator Niles reintroduced his bill for a grant of 75,000,000 acres of New West land to Asa Whitney to finance construction of the Pacific Railway. Newspaper accounts of the terrible deserts encountered by.General Kearney's Army of the West, plus lively promotion of John C. Frémont's book, *Report of the Exploring Expedition to the Rocky Mountains in 1842 and to Oregon and North California in 1843–44,* had kept Whitney in demand as a lyceum lecturer.

A score of other railroad plans achieved glory moments too. John Plumbe of Dubuque, Iowa, reminded newspapers of the time and money he had invested between 1838 and 1840 while trying to persuade Congress to appropriate a few thousands of dollars for surveys of a railroad route between Lake Michigan and Oregon. A Massachusetts Congressman dug out the article written by Dr. Samuel B. Barlow in 1834, which proposed Federal subsidies of "from six to fifteen million dollars a year" for construction of a Pacific railway. During 1847, Hartwell Carver of Rochester, New York, offered to finance a Lake Michigan–South Pass–California railroad from a land grant of only 8,000,000 acres; he advocated a track gauge of 8 or 10 feet, with the rails "to be laid on felt to lessen the vibration of the cars" and the locomotives on the Rocky Mountain divisions to be equipped with cogwheels that "would engage holes in the rails." Josiah Perman of Boston proposed the People's Pacific Railroad, to be financed through the sale of a million $100 bonds.

Senator Niles' new bill survived committee hearings in the summer of 1848, and moved on toward a floor vote. The South and North were deadlocked over the issue of slavery in the New West. Obviously the bias would extend to any route for a transcontinental railway. The deciding votes on the Niles bill were controlled by Thomas Hart Benton.

But Benton was staring hard at his prospects for re-election. His decision to edge toward the Abolitionists and favor gradual abolishment of slavery had cost him thousands of votes throughout Missouri. Now, if he voted for a plan to finance a Pacific railway that would be terminaled at Chicago, St. Louis merchants would join the slave owners of "Swampeast" and western Missouri in defeating him for a sixth Senate term. Frémont was leading another expedition into the central Rockies to locate passes for a St. Louis–San Francisco railway route. Benton desperately needed that throughway to California via St. Louis and the Missouri Valley. He voted against the Niles bill.

Benton influenced the votes of some of the North's Senators too. They were already worried about Whitney's cost estimates and the huge swathe of land—most of which had been promised to the Indians as "eternal hunting grounds"—that would be turned over to him. The new treaty with Colombia, they pointed out, guaranteed the United States right of transit across the Isthmus of Panama; the Pacific Mail Steamship Company was organizing fleets of steamers to operate in the Atlantic between New York and the Isthmus, and in the Pacific between San Francisco and the Isthmus. Construction of steamship piers and a trans-Panama cart road began in the spring of 1847.

This route, they believed, could handle freight and passenger services between the East and West Coasts for another decade or so. Meanwhile, exhaustive surveys should be made to determine the best overland route. So the Senate denied Asa Whitney the challenge of building the Pacific Railway.

On August 19, 1848, the New York *Herald* reported the rumor of a gold strike somewhere in John Sutter's New Helvetia. The War and Interior Departments officially denied it. But on September 16, Lieutenant Edward F. Beale hurried up the War Department steps, carrying a trail-stained knapsack, and an hour or two later was whisked over to the White House through a side door.

The news spread across Capitol Hill during the next week. Lieutenant Beale's knapsack had contained gold nuggets brought across the continent in a record-breaking ride. The gold found in the millrace northeast of Sutter's Fort on January 24 had been picayune. But all through the spring and early summer, prospectors made a series of strikes in the creek valleys toward the Sierra. On July 4 John Bidwell, the patient fruit farmer of the Bartleson-Bidwell pioneer trip across Utah in 1841, started a gold rush of sailors and traders out of San Francisco and Monterey by uncovering a ridge of gold-studded gravel near the South Fork of the Feather River.

Thomas Hart Benton heard Lieutenant Beale's story, considered it, then reread all the notes he had taken during the hearings on the Whitney Plan. Whenever the White House announced the existence of a gold field in California it would be "devil take the hindmost." Then he could launch his 1850 election campaign with the proposal for a National Road—via Missouri, of course.

CHAPTER **5**

THE TREASURE ROADS

> *The scum of Polynesia, desperadoes from Australia,*
> *bullies and blackguards from the wild state of Mis-*
> *souri, Spanish cut-throats from the cities of the*
> *Pacific Coast, dissolute women and reckless adven-*
> *turers from the slums of Europe congregated in San*
> *Francisco, and there plied their several avocations*
> *and followed their devious courses in defiance of the*
> *prohibitions of a law which had lost its terrors for*
> *them, and in disregard of any other check save the*
> *revolver or bowie-knife. At that time, San Francisco*
> *was one-half a brothel, and one-half a gaming hell.*
> *. . . W. F. Rae, Westward by Rail: The New Route to*
> *the East (1871).*

President Polk confirmed the California gold strikes in his final
message to Congress on December 5, 1848. By February 1,
the first shiploads of gold-seekers were at the shantytown of
Aspinwall on the Isthmus of Panama, preparing for the twenty-four mile jungle trip over the Chagres River Trail to the
new docks at Panama City on the Pacific. That same week,
Thomas Hart Benton introduced his bill for federal financing
of a "Buffalo Trail" highway west from St. Louis to a pass in
the central Rockies and on "down a central valley" to Great
Salt Lake and the Bartleson-Bidwell route into California.

The Buffalo Trail should be built, he urged, as a year-round gravel road, with bridges across the rivers and a network of Army posts to provide protection against Indians. Tollgates, staffed by the Army, would collect fees from pack trains and wagons, just as the states obtained maintenance funds from traffic over the National Road. Within a decade or two, Benton believed, the Buffalo Trail's profits would enable constructon of a paralleling railroad. This trackage, too, would remain a Federal property, controlled by a commission of managers. The various railroads operating into St. Louis from the east, and into Sutter's Fort from the west, by 1860 or 1870 would pay tolls to the Buffalo Trail Railroad for each trans-Rockies trip by a freight or passenger train.

The bill merely reflamed Congress' arguments about the route. The South stood firm for an extension of the Santa Fe Trail through El Paso to Los Angeles. A contingent led by New York's Senator William H. Seward orated, again, for Asa Whitney's Chicago–South Pass route. Benton's backers organized a railroad convention at St. Louis in October, with Stephen A. Douglas as chairman. But, like the Senate hearings, it ended in an argument. The Buffalo Trail plan died in committee.

Benton lost the election for a sixth term in 1850, and passed from the United States' Senate scene. New champions for the Pacific Railway would not appear in Congress until the eve of the Civil War. In 1852, even Asa Whitney bowed to the South's inflexible bloc by offering to build the Pacific Railway via an all-slavery route from Memphis through Arkansas and Texas. His proposal was referred to the Committee on Roads and Canals—and tabled.

But while Congress dallied, the Argonauts of the 1849 Gold Rush gritted through the two overland treasure roads to California that would serve as tenuous links between the Union's Atlantic and Pacific coasts for exactly twenty years: the all-South Ox Bow Trail followed Gadsden's South and Pacific Railroad route through El Paso; the California Trail used

South Pass and the Bartleson-Bidwell route via the Humboldt. Charles Crocker helped pioneer the California Trail and gained experiences that would prove invaluable to the Central Pacific Railroad. But eager Collis P. Huntington took the Panama Isthmus route and sharpened his instinctive trader's sense for the future task of outwitting the United States Army and Navy and Thomas C. Durant while maintaining a flow of supplies to "Cholley" Crocker and 15,000 "coolie" heroes through the desperate last years of the Civil War.

Collis Huntington, at twenty-seven, was as keen in ferreting out a profitable "swap" as Senator Benton was in detecting New West destiny. The Oneonta general store provided a comfortable living, but the excitement about "gold for the picking up in California" convinced him that the picking up would be far simpler for a wholesale grocer. The California adventurers would want three massive meals a day. When they hit pay dirt their appetites would go "on up the hog"; whisky, sugar, smoked meats, spices and white flour should bring high prices. Collis stashed $2,000 in a money belt, hurried to New York, and engaged the largest stateroom available on the Pacific Mail's S. S. *Crescent City*. He filled it, ceiling high, with kegs of bourbon and French brandy, sacks of sugar and white flour, chests of spices and wholesaler tins of saleratus.

At Panama he swapped some of the whisky for a string of burros, freighted his grocer supplies over the Chagres Trail, and tripled his investment. Then, as he proudly recalled for H. H. Bancroft's researchers in 1890, "I went down to Estebula and bought a little schooner called the *Emma,* and filled her up with jerked beef, potatoes, rice, sugar and syrup . . . and brought them up to Panama and sold them." In all, he told, he crossed the Chagres Trail twenty times; "It was only twenty-four miles." Improvements in the road and Panama Mail's belated development of freight and passenger service between Aspinwall and Panama City convinced him that the heyday of "easy pickings" was over on the Isthmus. He shipped on to

San Francisco during the spring of 1850. This cabin, too, was jam-packed with groceries and "gimcrack" trade goods. He had already parlayed the gold eagles in his money belt to $5,000.

Indiana farm life palled on Charles Crocker three years after he moved west from Troy. He left Father Isaac's clearing in 1840 with, he recalled, "a pair of woolen socks, a cotton shirt and a linen dickey tied up in a cotton handkerchief," then wandered across Indiana from job to job for eight years—sawyer, wagonman and ironmonger. When the news about California gold was telegraphed down from Chicago, general-store talk buzzed into plans for a California Miners' Company.

Crocker, too, was twenty-seven years old when he and a brother joined the company. A canvas-topped, boat-bottomed "prairie schooner" required six to twelve oxen to lumber it up the river valleys and over the mountains and cost $5,000. Oxen averaged two miles an hour or, roughly, 1,000 hours of walking from the Missouri to Sacramento. Horses might make it in half that time. But horses gave out on the mighty tug through the Rockies; or died of thirst on the deserts. Moreover, veteran wagonmen and trappers told them, most of the Indian bucks out there were delighted at the prospect of stealing a horse. A good horse meant prestige and wealth and love-songs in the wickiups. Play it safe with oxen, the old men warned; and load up enough flour, saleratus and sweetening for a six months' walk.

From Quincy, Illinois, the Hoosiers rafted down the Mississippi to St. Louis. There they located a steamboat captain who promised to carry them as far as the Iowa village of Council Bluffs on the Upper Missouri. Thirty miles west of the Bluffs, following the two-year-old ruts of the Mormons, their wagon train reached the ridge of the Platte River Valley. Francis Parkman had described the scene in *The Oregon Trail:*

> For league after league, a plain as level as a lake was outspread beneath us; here and there the Platte, dividing into a

dozen thread-like sluices, was traversing it, and an occasional clump of wood, rising in the midst like a shadowy island, relieved the monotony of the waste. No living thing was moving throughout the vast landscape, except the lizards that darted over the sand and through the rank grass and prickly pears at our feet . . . Skulls and whitening bones of buffalo were scattered everywhere; the ground was tracked by myriads of them, and often covered with the circular indentations where the bulls had wallowed in the hot weather. From every gorge and ravine opening from the hills, descended deep, well worn paths, where the buffalo issue twice a day in regular procession to drink from the Platte.

Up four hundred miles of the Platte and North Platte valleys, the route came finally to Fort Laramie—if the skulking Pawnee or Sioux or Blackfeet hadn't caught you at dawn, with guards drowsing and wagons parked helter-skelter. Behind Fort Laramie the Rockies cut the midafternoon sun to a green dusk.

We passed between precipices, sharp and splintering at the top [Parkman had reported]. On our left they rose close to us like a wall, but on the right a winding brook with a narrow strip of marshy soil intervened. The stream was clogged with old beaver dams and spread frequently into wide pools. There were thick bushes and many dead and blasted trees along its course, though frequently nothing remained but stumps cut close to the ground by beaver, and marked with the sharp chisel-like teeth of those indefatigable laborers.

Toward South Pass the trail led up taffy-colored crevices and creek valleys to a desolate land where trees could not grow and the oxen, eyes blodshot and bulging, made retching noises each time they breathed. Charles Crocker's training as a blacksmith and handy man now made him invaluable to the train. Wooden axles snapped against rock; iron tires ground to wisps of rust; several times the wagons had to be windlassed up hundred-foot bluffs.

Beyond South Pass the Oregon Trail blurred north toward the Valley of the Snake, but the scuff marks and litter of the

Argonauts veered southwest across sagebrush, desert, and alkali-poisoned pools to Jim Bridger's trading post in the Green River Valley on the Wasatch Mountains' east slope. Another Mountain Man veteran, Bridger had directed the Mormons through the Wasatch red canyons to the valley of Great Salt Lake. Through the summer and fall of 1849 he guided California Trail wagon trains over the same route. Farther west, veterans of the Mormon Battalion charged $5 a day "and keep" to guide companies through the desert north of Great Salt Lake and over the Nevada passes to the Humboldt.

Crocker's wagon train teetered across the Sierra during April, 1850; that same month Collis Huntington landed in San Francisco. After a few futile "digs" in sand bars and gravel pits along the American River, the Crocker Brothers opened a hardware store at Sacramento City—the brawling trade center being developed by John Sutter's son a mile north of the Fort.

Before midsummer, 1850, more than 55,000 men, women, and children survived the overland trail crossings to California; another 25,000 arrived by sea. Totting up the census figures that winter, statisticians discovered that more than 1,500,000 whites and Negroes had migrated west of the Mississippi—about 8 per cent of the nation's total. Missouri, with 682,044 citizens, had almost as many residents as New Hampshire and Connecticut combined. Now there were 212,592 Texans, 209,897 Arkansans, 192,214 Iowans, 61,547 New Mexicans, 13,294 Oregonians and 6,077 Minnesotans. In brief, there were 55 per cent as many New Westerners as there were New Englanders. Oregon, despite the exhortations of Whitman and Benton, had won only a little more than 13,000 settlers in fourteen years; the zany stories about "free gold" drew 80,000 to California in one year.

Then add the trans-Allegheny populace. Illinois was now "the home place" for 851,470. There were 988,416 Hoosiers, 397,564 Michiganders, 1,980,329 Buckeyes. From Alabama's

771,623 and Mississippi's 606,526, north through Wisconsin's 305,391, more than 10,000,000 Americans lived west of the Alleghenies. The mother states of the Atlantic seaboard, including the giant throughway "funnel" of New York, now held only 57 per cent of the population.

These statistics, plus the Yankees' success in barring slavery in California, the popularity of the all-north California Trail, the railroads racing toward Chicago and St. Louis, worried the leaders of the Old South bloc in Congress. Their anxiety grew when the Legislature of the Mormons' Territory of Deseret presented an official "Memorial" to Congress. More than 5,000 immigrants had needlessly died from starvation, accident, and Indian attacks on the overland trails to California in 1849–50–51, the Mormons pointed out, then added: "There is no great obstacle to a railroad route from Salt Lake to San Diego. A national central railroad from the Mississippi or Missouri rivers to San Diego or San Francisco would [end the needless suffering and open the high plains to settlement] . . . On completion of the line the entire trade of China and the East Indies will pass through the United States."

That summer of 1852 the Democrats lured ex-Senator Franklin Pierce away from his New Hampshire law office and drilled him as a "compromise candidate." He beat Winfield Scott, 254 electoral votes to 42. The cabinet imposed on him in 1853 was a hopeless compromise too. William L. Marcy, former governor of New York, became Secretary of State. Jefferson Davis, a Mississippian by adoption, went in as Secretary of War. Marcy and Davis were devoted enemies.

Davis soon became the mouthpiece for a plan to win the New West's trade and allegiance for the South via the Gadsden-Calhoun vision of a South & Pacific Railroad. The Treaty of Guadalupe Hidalgo gave only vague descriptions of the permanent boundary between the Republic of Mexico and New Mexico Territory. Furthermore, army surveys indicated that the best route for the South & Pacific Railroad veered up the Rio Grande Valley from El Paso, then cut west through the desert to the Gila River Valley. Who, Davis suggested, would be a better ambassador than James Gadsden to negotiate permanent boundaries with Mexico and obtain the Upper Rio Grande and Gila Valleys for the United States? The matter was brought to President Pierce's attention with testimony of its "dire importance to national defense." The President agreed.

On December 30, 1853, James Gadsden and President Santa Anna of Mexico signed a treaty for the United States' purchase of 45,535 square miles of land south of the Gila River and east to El Paso del Norte. Thus, to the future delight of battalions of Western novelists and movie scriptmen, the strongholds of the Apache, the pueblo of Tucson, the sites of Tombstone, the O.K. Corral and the Lincoln County War all became part of the United States at a cost of $10,000,000.

The Gadsden Purchase, Secretary Davis reasoned, assured the future. What the South & Pacific route now needed was a demonstration to convince California immigrants of its superiority over the California-Mormon Trail. A United States Army Camel corps, he recommended to the House and Senate Committees on Appropriations, would provide splendid transportation for "troops moving rapidly across the country." A camel corps could patrol the New Mexico and California Deserts effortlessly, rescue immigrants stranded there, and follow Apache and Navaho raiders into the most desolate hideaways. Moreover, the grotesque beasts might frighten the Indians as thoroughly as Cortez' horses had terrified Montezuma and his subjects.

Congress voted to take the idea "under advisement." First, steps must be taken to placate California on this matter of a Pacific railroad. A delegation had just presented an angry petition signed by leading California businessmen. The route from San Francisco to the East Coast via Cape Horn, the petition said, was longer than the entire circumference of earth at San Francisco's latitude of 38 degrees; the route via Panama was as long as the trip from Chesapeake Bay to Hong Kong.

Canada was building a railroad that would run west from Halifax for 1,600 miles. "Shall we who have beaten them in clipper ships, swift steamers, and other useful notions," the petition challenged, "yield to them the plan of building the longest railroad on the American continent? Never!"

The Secretary of War, Congress ordered, would immediately take steps to survey the likeliest railroad routes between the Mississippi River and the Pacific and prepare reports on their respective merits. Davis purred; the surveys would undoubtedly prove the superiorities of the South & Pacific route. Five expeditions left for the West that fall. They were led by promising young officers and enginers including Lieutenant John B. McClellan, Lieutenant John Pope, and Frederick Lander, the Massachusetts engineer who eight summers before had persuaded his mother's farmhand, Grenville Dodge, to enroll at Norwich University.

Government surveys were one thing. Action was something else. By 1853, the gold rush brought 200,000 adventurers to California. The sand bars and gravel pits between Sacramento and the Sierra Nevada yielded $50,000,000 in gold each year. But the entire economy depended on mule teams, stages and steamboats. California needed railroads. In January, 1854, C. L. Wilson of Sacramento requested an appointment with New York's new governor, Horatio Seymour. His organization, he explained, planned to build a railroad between Sacramento and the gold fields. No engineer then in California had experience in this type of construction. In view of New York's network of rails, plus the splendid comments he heard about the governor's brother, would Governor Seymour help him locate a competent youngster who might be interested in building the first railroad on the Pacific Coast?

Governor Seymour suggested a luncheon meeting with brother Silas. Selection of a young man devoted to Northern interests could prove most useful, he observed. Silas knew of just such a young man. His name was Theodore Dehone Judah. Although he was still under thirty, he had shown amazing skill as a location engineer on both the Niagara Gorge and Erie lines. A telegram went off to Buffalo, asking Judah to come downstate at once for conference.

A week later Anna Judah stared speechless at another telegram. It read: BE HOME TONIGHT. WE SAIL FOR CALIFORNIA APRIL 2. LOVE. TED.

The Challengers

These machines are but just being brought into use; and he is a bold man who, casting his eye 100 years into the future, shall undertake to tell the present generation what will be their effect on our North American valley, when their energies shall be brought to bear over all its broad surface. . . .

—Jessup W. Scott in the Toledo, Ohio, *Blade* (1850)

CHAPTER 6

CHICAGO'S REACH

> *The train calls at stations in the woods, where the wild impossibility of anybody having the smallest reason to get out is only to be equalled by the apparently desperate hopelessness of there being anybody to get in. It rushes across the turnpike road, where there is no gate, no policeman, no signal; nothing but a rough wooden arch, on which is painted "WHEN THE BELL RINGS, LOOK OUT FOR THE LOCOMOTIVE." On it whirls headlong, dives through the woods again, emerges in the light, clatters over frail arches, rumbles upon the heavy ground, shoots beneath a wooden bridge—dashes on haphazard, pell-mell, neck-or-nothing. . . .* Charles Dickens, *American Notes* (1842).

"Chicago on the beam," a deck hand bellowed one summer afternoon in 1851. Grenville Dodge hurried to the railing for a first look. South, a ridge of sand hills blended enticingly with the bright blue sheen of Lake Michigan. Dodge felt a twinge of homesickness for the sand beaches and piney headlands around Salem. The nostalgia deepened as his eyes moved north across a gloomy bog to the cluster of unpainted grain elevators and hound-yellow brick warehouses dead ahead.

The Indians called the spot *Eschikagou*. The translation varied with the mood of the translator. The word could mean

Place of the Chief. It could also mean, avowed linguists, Smells-like-a-skunk or Wild Onions. All three definitions were appropriate. Strategically, the murky inlet at the bog's center was the best throughway between the Great Lakes and the Mississippi. Exalted by the title of Chicago River, it oozed southwest toward a clay ridge that marked the westernmost rush of Lake Michigan's storm waves. An Indian portage trail crossed the ridge to the Illinois River; the Illinois roiled almost due west for 50 miles, then veered southwest to join the Mississippi 15 miles above its Missouri River junction.

Chicago was a stepchild of the Erie Canal. As Secretary of War in 1819, John C. Calhoun had urged construction of a Lake Michigan–Illinois river canal as an "urgency of the national defense." The canal company was incorporated in 1829 when only 25 or 30 families lived on the miasmic claybank alongside Fort Dearborn. Four years later Congress granted $30,000 to dredge a sloop channel up the Chicago River. The village attracted speculators who began to ballyhoo it as "the Garden City." In 1836, when there were 3,820 residents, construction started on the Chicago River–Illinois River Canal.

Muck and sand tossed up from the dredging enabled bog fill for new homesites. Engineers recommended that the swamp be filled in with rock and soil to a level of at least 6 feet above Lake Michigan's spring-freshet tides. The prospect of hauling fill 4 or 5 miles by oxcart brought grunts and headshakes from most settlers; the town was too much of a gamble for all that work. Milwaukee, 100 miles up the lake, was a "boomer" too; so were half a dozen other communities on the Indiana and Wisconsin shores. Any of them might start a settlers' rush that would spell "bust" for Chicago real estate. The boardwalks that began to hammer out from South Water Street and North Water Street in the 1840s had to arc like chute-the-chutes: up to a store built on a 6-foot fill; down to a cabin (with front-room grocery) built on a 2-foot fill; back up to a false-front harness shop built on a 4-foot fill.

The whole crazy patch might have been abandoned to the skunks and wild onions during the Van Buren depression of 1837–40, if the prairie plow hadn't come to the rescue. Intensive crop farming was impossible in Illinois and much of Wisconsin and Iowa until John Deere and other frontier blacksmiths developed plows with sheet-steel faces. The early ones were usually made from old saw blades, heat-molded to a wood or cast-iron base. These enabled the first crops of corn and wheat. In 1839, sloops at the Chicago piers loaded 4,000 bushels for Detroit and Buffalo, plus 3,000 grain-fat cattle driven in from prairie farms. In 1842, almost 600,000 bushels of wheat hissed into ship bottoms from raw-wood bins along Water Street. The population, now under city charter, passed 6,500. The first markethouse went up at Lake and State Streets. The Illinois–Michigan ditch was halfway through the ridge toward Joliet. Wheat, corn and cattle fixed Chicago's destiny. Plank roads were built south and west over the Indian portage trails, north toward Milwaukee, northwest to the Rock River–Mississippi junction at Rock Island.

In 1846, Chicago's first mayor, William B. Ogden, resurrected the decade-old plan for a Chicago and Galena railroad. Ten miles of track into Chicago were ready for grain shipments during the fall of 1848; the line averaged a gross revenue of $2,000 a month during its first year. Ogden raised funds to build on west toward Elgin. At Aurora, 38 miles out on the prairie, businessmen organized the Aurora branch to build a 12-mile spur to the Galena & Chicago Union's line. By the fall of 1850, the two roads operated three locomotives: the Pioneer, 10 tons; the Whittlesey, a 12-tonner with four drivers, built by Norris and Brothers of Philadelphia; and the Pigeon, a 14-tonner built by Josiah Baldwin in 1837 for the Detroit & Pontiac.

Grenville Dodge, conditioned to Boston and the North Shore, plus the bumptious four years at Norwich University, must have reacted to Chicago that afternoon of 1851 much as young William Corkran would in 1868 when he arrived from New York City to begin his duties as librarian of the Chicago Historical Society:

> The city of Chicago [Corkran wrote] was laid out in three great divisions or sides. These were the North Side, South Side and West Side, so-called from their being divided by the Chicago River, a dirty narrow stream emitting an effluvium that would have puzzled any scientist to analyze. We were assured however that this vast sink of black greasy waters was not unhealthy and that we would soon become so accustomed to it as not to mind it at all.
>
> To a new arrival, a walk through the streets of Chicago was anything but agreeable. So long as he kept in the great thorough-fares it was well enough, but if it was necessary to go through any of the side streets, then began a system of clambering up or down six or seven steep little steps, or running down a plank or up another. This system was called grading or leveling, or in other words, when you stood below, you stood just two feet above the original level of Chicago, but when above, the proper level of six feet.
>
> The main thoroughfares such as North and South Clark Street, which was the vertebra of Chicago running from one end to the other of the city, and changing name as it was separated by the river, was a broad street whose wooden pavement, when not broken, was pleasant to drive upon . . . The stores on either side of the street were mostly low wooden houses whose fronts were anything but prepossessing, whilst their rears were utterly misera-ble. This street was the great center for lager-beer saloons, Turner Halls, concert rooms, small groceries, drug stores, and numerous other stores, kept mostly by Germans, of which Jews predomi-nated. It was a thorough Western street in every sense of the words, for here were found numerous small dealers in every branch of trade, running a business on small capital, sleeping and living in the rear of their stores, whilst the upper floor was rented to boarders and lodgers, and as prices were generally as high as in the first stores of the city, it is no wonder that a great num-ber of these people succeeded soon in buying up a house and lot of their own, and becoming property owners."

Chicago, under a coppery midsummer sky in 1851, was smaller, smellier and dirtier—with more hogs, cows, geese and chickens wallowing in the streets.

Stephen A. Douglas, five years wiser than he had been in the harangue with Asa Whitney, had recently secured a land grant of 2,200,000 acres from Congress for construction of an Illinois Central Railroad that would cross the 440 miles of prairie and coal-rich hillocks between Galena and the Ohio-Mississippi junction at Cairo. (Thomas Benton voted "aye" on the bill because it would open all of Illinois to St. Louis merchants. Henry Clay voted for it because it bode new outlets for Kentucky tobacco, whisky, sorghum and hardwood. The Southerners didn't pay it much mind; it was intrastate and evinced no ambitions of snooping across the Mississippi.)

State and Federal legislation specified that the Illinois Central was to build its high iron as its name implied, down the center of Illinois. But Stephen A. Douglas had become a resident of Chicago and an enthusiast about its future. He persuaded Illinois Central's directors to approve a branch line from the Illinois River crossing at La Salle into Chicago.

Meanwhile, Chicago's City Council debated tax assessments to finance construction of a stone breakwater south across the bog from the Chicago River, thus enabling more muckland to be filled in as lakefront properties. During the spring of 1851, the council offered Illinois Central a right of way up the lakeshore to a South Water Street terminal, if it would also build the stone breakwater and haul in clay and black prairie earth for bog fill. Illinois Central's directors accepted; their engineers and bogtrotters created the land that, under the title of "Michigan Boulevard," would rank with New York City's Grand Central Terminal area as the most valuable real estate in North America.

To Grenville Dodge and other young engineers debarking at Chicago that summer, the breakwater project and the vision of a railroad operating 440 miles across the Prairie State were symbolic of opportunities in the New West. The prairie was a railroader's dreamland; gradients to Rock Island, to Quincy and even to remote Council Bluffs would be almost as simple as Illinois Central's clang to Cairo. Dodge stared down the wharf at a family of Germans squatting patiently atop their baggage. Beyond them, six flaxen-haired Swedes pushed their cartload of trunks and boxes toward the canalboat that would float them through the new Summit Lock and down the Illinois to a Mississippi steamer connection for St. Paul. Thousands of Germans, Swedes, Hollanders and Finlanders trekked West each year now. Many were refugees from that savage 1848 Revolution against Germany's Junkers; others were lured by descriptions of the land being offered for $1 an acre in Wisconsin and Minnesota Territory. The Finlanders, like the Cornish and Welsh, sought the $30-a-month jobs and homesteader privileges promised by the lead-mine, coal-pit and rock-quarry operators in the upper Mississippi Valley. This was a type of gold rush as positive and passionate as the Forty-Niners' roar toward California. And, as any twenty-year-old engineer could sense, it was more durable than California's. The "gold" sought here was the good earth and an opportunity to wrest a living plus 5 per cent from it, in fee simple, without quitrents or military conscription.

Lumber, cheese, butter, beef, pork, leather and grains would flood out of this Midwest when these North Europeans began to apply their historic land skills. Then they would be a market for plows, reapers, barn tools, seed, twine, wagons, cloth and such ready-mades as their frugality permitted. Neither steamboats nor the Erie Canal would be able to handle such vast two-way traffic; the railroad would be—must be—the lifeline of the New West.

These were the urgencies that had drawn Grenville Dodge to Illinois two months after his graduation from Norwich. His engineering instructors there, Dodge would recall in his autobiographies, were "filled with enthusiasm for steam transportation and expansion of railroads from the Atlantic to the Pacific." During the fall of his senior year Dodge wrote in his diary: "Forty-three years ago today, October 12, 1807, Fulton made his first steamboat trip up the Hudson River. How wonderful has been the effect of his discovery. In the short space

of forty-three years steam power has revolutionized the world."
The predestiny of motherly interest by the widow of Colonel
Trueman B. Ransom sent Grenville Dodge to Illinois, just as
the interest of the Widow Lander had stimulated him toward
Civil Engineering. Colonel Ransom had initiated the Civil Engineering course while president of Norwich University, but
led the school's Cadet Brigade off to the War with Mexico and
was killed in the assault on Chapultepec. The era of Federal
pensions was a generation away; his widow began to take in university students as boarders. Grenville Dodge boarded at Mrs.
Ransom's during his junior and senior years. She urged him
to join her sons on the land survey being directed by her
brother George W. Gilson at Peru, Illinois. Gilson, a State
Senator and land agent, was developing home and factory sites
for the "boom" bound to occur in the Illinois River's midvalley
when the Illinois Central Railroad pushed through. He predicted that Peru, with its sister community La Salle, would
soon surpass Chicago in population.

Grenville Dodge took a canal packet from Chicago to La
Salle, witnessed his first gun fight, and reported for duty at
Senator Gilson's office. A few weeks later he wrote his father:
"I can double any money you've got within six months. To
start with, buy up a couple of Mexican land warrants, send
them out and I'll locate them in places where land is selling at
this minute for $2.50 an acre. The warrants are for a quarter-
section each and can be bought back east for about a dollar.
Now this is no gun-game, but the truth. They will pay better
than all the post-offices and book stores in the kingdom." But
by snowfall he was applying to the Illinois Central for assignment to a survey crew.

Thomas C. Durant promoted stock sales in New York City
to launch the Michigan Southern Railroad's race toward Chicago. John B. Jervis signed on as chief engineer. Henry Farnam and Joseph Sheffield shipped to Chicago during the spring
of 1850, leased a carriage, and explored the swamps, creek

channels and sand hills of Lake Michigan's South Shore before bidding for the contract to build the 200-mile extension to a Chicago River terminal.

The Michigan Central Railroad operated between Detroit, Ann Arbor and Jackson. When Michigan Southern announced award of its contract to Farnam and Sheffield, the Boston bankers backing Michigan Central decided to extend its trackage to Chicago too. (Robert Casement's son Jack went with the Michigan Central as a trackhand shortly after the family moved from Geneva, New York, to a farm near Ann Arbor, Michigan. But the line's decision to build on to Chicago came too late for Jack Casement to participate in the race. In the spring of 1850 he went to Cleveland as the twenty-one-year-old foreman of a track gang on the Cleveland, Columbus & Cincinnati Railroad.)

Samuel B. Reed, the young Vermonter who had worked as a location engineer on the Erie Canal's deeper channel through the Montezuma Swamp, was one of the first location engineers hired for Michigan Southern by Jervis. The line, having pacified the Indiana Legislature by adding "& Northern Indiana" to its title, hammered track to the Illinois state border in the late fall of 1851, then when the Calumet swamp froze up, built willy-nilly on by laying ties and track on the ice and frozen muck. On February 20, 1852, Michigan Southern's first passenger train into Chicago tied down the whistle while it chuffed up Clark Street. The Michigan Central wailed into town a few weeks later.

Farnam and Sheffield, like the contractors for Michigan Central, regarded Chicago as a steppingstone toward the Mississippi and Missouri river valleys. It was good sense to "be at the gate with the wagon hitched" whenever Congress compromised the slavery and States'-rights snarl and made the essential $50,000,000 to $100,000,000 appropriation for a Pacific railway. Meanwhile the prairie farms guaranteed a brisk freight and passenger business; enough, anyway, to pay stock dividends. Also, land inflation along the rail lines was proving a rich bonus. Durant, Farnam and Sheffield bought the charter for a La Salle–Rock Island rail route. Michigan Central made a stock swap with The Aurora Branch. Consequently the La Salle & Rock Island became the Chicago & Rock Island, while The Aurora Branch merged with other charter dreams into the Chicago, Burlington & Quincy. John Jervis became the chief engineer for the Chicago & Rock Island, with Samuel B. Reed as one of his location engineers; Farnam and Sheffield assumed the contract for construction to the Mississippi-Rock River junction.

During 1852, then, Chicago—the lake and canal terminal—became Chicago—the railroad center. During the next five years another dozen railroads entered its roller-coaster bog from Cleveland, Pittsburgh, St. Louis and Milwaukee.

Grenville Dodge's offer from the Illinois Central came in January, 1852. He worked on a survey for a month or two, resigned, and went back with Gilson's house-lot crew. "A dispatch was received here," he wrote in explanation to his father, "with the important intelligence that the Rock Island Railroad, 200 miles long, and separate from the Illinois Central is to be built . . . We will have direct communication by the Rock Island with Iowa and the far west; for this is the true Pacific Road and will be built to Council Bluffs."

He guessed correctly. Farnam, Sheffield and Durant made plans early in 1852 for a gradient survey across Iowa to Council Bluffs. Again there was a six months' wait for Engineer Dodge until the call came from Peter A. Dey, the chief surveyor hired by Farnam, Sheffield and Durant. Dey recalled the incident nearly forty years later: "Dodge made application to me and I took him into one of my parties. That was in the fall of 1852. Very soon I discovered that there was a good deal in him. I discovered a wonderful energy: for instance, if I told him to do anything he did it under any and all circumstances. That feature was particularly marked. In the spring of 1853, I made a survey of what was called the Bureau Valley

& Peoria, and I gave Dodge the use of one instrument. He then developed a great deal of energy and so enhanced my opinion of him that in May, 1853, when I came out to Iowa City to make serveys from Davenport west, I took him with me."

When Chicago mushroomed as the terminal for the rail gambles out of Detroit, Buffalo and Pittsburgh, three new villages on the Missouri River became potential terminals for a Pacific railway over the California-Mormon Trail. In Iowa, Council Bluffs was the sole candidate. St. Joseph clung on the Missouri's east bank bluffs 150 miles south. West, the Kansas plains tilted gently up the 500-mile hill to the Continental Divide. Justice John Clemens and his Hannibal neighbors had visualized this portal route when they drew up a charter for the Hannibal & St. Joseph Railroad Company in 1847. But Justice Clemens died a few months later; the charter was still tucked in a lawyer's strongbox. Another 50 miles south, where the Missouri curved its mud southeast to the Ozark foothills, the hamlet of West Port sat on the cliffs. It also offered access to the Santa Fe Trail, via Independence, Kansas Territory. Council Bluffs and St. Joseph became the terminal goals for railroads keening west out of Chicago, with tiny West Port as a third choice.

The Michigan Central's backers, by developing the Chicago, Burlington & Quincy, were building toward all three of these Missouri River terminals. The Chicago & Quincy branch, arching southwest beyond Aurora, reached the Mississippi's shore only 20 miles north of Hannibal; a train ferry and spur track down the west shore would connect with the Hannibal & St. Joseph route. The Chicago & Burlington branch, veering through Galesburg, reached the Mississippi's shore opposite Burlington, Iowa. Burlington's businessmen were as ambitious as Hannibal's. In 1851, they built a plank road 28 miles over the bluffs to Mt. Pleasant, and resolved during the celebration ceremonies that "while we regard our plank roads as emphatically the farmer's highway to market and prosperity, yet we ardently look for the time when the Mississippi shall be connected with the Missouri by railway, thus facilitating communication between remote points and constituting a part of the railroad to the Pacific Ocean through Southern Iowa."

During the months that Farnam, Sheffield and Durant reached the decision to jockey with the Iowa legislators and peddle bonds for a Rock Island extension toward Council Bluffs via Davenport, Iowa City, and Fort Des Moines, the Michigan Central—Chicago, Burlington & Quincy strategists maneuvered incorporation of a Burlington & Missouri Railroad and began negotiations with the charter owners of the Hannibal & St. Joseph.

The Rock Island incorporated in Iowa as the Mississippi & Missouri Railroad, then allied with a chartered, but unbuilt, Davenport & Iowa City Railroad Company. Farnam, Sheffield and Durant pledged to lay trackage between Davenport and Iowa City before 1855. Other trans-Iowa competition developed. Promoters bought the decade-old charter for a Lyons & Iowa Central line, reorganized it as the Iowa Air Line, and announced plans to run surveys on to Council Bluffs. Grenville Dodge and Peter Dey reached Iowa City in May, 1853. Dodge learned that the race with Iowa Air Line across the prairie would have an element of intramural rivalry; the chief surveyor for Iowa Air Line was a Norwich University alumnus too. Dodge wrote his father:

> Yesterday I started my line west of Iowa City and tomorrow I leave for good. Today I bought a saddle horse for $125.00. I have one wagon for camp chest and provisions and one for stocks and baggage. We have in all, six horses and fourteen men, including the cook and hunter. The season is late and we cannot look ahead without seeing hardships and exposures never experienced by any of us. The snows on the Missouri are unusually severe, nor can we expect to arrive before they come on. There is also a probability, after arriving at Fort Des Moines, of our locating several hundred miles in order to keep ahead of the so-called Lyons Road which is nearly parallel with ours west of Iowa City. The projectors have no money but they are pushing lines through the state and making a cry to get the counties to

take stock. We have moneyed men to back us. My expenses reach $1,000 a month. Oh, that you could come out and overtake me on the prairies of Iowa and take a week's trip with us, look at the country and see how we live. We shall make an examination of the great Platte as far into Nebraska as we think fit.

Dey now had complete confidence in his tall and scowlingly serious Yankee assistant. He stayed in Iowa City for the word battles with legislative committees, while Dodge wigwagged transit sightings and drove flagged stakes toward the crest of the ridge that divides the Cedar and Des Moines river valleys. On this summit, near the end of September, Dodge ordered a tall flagpole to be erected. A year later he suggested to the consumptive New York preacher, J. B. Grinnell, that the summit would be ideal for the farm colony and agricultural institute that Grinnell wanted to locate in the Iowa wilderness. This survey flagpole became the site of Grinnell College.

Sumac shrilled fall's approach with scarlet leaves when the crew's wagons crunched down the Des Moines River bank. Dodge paused long enough to lay out a forty-acre site for a station, roundhouse and wagon park, then ordered his chainmen to route due west; word came through from Peter Dey that they were running a week ahead of the Iowa Air Line crews. In the Raccoon River country, with hoarfrost on the buffalo grass and the oaks massive flames of gold, some of the crew came down with "the chills." Dodge arranged bed and keep for them at cabin homes, then scouted the valley to hire substitute axmen and drivers. One youngster he signed on was "a strong axman, well up in all woodcraft and a bee hunter. He could follow a bee to its hive in a tree, so he kept us in honey all the way to Missouri."

Peter Dey rode in one November afternoon. The Mississippi & Missouri was holding its lead over the Air Line. "Let's keep it that way. Don't take time to revise the line now. Just beat them into the Bluffs." They did. On November 22, Dey and Dodge took alternate whacks at the stakes on the Missouri's brown bank. The townspeople cheered and led the way to the nearest tavern. The Iowa Air Line crew reached town a week later. Everybody shook hands, and there was another rousing party. A Burlington & Missouri team, it was reported, was working north up the flats, somewhere across from the Platte's mouth.

Back across Iowa, Henry Farnam began work on the great wood and stone bridge scheduled to straddle the Mississippi via Rock Island. Antoine Le Claire, a half-breed of the Sac-Foxes, stopped grumbling about the plat line for it that Grenville Dodge and Peter Dey had run through his Rock Island apple orchard. In 1855, Ralph Waldo Emerson would report, after an Iowa lecture tour, "Le Claire chose his lot 30 years ago, and now the railroad to the Pacific runs directly through his log house, which is occupied by the company for wood and other purposes. His property has risen to the value of five or six hundred thousand dollars."

In Chicago, when ice closed the Mackinac Strait to steamboats again, the lobbyists and bond salesmen for the Chicago, Burlington & Quincy and the Chicago & Rock Island could all smile. The Rock Island was surveyed through to the Missouri Valley; its Pacific wagon was hitched. Chicago, Burlington & Quincy had quietly arranged ownership for more than half of the Hannibal & St. Joseph Railroad's stock among "friends," and planned to start trans-Missouri construction in 1856. The North's railroads, at long last, were invading the New West.

In Washington, Secretary of War Davis studied the packets of charts couriered back by the Pacific Road Survey and Exploration teams.

CHAPTER 7

EL PASO OR SALT LAKE?

Neither current events nor history show that the majority rules, or ever did. . . . Jefferson Davis (1864).

The wagon trains sent out in 1853 to explore the five possible routes for a Pacific Railway carried surveyor instruments, geologist's tools and artist supplies. The first field notes reached Washington during the fall of 1854, followed by oilcloth packets of topographic estimates and on-the-scene paintings and sketches.

One school of historians maintains that Secretary of War Jefferson Davis researched this material with "great integrity" and "complete honesty." Another school, viewing the outcome as a Civil War prelude, concludes that, "The decision was rigged." In any case, the Secretary's decision was that the all-South Oxbow, running from the Red River Valley via El Paso and the Gadsden Purchase lands, was only 1,618 miles long and would cost $35,000,000 less than any other route.

The Northern Pacific Trail, based on the Lewis and Clark route plus Thomas Hart Benton's original plan for a Missouri–Columbia Canal, was given an official cost estimate of $130,781,000. (The field notes estimated $117,121,000, but the War Department discovered another $13,660,000 of "unavoidable" expense.)

The Benton-Frémont Buffalo Trail took 2,080 miles to cross from West Port to San Francisco, the survey concluded; Secretary Davis dismissed it because of "impracticable" costs and terrain.

The 35th Parallel route crossed the Raton Pass into Santa Fe, then followed the Spanish trails used by the Army of the West in 1846. But the 1853-4 survey, as published, alleged it to be 1,892 miles long and gave it the highest cost estimate of all—$169,210,255.

The California-Mormon Trail, according to the War Department, snaked 2,032 miles from Council Bluffs to San Francisco; a railroad over it would cost a minimum of $116,-095,000. Moreover, the report gloomed, the route was impassable six or seven months of the year because of snowdrifts, the fierce "northers" and springtime floods.

But the Oxbow felt only occasional snows, was 414 miles shorter; the South & Pacific Railway could be built for less than $70,000,000, or only $5,000,000 more than Asa Whitney's initial estimate for the Chicago–Oregon Railway.

The War Department published its reports in twelve volumes titled *Exploration and Surveys, RailRoad Route Mississippi River to the Pacific Ocean.* "The Government expended hundreds of thousands of dollars in explorations," Ted Judah's friend, John C. Burch, would write about them a few years later, "and elaborate reports thereof had been made and published in immense volumes, containing beautiful and expensive engravings showing the most picturesque and wonderful scenery in the world on the route of the exploration . . . yet all of this did not demonstrate the practicability of a route, nor show the surveys, elevations, profiles, grades or estimates of the cost of constructing the road over the route finally adopted."

The volumes were still being edited when Secretary Davis persuaded a $30,000 appropriation through Congress for development of the United States Army Camel Corps. Edward Fitzgerald Beale, the Navy officer who had made the spectacular transcontinental ride with New Helvetia gold, and was currently superintendent of Indian Affairs for California and Nevada, was appointed commander of the procurement expedition to Africa. Beale's ship, the Army transport *Supply*, reached Tunis in the fall of 1855, received a gift of two Bactrian camels from the Bey, and coasted on to Balaklava. There British quartermasters related their experiences with these animals during the Crimean War and convinced Beale and his associates that a United States Camel Corps would be ideal for operations against the Apache, Navajo and Comanche along the Oxbow.

The *Supply* returned to Indianola, Texas, in the spring of 1856 with a cargo of 38 adult and 2 baby camels. Commander Beale established a training camp at Green Valley near San Antonio and began a series of field tests. Thus, that year the hopes of the South & Pacific Railway's promoters reached their highest tide. The theory of "squatter sovereignty" propounded by Stephen A. Douglas' Kansas-Nebraska Compromise had exploded into guerilla raids throughout the Missouri-Kansas frontier. If the fighting spread north into new Nebraska Territory, Council Bluffs would be blocked just as effectively as West Port and St. Joseph for terminals of any Pacific railway approved by Congress. And now the Camel Corps was readying a new form of traveler security for the Oxbow.

In the early summer of 1856, the future seemed bright for the South & Pacific Railway. Secretary Davis began campaigning for his former post as United States Senator from Mississippi. The Democrats had nominated James Buchanan of Pennsylvania as their Presidential candidate; he had proven such a bumptious reactionary, in Congress and as ambassador to Russia and Great Britain, that he should be easy to maneuver. Governor John B. Floyd of Virginia wanted to be Secretary of War if the Democrats could defeat that radical, new

Republican party and its "Pathfinder" candidate, John C. Frémont.

Grenville Dodge's urgency to finish the Mississippi & Missouri survey into Council Bluffs was not solely due to his loyalty to Farnam, Sheffield and Durant; or even for the pleasure of beating the Iowa Air Line transit men. At Peru, Illinois, during 1853, he had fallen in love with Anne Brown. The couple announced their engagement before the survey race began out of Iowa City; Miss Brown went to Danvers that fall to meet the rest of the Dodge family and spend the winter as Sylvanus' assistant at the bookstore post office.

Since 1852, wagons had straggled into Council Bluffs in anticipation of agreement between Federal commissioners and the Omaha Indians on the treaty that would enable the great prairie trough of the Platte Valley to become the Territory of Nebraska. During December, 1853, Dodge and Dey joined the hundreds of men searching for future homesites along the Missouri's west bank. They rode due west twenty miles behind the traders' post of Omaha to Elkhorn Creek. Here the north-south ridges formed by glaciers and prehistoric flood channels gave way to the east-west sweep of the Platte Valley. The Elkhorn rippled down from the northwest through groves of hickory, beech and cottonwood. Congress was giving assurance that Nebraska Territory would be created during 1854; Dodge decided to build his cabin on the Elkhorn, and asked Dey for a leave of absence to return to Danvers.

Anne and Grenville were married in Danvers on May 28, 1854, two days before Congress opened Nebraska for homesteading. They spent the summer tenting beside the Elkhorn and finished their cabin before fall. In the spring of 1855, Sylvanus, and Grenville's brother Nathan located an adjoining claim, built a second cabin, and began bull-plowing bottom land.

That summer, too, William Farnam and Thomas Durant buggied across Iowa, arguing with bankers and local politicians about the urgency for organizing Pacific Railway rallies in each community. The speeches at these affairs always preceded the barbecue; politicians had demonstrated for a century that the tantalizing odor of roasting ox held crowds through two-hour speeches. There was enthusiasm enough for the Mississippi & Missouri's extension from Fort Des Moines to Council Bluffs. But it came from farmers, peddlers and crossroads merchants who could afford only a few shares of stock. The bankers and legislators, like the New York and Boston stockholders, muttered pre-election fears: Times are bad; the Kansas war may set the whole Missouri Valley ablaze; Des Moines is far enough; Wait and see what the next Congress will do.

Dey stubbornly kept Dodge on the pay roll, allotting him $1,500 a year to explore potential gradients through Omaha to the Platte Valley and west toward South Pass. Thus it was that Dodge, taking sights far up the Platte one summer afternoon in 1855, saw two brown specks on the plain. They loomed into white men astride gaunt ponies. He held his rifle at the cock and jogged toward them. A hundred yards away, one of the strangers threw his arms above his head, shouted, and spurred his pony. Dodge howled back. The horses slid together in a cloud of dust, and the riders embraced.

Fred Lander and an assistant were returning from the War Department's survey of the North Pacific route to Puget Sound. They had started West with a seven-man expedition. The other five had died in accidents and Indian fights and from mountain fever. The Pacific Railway dominated the conversations around the Dodges' fireplace during the next two weeks. "It's bound to come right through this valley," Lander prophesied.

Most of Lander's report to Washington had been routed by Panama Isthmus mail from Oregon. But, he decided, he would go on to Washington and attempt an audience with Mr. Davis. News of the Oxbow route estimates had been gossiped back to the frontier forts. Officers who knew Fitzpatrick, Carson, Bridger and other veterans of the South Pass and Wasatch Crossings snorted disagreement. A Pacific railroad, they said, might cost more than $100,000,000 by any route. But the California-Mormon Trail would assuredly not cost more than the Oxbow and would be easier to build. Fred Lander rode on to Washington and urged another survey of the California-Mormon Trail. It netted him a frosty "Thank you."

The ancient feud between the Omaha and Sioux Indians resumed with a series of murders during the fall and winter of 1855. Friends in both tribes came to the Dodge cabins and urged them to move into Council Bluffs before "big war come" in the spring. Anne leased a house in Council Bluffs and settled in while the three men sledged crops and furniture across the Missouri ridge. Grenville spent the spring of 1856 helping Durant and Farnam organize another series of Pacific Railway rallies at Council Bluffs, Omaha and Florence.

It was Durant, historians agree, who slyly introduced the element of "civic pride" into the system of stock sales for the Mississippi & Missouri and its extension to the Pacific Ocean. Florence, Nebraska, was six miles down-river from Omaha and closer to the Platte Valley. Some of the Mississippi & Missouri stockholders at Davenport and Iowa City favored Florence as the Nebraska terminal of the line. Farnam, "the bluff engineer," made a better impression on frontier audiences than Durant, "the New York slicker." Durant coached Farnam in the "pitch" to be made to each community. If Council Bluffs would subscribe for $300,000 in bonds, grading would begin at once toward the line's end-of-track at Fort Des Moines. If Florence bettered the bid, grading would start from the Iowa River bluff opposite that town.

During the conferences at Florence, Dodge and Farnam visited with the Cornish, Welsh, Manx and English Midland families gathering for a summer migration to the "Promised Land" in the Great Salt Lake Valley. Partly because of disquieting rumors ebbing out of Washington, these converts to the Book of Mormon would attempt the trip over the Rockies without wagon trains. They were building two-wheel handcarts to hold their luggage and foodstuffs. As they whittled spokes

for the handcarts' wheels and forged bar iron into tires they
sang the rollicking song they had just composed:

> For ye must cross the raging main
> Before the Promised Land you gain
> And with the faithful make a start
> To cross the plains with your handcart.
> For some must push and some must pull
> As we go marching up the hill,
> So merrily on our way we go
> Until we reach The Valley, oh!

If these innocents could be inspired to attempt the 1,200-
mile trek to their Promised Land with handcarts, Dodge
thought, comparable faith and persistence by a few engineers,
contractors and politicians could win the Pacific Railway for
the same route.

The course taken by the pilot of the steamboat *Effie Afton*
as she swung down the Rock Island channel of the Mississippi
one afternoon that summer was even more fateful for the final
route of the Pacific Railway. An eddy whipped her across
channel into one of the piers of the Mississippi & Missouri
bridge. She tilted, attempted to back off, and columns of flame
shot into the wooden fretwork of the bridge. Henry Farnam's
masterpiece blazed like a haystack. Volunteer firemen from
Rock Island and Davenport pumped and chopped desperately
and saved everything but the central span.

The *Effie Afton*'s owners refused to pay damages. The
bridge was a menace to navigation, they charged; the railroad
should pay them for the steamboat's stoved-in woodwork and
scraped paint. Norman Judd, the line's attorney, recommended
to Farnam and Durant that he engage the services of an old
friend at Springfield, Illinois—a trial lawyer who had served
the Illinois Central well during lawsuits—whose name was
Abraham Lincoln.

Lincoln accepted the case and based his argument on the
prophetic fact that "people have as much right to travel east

and west as north and south." The suit crept through Iowa courts, went on to the United States Supreme Court, and was eventually decided in favor of the railroad. Its importance is that it introduced Abraham Lincoln to the California-Mormon Trail route for the Pacific Railway.

On July 22, 1856, Congress authorized appropriations for expeditions to build bridges, blast boulders and grade the more dangerous wheel tracks along the Oxbow, Santa Fe and California-Mormon Trails. The organization of field crews began that fall; Frederick Lander was appointed chief engineer and field superintendent for California-Mormon Trail improvements.

As Jefferson Davis had forecast, John B. Floyd became Secretary of War in the Buchanan Cabinet. Officers at Fort Kearney warned Lander against possible ambushes by the Mormons on the desert crossing between South Pass and the Wasatch; at Fort Laramie, Lander learned that a Utah Expeditionary Force was organizing to "give the Mormons a lesson they'd never forget."

Secretary Floyd's preparations for the Mormon War were so furtively clumsy that the 5,000 infantry and cavalry didn't leave Fort Leavenworth until mid-July. Russell, Majors & Waddell, the freighting firm that held the Army's contract to haul supplies to all the forts west of the Missouri, received its first notification of the Utah Expeditionary Force in late June; Floyd gave them five weeks to round up 3,000,000 pounds of supplies, load it, and get their ox trains rolling toward South Pass. General William S. Harney, assigned to command the force, was a towering Indian Wars veteran who knew the treachery of October and November weather on the Rockies' plateaus, and furthermore did not share the Buchanan-Floyd views about "the polygamous, ungodly Mormons." (He had recently been transferred from Oregon where in addition to conducting a masterly campaign against the Cayuse and neighboring tribes, he had instilled some reverence in Lieutenant

Philip Henry Sheridan—still almost as brash as he had been on Albany's Rose Hill in 1836.) No ox trains and barracks-soft infantry could reach the Wasatch passes before snowfall, Harney predicted in dispatches to Washington.

Before the column was halfway up the Platte a messenger reined in with a letter from Mr. Floyd. Harney was relieved as commander. He would be replaced by Colonel Albert Sidney Johnston, former Secretary of War of the Republic of Texas. (Colonel Johnston's assignment as commander of a Texas cavalry regiment would be filled temporarily by his Lieutenant Colonel—Robert E. Lee.)

The next five years would prove John B. Floyd a traitor, liar and thief. The temptation is to ascribe his 1857 activities to the Secession plotting of his 1859–60 deceits. The temptation grows during an examination of 1857 developments in the Slavery-Free Soil struggle. In Nicaragua the proslavery pirate William Walker again tried to take over the government and thus gain control of its trans-isthmus route to California. The proslavers of Kansas rigged the Le Compton Constitution that recognized as "legal property" the slaves already in the territory. President Buchanan studied—with astute Southern coaching—a proposal to occupy the Mexican states of Chihuahua and Sonora, allocate Federal funds to purchase Cuba from Spain, and turn all three into slave territories. The Mormon War and the appointment of Albert Sidney Johnston as the Utah Expeditionary Force commander fits snugly into this pre-Secession pattern; the Utah war could delay Congressional bills seeking Federal appropriations for the Pacific Railway via the California-Mormon Trail; Colonel Johnston was an avowed "slaver," a Virginian by birth, and a Texan by fierce adoption.

The Force crept up the North Platte's ridge toward South Pass that August week when Ohio banks closed their doors and set off "the Buchanan Panic"; fears about the Mormon War and guerilla fighting in Kansas Territory contributed to the 4,392 business bankruptcies that fall and winter. But the

Mormons did not panic. Their Nauvoo Legion defeated the Utah Expeditionary Force without the loss of a man.

Two of the Russell, Majors & Waddell ox trains pulled into Simpson Hollow east of Jim Bridger's fort on the afternoon of October 4. Another train was fifteen miles east. A regiment of United States dragoons camped on the west bank of the Green River a few miles west. About midnight forty Nauvoo Legionaires surrounded the Simpson Hollow wagons, disarmed the guards, and ordered the bullwhackers to "Get your clothes on and start walkin'." By the time a scouting force of Dragoons forded the Green to investigate the transriver fire cloud, the raiders were slapping leather east toward the next wagon train. Before dawn 75 wagons and 300,000 pounds of meat, flour, sugar and grain were charred circles in the forests. As a final insulting filip, the Legionaires drove 700 of the wagon trains' oxen home to the City of Great Salt Lake via a back trail.

Similar raids on livestock and supplies slowed Johnston's march to a crippled crawl. The Mormons burned stands of grass along the route. The snows came. Johnston finally ordered his troops to hole up for the winter at Fort Bridger. When President Buchanan went before Congress on December 8 with a shrill plea for "more troops to reassert Federal authority in Utah" the Mormon War was over. During the spring of 1859, after abject promises that not a soldier would be stationed in the City of Great Salt Lake, Johnston marched his columns down to the desert edge forty miles west of town. The Mormons baked the bricks and cut the lumber for the barracks built there—on contract and at good prices. Johnston named the place Camp Floyd.

Through it all, the Mormons and their leaders evinced faith that their struggle was with "a power clique in Washington," but not with "dear Uncle Sam." Frederick Lander's reports on the South Pass wagon road construction bear this out. He wrote to Washington:

"The passage up the Platte and into the mountains was made without any difficulty whatever, so far as the Utah population was concerned. John Justus, my messenger to Salt Lake City to procure men, was enabled to proceed in the business of hiring them without interruption immediately upon the arrival of Colonel Johnston's command . . . I was assured by ex-Governor Young, whom I visited while in Salt Lake City, that . . . he would be very glad to have his people employed by me, not only because the work was one of public utility, but because it aided the people in getting a little money for the purchase of groceries and what they termed 'settlement supplies.' The Mormons who worked upon the wagon road were very much pleased with their engagement, and returned to the city comfortably clad from the stock of clothing which had been taken to the mountains by the expedition. The existence of this Mormon population, and the supplies they are enabled to furnish, is a most important matter in making estimates for any public work to be carried on in that section of the country. They are very excellent laborers, many of them Cornish miners who understand all sorts of ledge work, masonry, & c. They will prove of remarkable service should the proposed line of the Pacific railroad pass anywhere in the vicinity of their settlements. I paid them a dollar a day for work, but the next season I shall probably have to pay them at higher rates. Ex-Governor Young told me that he would engage to find laborers and mechanics to build that portion of a Pacific railroad which should extend across the Territory of Utah.

Another 4,225 business firms went into bankruptcy in 1858, and 3,913 more gave up in 1859. Farnam, Sheffield and Durant succeeded in saving the Chicago & Rock Island, but the Mississippi & Missouri failed. Durant and Farnam hurried to Iowa City, argued with politicians, and succeeded in having the Chicago & Rock Island named receiver for the Mississippi & Missouri's trackage and surveyed route.

John B. Jervis resigned and went East to supervise construction of the Hudson River Railroad between New York City and Poughkeepsie. Peter Dey succeeded him as chief engineer. Grenville Dodge rode out the "Buchanan Panic" by opening a Council Bluffs office that peddled real estate, undertook contract freighting, and sold contract lumber to home builders.

The Chicago, Burlington & Quincy managed to survive too.

General "Jack" Casement. *Union Pacific Railroad*

Grenville M. Dodge
in dress uniform as
a Major General.
Union Pacific Railroad

HANNIBAL & ST. JOSEPH RAILROAD.

TIME TABLE NO. 38.

To take effect on THURSDAY, JUNE 9th, 1864, at 11 o'clock, P. M. Bound East.

For the information and government of Employees ONLY—the Company reserving the right to vary therefrom as circumstances may require.

(detailed train schedule table — columns: No. 7 Coal Express, No. 5 Express Freight, No. 3 Express Freight, No. 1 Passenger Express, STATIONS, No. 2 Passenger Express, No. 4 Express Freight, No. 6 Express Freight, No. 8 Coal Express, No. 10 Express Freight)

Timetable for the Hannibal & St. Joseph Railroad, June 9, 1864.

UNION PACIFIC RAIL ROAD.

TIME TABLE

For Construction Trains,

TO TAKE EFFECT

MONDAY, JUNE 11TH, 12 O'CLOCK NOON.

STATIONS.	Going West.		Going East.	
	TRAIN No. 1.	TRAIN No. 2.	TRAIN No. 3.	TRAIN No. 4.
OMAHA,	12.00 M.	6.00 P. M.	8.15 P. M.	4.30 A. M.
PAPILLION,	1.30 P. M.	**7.20** "	**7.20** "	3.30 "
ELKHORN,	3.00 "	9.00 "	6.00 "	2.15 "
FREMONT,	**4.30** "	10.30 "	**4.30** "	12.50 "
NORTH BEND,	5.45 "	**11.40** "	3.00 "	**11.40** P. M.
SHELL CREEK,	6.50 "	12.50 A. M.	1.40 "	9.50 "
COLUMBUS,	8.00 "	2.00 "	12.00 M.	8.00 "

THE FULL-FACED FIGURES DENOTE MEETING PLACES.

RULES & REGULATIONS:

1. The Clock in the Cashier's Office at Omaha will be the standard time, and Conductors will regulate their time pieces by it.

2. Trains going West will have the right to Track for one hour behind time. If not then at meeting point, Trains going East, will proceed, keeping one hour behind card time until meeting Westward bound trains.

3. At meeting points Conductors will allow five minutes for variation of time if Trains due have not arrived.

4. Trains going East will Side Track at meeting points.

5. Trains will leave Omaha and Columbus on time whether Trains due have not arrived or not.

Sam'l B. Reed,
General Superintendent.

OMAHA, JUNE 9th, 1866.

OMAHA DAILY HERALD PRINT.

Timetable for the
Union Pacific Railroad,
June 9, 1866.
Union Pacific Railroad

The Union Pacific Railroad's Locomotive Number 1, later named "The General Sherman." *Union Pacific Railroad*

The *Denver* and the *Colorado* tied up at the Omaha wharf, after the trip up the Missouri with the Grand Excursion to the Hundredth Meridian Party. *Union Pacific Railroad*

Casement train on a siding either at Cheyenne or Laramie, 1867–68. *Union Pacific Railroad*

Bear River City, Wyoming Territory, where the *Frontier Index* plant was burned by a mob and the Freemans were threatened with a "necktie party." *Union Pacific Railroad*

General U. S. Grant and party at Fort Saunders, Wyoming, at the time of the "showdown" between Dodge and Durant, summer, 1868. Some of those in the picture are: General Phil Sheridan (second from the left with his hands in his pockets), General U. S. Grant (seventh from the left with his hands on the fence), General Sherman (at the center with his coat over his arm), General Harney (the tall bearded man in the cape), and Thomas C. Durant (slouched behind General Harney in the black suit and sailor hat). *Union Pacific Railroad*

The Devil's Gate Bridge, at Devil's Gate, the Utah crossing of the Weber River. Wreckage of the original wooden span is visible in the river and along the banks. The Howe-Truss span was installed during the summer of 1869. *Union Pacific Railroad*

A sightseeing party in Weber Canyon, Utah, 1869. *Union Pacific Railroad*

The *L. L. Robinson*, the first steam locomotive on the Pacific Coast, was used by the Sacramento Valley Railroad. The man standing in front of the tender in the gray top hat is Ted Judah, then Chief Engineer of the line.

→

Snow plow of the Central Pacific Railroad at Cisco in 1867. *Southern Pacific Historical Collection*

→

Snowshed under construction near Summit in the Sierras on the Central Pacific line in 1868. *Southern Pacific Historical Collection*

The high Secrettown trestle in the California Sierras being filled with dirt in 1877. Note the meager tools with which the Central Pacific's coolies had to work. *Southern Pacific Historical Collection*

A painting by the Chinese artist Jake Lee, one of a series on Chinese-American history produced for Kan's Restaurant in San Francisco, depicting the wicker baskets used by coolies on the Central Pacific Railroad. *Kem Lee Studio, San Francisco, California*

Camp "Victory" for the Central Pacific Railroad construction forces on April 28, 1869. On that day more than ten miles of track were laid to set a record. "Victory" was just west of Promontory Point, Utah, where the last spike was driven on May 10, 1869. *Southern Pacific Historical Collection*

The scene at Promontory Point, Utah, a few minutes before the Golden Spike ceremonies were begun.

The Golden Spike Ceremony at Promontory Point. *Utah State Historical Society*

The monument erected at the site of the driving of the Golden Spike.
Utah State Historical Society

Interior of Pullman's Palace Car, 1867–70. *Union Pacific Railroad*

Interior of a Union Pacific Railroad coach, 1870. *Union Pacific Railroad*

Samuel Reed shifted to its Burlington and Missouri route and was assigned to start location surveys toward Ottumwa, 75 miles west of the Mississippi. Europeans bought the bonds that enabled the Hannibal & St. Joseph to build across Missouri; on February 13, 1859, its rails joined at Cream Ridge, Missouri. Thomas Hart Benton died in 1858, but his ghost must have led the Grand Marches at the St. Joseph and Hannibal receptions that week; railroads had finally linked 1,200 miles of his Road to India, from the Hudson to the Kansas prairie, just thirty years after his prophetic series of editorials in the St. Louis *Enquirer*.

As though in justification of the old warrior's crusades for the New West, a gold strike that seemed as dazzling as California's sent thousands of wagons, daubed with PIKES PEAK OR BUST legends, west out of Missouri valley towns. Grenville Dodge opened a trading station for them on the Elkhorn and persuaded his father and brother to go out and operate it. This traffic up the South Platte encouraged Chicago & Rock Island's backers. They approved Dey's request to put Dodge back on the pay roll and send him on a Pacific railroad survey all the way to South Pass.

Dodge arrived home from this survey on August 12, 1859, and saw a crowd gawking around the Pacific House in Council Bluffs. Anne drew back from their first embrace to gasp, "You're just in time. Abraham Lincoln is here. He's promised to make a speech tonight."

The Mississippi & Missouri's attorney, Norman Judd, wanted a loan on a plot of land Dodge had purchased for him on the Missouri flats. He asked Lincoln to take the mortgage. Lincoln, returning from a lecture tour in Missouri, had come upriver to look at the property. But Dodge sensed another reason for the visit as he listened to the speech that night. The debates with Senator Douglas the year before had made Lincoln the favorite son of the Illinois Republicans. Frémont was washed up. Senator Seward of New York and Abraham Lincoln would probably be East-West rivals for the Presidential candidacy in 1860. Lincoln, by sauntering into Council Bluffs to inspect the mortgage value on land owned by a man he had known and trusted for a decade, was playing the fox again. This could be a bid for the convention votes of the Iowa delegation. It showed in his speech. "The clear and lucid manner in which he set forth the true principles of the Republican Party," reported the Council Bluffs *Non Pareil* the next day, "the dexterity with which he applied the political scalpel to the Democratic carcass, beggars all description at our hands." The loudest cheer of the evening came when Lincoln, poking a finger toward the Missouri, twanged, "Not one, but many railroads will center here."

Dodge walked down to the Pacific House next morning to see whether Lincoln would expound on that railroad prophecy. W. H. M. Pusey, Lincoln's official host, saw Dodge in the crowd, tugged Lincoln's arm, and said, "That black-whiskered fellow down there is Grenville Dodge. He knows more about railroads than any two men in the country."

J. R. Perkins, Dodge's official biographer, described the interview that followed Pusey's brag: "Lincoln studied Dodge intently for a moment, and then slowly crossed the porch to where he sat on a bench, crossed his long legs, swung his foot for a moment and said, 'Dodge, what's the best route for a Pacific railroad to the West?' 'From this town out the Platte Valley,' was the instant rejoinder."

During the next hour, as Dodge himself expressed it later, "he shelled my woods completely and got all the information I'd collected for Henry Farnam, my employer." Extolling the California-Mormon Trail and the engineering facts Frederick Lander had given him about the Wasatch and Nevada, Dodge pointed out the importance the route already had in the rush to the Pike's Peak gold fields. "In 1857 alone, at the height of the fears about Johnston's Utah Expedition," he quoted from Lander's field report, "more than seventy thousand cattle were driven through South Pass and over the deserts to Utah. If cows can make it, a railroad certainly can." And he had picked up another rumor. Word of a new gold and silver strike somewhere on the Nevada side of the Sierras had reached Fort Kearney. Pikes Peak gold . . . City of the Great Salt Lake . . . Nevada gold and silver. All three were located directly over the California-Mormon Trail.

Abe Lincoln nodded. He had some news too. Some young engineer was preaching from San Francisco to Sacramento that the logical route for a Pacific railroad was up the passes out of Sacramento to Salt Lake. He had stirred up such a fuss that a Pacific Railroad convention was scheduled to be held in San Francisco sometime during the summer. For all Lincoln knew it might be going on right then.

CHAPTER **8**

"CRAZY" JUDAH

How beautiful to think of lean tough Yankee settlers tough as gutta percha, with most occult unsubduable fire in their belly, steering over the Western Mountains to annihilate the jungle, and bring bacon and corn out of it for the posterity of Adam. . . .
Thomas Carlyle (1849).

"He had always talked, read and studied the problem of the railway to the Pacific," Anna Judah later reminisced. "He would say, 'It is going to be built and I'm going to have something to do with it.' " This faith, asserted in the cottage overlooking the Niagara gorge, was compounded by the time the Judahs reached Sacramento in mid-May, 1854.

They sailed from New York in early April on one of Cornelius Vanderbilt's new ships. The icy blue eyes of the Staten Island ferryboat king—he still signed his name Van Derbilt—had observed that the Lake of Nicaragua empties into the Atlantic via the San Juan River. A road from the lake's west shore required only twelve miles of grading to loop down to the Pacific's beach. Vanderbilt ordered his bankers to transfer some of his ferry and Hudson River steamboat profits into a Nicaragua route fund. He negotiated a lease with the Nicaragua government and built a road, pleasantly surfaced with

McAdam's composition, from Virgin Bay over the Cordillera. The trip via Nicaragua saved two days on the New York–San Francisco run via Panama. Vanderbilt's rates were lower than the United States Mail Line's. His boats were new, with better staterooms and meals.

Still the trip took five to six weeks, barring hurricanes and gales in the Atlantic, tropical floods in the San Juan River, mud or rock slides in the Cordillera, monsoons and fog on the Pacific sail. Ever present, too, was the likelihood of tropical disease, especially the mysterious and deadly yellow fever. Nevertheless, every cabin was filled and the holds were stacked with the ironware, yard goods, flour, and other commodities needed by the Californians. Judah introduced himself to the ship's officers as "the engineer engaged to build California's first railroad," and soon had the run of the ship. Prowling from boiler room to crow's-nest, his amiability enabled him to launch discussions with anyone from a cabin boy to a seasick missionary.

Continental maps were an old passion of Judah's. On the Pacific Mail run north past Acapulco and the misty fangs of the Baja California Sierras, Judah unrolled his topographic charts to restudy San Francisco's Bay, the twisting ship route to Sacramento, and the dappled black lines that marked the Sierra Nevada. San Francisco, he mused, had topographic parallels with New York City. Its throughway to the interior, comparable to the Hudson–Mohawk throughway, was the great bay fed by the Sacramento and San Joaquin rivers. The bay, roughly parallel with the Pacific shore, runs southeast by northwest to form a harbor 50 miles long and up to 10 miles wide. The city lies on the southern slopes of the Golden Gate, the bay's only channel. Thus any railroad from the east must swing across the California desert and Santa Lucia Range, then come up the peninsula from the south; or it must dead-end across the bay at the village of Oakland.

A bird, he mused, need fly only 75 miles from San Francisco to Sacramento. But steamboats, twisting through the estuary at the north end of the Bay, then dodging sand bars up the Sacramento River channel, groaned and shivered for twelve hours and traveled 150 miles. A railroad from the Bay to Sacramento could almost match the birdline.

East of Sacramento the Sierra Nevada leaped toward the sky. Sacramento was only 50 feet above sea level. East for another 10 miles the American River Valley crossed a gentle plain with a rise of only about 100 feet. The 1,000-foot elevation lay 30 to 35 miles east of Sacramento. But over the next 60 miles the Sierra soared its coastal wall to peaks the Army's engineers estimated as 11,000 and 12,000 feet high. The descent to the 4,250-foot average of the Nevada and Utah high plain was almost as much of a toboggan. Yet, it was less than 200 miles from Sacramento to the Nevada desert. That was the great challenge: To find a rail route through the Sierra's Gargantuan wall. The grade across Nevada and Utah to the Wasatch seemed to be child's play.

Judah's eagerness to finally see and gauge the Sierra Nevada made him as restless as a saddled colt when they crossed the gangplank to the Sacramento wharf. Several of the backers of the Sacramento Valley Railroad were waiting. Colonel Wilson made the introductions. Most of them were New Englanders or New Yorkers who had been to Greenfield and Troy too.

Judah beamed shamelessly during luncheon when one of the stockholders suggested that it might be helpful to promotion if some estimate could be obtained of potential traffic over the route. Splendid idea, the engineer agreed; it could be secured during the preliminary survey. If the directors wished to place a half-dozen men at his disposal he would begin both the traffic count and the survey the next day.

The first division of the Sacramento Valley Railroad would operate only 21 miles up the American River to Folsom. The best that could be said for it was that it would save wagon trains a day's haul from the steamboat wharves. The real challenge was the Sierra Nevada, hulking 20 miles beyond Folsom. Judah took a wandering route to Folsom, zigzagging between the roads to Placerville, Grass Valley, and other mining centers of the Mother Lode. He ordered a man out at each road intersection and told him to camp there for a week to count each wagon that passed and make an estimate of its load. He left the rest of the crew at Folsom, then cantered east toward the mountains. At sunset he stood on a rise behind Placerville. In 1894, John Muir recorded the emotions experienced by Judah and other sensitive pioneers in that first sunset view of the Pacific's guardian range: "From the eastern boundary of this vast golden flowerbed rose the mighty Sierra, miles in height and so gloriously colored and so radiant, it seemed not clothed with light, but wholly composed of it, like the wall of some celestial city . . . It seemed to me that the Sierra should be called, not the Nevada or Snowy Range, but the Range of Light."

The Sierra Nevada became Judah's Range of Light too. He was, by birth and conviction, a Northerner and a devout Episcopalian. He perceived the utter impossibility of human "equality." Heredity and environment both denied that, and would keep on denying it. But freedom and equal rights to improve both individual and community environment were human birthrights. A Pacific railroad, as a technologic instrument that bound the Union to its Pacific states and territories, was a vital step toward the achievement of freedom and equality of opportunity. The railway, then, was a project in ethical goals as well as military expediency and the economic realization of Northwest Passage. As such, it must run through the freemen's territory of the North, rather than through the lands of the slavers.

The survey for the Sacramento Valley Railroad was a pleasure after that first view of the Sierra. The tallies of the crossroads scouts totted up heavier traffic to the mines than the directors had anticipated. The explanation was simple. Most of the $200,000,000 worth of gold taken out of the creek beds and sand bars since 1848 had been mined by hand operations. A prospector could hike toward the mountains with a shovel, pick and tin pan, then set to work at the first spot that appealed to him. By 1854 most of this "placer" treasure had been recovered. California's gold mines settled into the prosaic, and expensive, routines of washing down dirt banks with high-pressure water jets, or rock-mining the ore by the techniques used in lead and coal mines. Both hydraulic mining and quartz mining required heavy equipment. The railroad could do a splendid job of filling this demand.

On May 28, 1854—the day Grenville Dodge married Anne Brown in Danvers, Massachusetts—Judah began the final draft of his survey report. The report was approved. The house-to-house and meeting-to-meeting chores of stock sales began. Decision was reached to engage the New York firm of Robinson, Seymour & Company to do the construction work and provide the rails, locomotives and cars. This was not too surprising. The Seymour in the firm was Governor Horatio Seymour's brother Silas—the engineer who had recommended Judah to Colonel Wilson.

The final surveys began in midsummer. The Judahs rode east out of camp almost every weekend to picnic on the Sierra slopes, hike up gullies, and take endless measurements of the terrain. Hopefully, Judah pushed the survey a few miles beyond Folsom to the settlement of Mormon Bar. It would be ready and waiting, he reasoned, when the day came to build the Pacific Railway.

A locomotive and 400 tons of rail were finally eased onto a Sacramento wharf after a 130-day sail around Cape Horn. (The clipper *Northern Light* set the all-time record that spring with a trip of 76 days and 6 hours from the San Francisco wharf to Boston Light.) On August 19, 1855, the locomotive L. L. Robinson, an eight-wheeler grossing twenty tons, hauled two flatcars loaded with stockholders and their families from Sacramento to Folsom. The Sacramento *Union* published a lavish report. San Francisco papers echoed. Business was brisk the first few weeks; families waiting in line agreed on the alibi: "We want our youngsters to have a ride on the thing." But the directors shook their heads against the notion of further construction "for the time being." There was a whopping debt of $700,000 to be paid off to Robinson, Seymour & Company. And Wells Fargo, having already lowered its wagon rates on direct hauls to the mines, now threatened to boycott hauls out of Folsom.

Judah's work was done. He had been hired as chief engineer for the construction of California's first railroad. The job was finished. The logical thing to do would be to go back East and sign on with one of the railroads building across the prairie. Jobs were available there for a man with his experience.

But Theodore Judah had fallen in love with the Sierra. Somehow, sometime, he knew that the first Pacific railroad would cross that Range of Light between Sacramento and Salt Lake. There would not be the three Pacific railroads proposed by Senator Gwin in the bill just passed by the Senate (but never let out of committee by the House). The first iron Northwest Passage would run down one of those ridges, send side spurs out to the Mother Lode, then sprint across the seventy-five miles of flatland to San Francisco Harbor. Sacramento had just succeeded Monterey as California's capital city. The San Joaquin Valley was already abawl with cattle; and wheat, fruit and dairy farmers were pushing in fast. Coal and copper deposits, kaolin clay pits, jet-black venation marbles, dolomite limestone, soapstone and scores of other minerals lay back in those mountains waiting for railroads to furnish bulk transport to markets. The Pacific slopes for a thousand miles gloried in forests of fir and redwood. Judah echoed Brigham Young: This is the place.

A few surveying jobs straggled in. But the stage lines, steamboats and bullwhackers were established, had credit at the banks, and fought shrewdly to retain their monopoly. ("Railroads are, of course, most desirable projects. But, *public* projects, young man! A matter for the Government.") He did find backing for the survey of a line from Sacramento to San Francisco Bay, and—some allege—for another line from San

Francisco down the coast to San Jose. These more than paid his living costs. Between assignments he sought interviews with legislators to urge state action on "the Great Pacific Railroad," or disappeared into the Sierras for weeks at a time—transit, barometer and gauges wrapped in chamois bundles and strapped to the lead mule's back.

In the fall of 1856 he and Anna stored their few possessions and sailed back to New York. The records are scant. Anna went home to Greenfield to visit her parents. Judah took the train to Washington. There is the little pamphlet titled "A Practical Plan for Building the Pacific Railroad" and signed by T. D. Judah, Civil Engineer, San Francisco. It was published in Washington on January 1, 1857, and advocates that the railroad should be built by private enterprise without government aid. "The General Government," Judah wrote, "is a house divided against itself; it cannot be done until the route is defined." He pleaded for a survey "on one selected route," estimating it would cost $200,000. The final railroad, he believed, would cost an average of $75,000 per mile, a total of $150,-000,000 from the Mississippi to the Pacific.

It was a gallant try but never got as far as a committee. Senator Gwin was still committed to the compromise of three Federal routes, to be named Northern Pacific, Central Pacific and Southern Pacific. No Congressman would lend his name to Judah's idea. By the summer of 1857 the Judahs were back in San Francisco again. The pattern resumed. The engineer drummed up enough odd jobs to pay the bills, then channeled the rest of his energy into speeches and interviews about "The Great Pacific Railroad." It became a simple, obvious reaction, whenever the subject came up at an Odd Fellows' meeting or a business luncheon to ask, "D'you know that crazy engineer Judah?"

The editors of the Sacramento *Union* proved a godsend. They had taken a liking to Judah during the survey for the Sacramento Valley Line. Time after time through the Buchanan Panic of 1857–58, Judah was lifted from gloom by editorials that urged "action about the railway," and by casual column mention that "We have just talked with Theodore Judah about plans for the Pacific Railway. This amiable engineer believes . . ."

The *Union* carried occasional advertisements, too, for "Fresh lots of the best merchandise" at Huntington & Hopkins' large brick store on K Street, the "Complete Mining Supplies" at Stanford Brothers Wholesale & Retail Groceries, and the "Wonderful new patterns in calico and dimity" at Crocker Brothers. During 1855, alongside a report of progress on the Sacramento Valley Line, the *Union* announced the return of Mr. Leland Stanford of Stanford Brothers from New York State with his lovely wife Jane, and their decision to build a permanent home "in our city." The next year, while the Judahs were packing for the trip East, the *Union* announced the elections of Leland Stanford and Mark Hopkins as city aldermen, and commented on the prominence of both in the new state organization of the Republican Party. During 1857, Leland Stanford paid for several modest advertisements proclaiming his virtues as the Republican candidate for state treasurer. Mr. Charles Crocker also scribbled some text about his qualifications as the Republican choice for assemblyman. The *Union* duly reported, with regrets, that both candidates were defeated.

There are no records of meetings between Stanford, Crocker, Hopkins, Huntington and Judah before 1860, despite the Republicans' 1856 campaign slogan of "Freedom, Frémont and the Railroad" and the *Union*'s continuing promotion of both Pacific Railway and Judah. Through the winter of 1858, Judah returned to Sacramento as a one-man lobby arguing for an official state-sanctioned convention that would consider plans —then prepare "memorials" to Congress—for the Pacific Railroad. California, he argued, was the western terminal for most of the routes being proposed to Congress. Therefore California should summarize her views on the railroad, decide which route it preferred, and thus possibly break the vicious deadlock between the Slavers and Freemen. The new Butterfield Stage route, he pointed out, had been assigned to an all-Slaver route by the Buchanan Administration. What would happen to its United States mails—especially if addressed to known Abolitionists? Furthermore, the coaches' 25 to 30 days for the run from St. Louis to El Paso, Los Angeles and San Francisco was little improvement over the Nicaragua and Panama routes.

Perhaps some of the assemblymen who voted Aye on the proposal to call a State convention on the Pacific Railroad were adopting the simplest method to "get shed of that Crazy Judah." However, on April 5, 1859, the resolution passed. Anna worked all spring and summer assembling Theodore's notes and clippings into tables of statistics that would prove, in a two-minute perusal, the advantages of the California-Mormon Trail route over all others. Back east at Latin School she had shown a flair for painting, so usually took a sketchbook or oils and easel along on the expeditions into the mountains. She packed some of her mountain scenes with the other materials for the convention. What was it that the *Union*'s editor had said? "A picture has a clearer voice than a headline!" Something like that.

The convention opened in San Francisco on September 20. More than a hundred delegates registered as official representatives from the assembly districts. Some were obvious stooges for the coach, freighter and steamboat lines, determined to scuttle all Pacific railroad proposals with sighs about "illogical thinking" or "a matter for Federal action." Yet Anna, after a day of seemingly inane chatting, reported that the majority favored the California-Mormon Trail route and were willing to back it in a floor vote.

She was right. The motion to formally approve the "Central route" won through. On October 11 the convention appointed Judah its accredited agent to carry its "memorial" to Congress. It just might be a good idea, some of the members advised, if the Judahs could book passage on the *Sonora*. She was scheduled to sail on the 20th. J. C. Burch, the new California Congressman, would be aboard. This would be Burch's first session. He might be looking for a nice hobbyhorse to ride.

John Burch proved to be intelligent and objective. Reminiscing years later on the shipboard meeting and the friendship that cemented during the five weeks' journey, he said: "Our introduction was immediately followed by a statement to me in detail of the objects and purposes of his mission . . . No day passed on the voyage to New York that we did not discuss the subject, lay plans for its success, and indulge pleasant anticipations of those wonderful benefits so certain to follow that success."

Senator Lane of Oregon was aboard, too, and occasionally entered into the discussions. He was bound, of course, to be cautious. His constituents favored Senator Gwin's compromise plan, since it included a Northern Pacific Railroad from St. Paul to Portland. Both he and Burch were intrigued, nonetheless, by an idea Anna shyly advanced one dinnertime. "Would there be any advantage," she asked with studied innocence, "in establishing a Pacific Railway Exhibit on Capitol Hill?" She had packed the charts used at the convention, as well as samples of ore, minerals and fossils she and Ted had picked up on their Sierra expeditions. Also, she had her sketchbook and a few paintings so that Greenfield relatives and friends might sense the majesty of Eastern California.

Ted gulped, then reached under the tablecloth to pat her hand. Senator Lane's eyebrows were up. His head was nodding agreement. Burch was saying, "Splendid idea." Thus in December, Judah secured an audience with John A. Logan, the Illinois Congressman who headed the House Committee on Contingent Expenses. Again the engineer displayed his mastery of the problem. Logan assigned Judah the use of a room in the Capitol for the Pacific Railway Museum. There during the tense weeks of John Brown's trial in nearby Charles Town, Virginia, and the glowering debates over Hinton Helper's book, *The Impending Crisis in the South,* hundreds of Congressmen, lobbyists and government clerks visited the display of charts, sketches, minerals and fossils—then argued the merits of Pacific railroad routes with the suave, brown-eyed custodian.

During the Christmas holidays, while John Brown's final challenge, "You are guilty of a great wrong against God and humanity," echoed in thunderous editorials throughout the North, Judah rejoined Anna in Greenfield for a few days, then headed West. Again details are scant. There is evidence that he traveled as far as Chicago and visited officials of the Rock Island and the Chicago, Burlington & Quincy railroads to discuss their plans for surveys west of St. Joseph and Council Bluffs. Here Judah could logically have heard rumors of the most exciting development yet for the California-Mormon Trail.

The whisper was out that a Pony Express service was being organized for weekly deliveries of mail and dispatches between St. Joseph and Sacramento. It was a foolhardy venture, railroad officials felt. Russell, Majors & Waddell had lost a fortune when the Mormons burned the Utah Expeditionary Force wagon trains in 1857, and had never been able to get a nickel of it back from Congress. The next year Russell borrowed heavily to establish a Leavenworth & Pikes Peak stage line. All in all, this Pony Express seemed a desperate last gamble to win a United States mail contract and save the firm from bankruptcy. Nevertheless, it bid to be a daredevil display that should win newspaper headlines. The Hannibal & St. Joseph Railroad was backing it to the hilt. Why not? They'd like to carry United States mail for the Pacific too!

On April 4, 1860, Judah sat gloomily at his Washington desk in the Pacific Railway Museum. Repeat and repeat. Burch had introduced a bill for a Central Pacific survey in the House. Senator Gwin, still wondering whether to plunk with the Slaver or Compromise blocs in the Democratic party, had recompromised his bill in the Senate and included an appropriation for surveys. But both measures were tabled in committee for "consideration next session." This was another election year.

Judah glanced at a morning newspaper and saw the headline Pony Express Starts. Ten days? He pulled the paper across the desk and began reading. The first run had set out from St. Joseph just before sunset on the 3rd. Another was scheduled to leave San Francisco at the same hour. Charles Russell, president of the firm, the report rumored, had placed a large wager that the dispatches carried on those initial runs would be delivered in San Francisco and St. Joseph, respectively, within 10 days. The relay stations linked across Kansas and a corner of Colorado to South Pass followed the Mormon Trail into Salt Lake, then headed arrow true toward Fort Carson, Lake Tahoe and the American River Gorge into Placerville.

April 14th's papers were jubilant. The eastbound run of the Pony Express reached St. Joseph five minutes before the expiration of the 10 days. The rider, an ex-jockey named John Fry, had heard that the Sierra relays bucked blizzards and deep drifts most of the way from Placerville to the Nevada line. There it was! Mail from California in 10 days. And via the California-Mormon Trail.

Judah folded the paper carefully, locked the Museum door, and walked down the hall to John Burch's office. He and Burch studied the Sierra Nevada maps again. A few days later in Greenfield, Anna received a letter, laughed, and began packing. The time was ripe, Theodore explained when he reached Greenfield. Every newspaper in the country was featuring Dispatches by Pony Express. The Central route and the gallantry of those blue-and-red clad horsemen were causing almost as much comment as the Democratic convention's split. Now was the time to determine a railroad route through the Shining Mountains and begin the struggle to actually incorporate a Central Pacific railroad.

CHAPTER **9**

GIFT OF THE WEST

> *Laboring Men! Remember that the Republican is
> the only national party committed to the policy of
> making the public lands free in quartersections to
> actual settlers, whereby every worker will be en-
> abled to hew out for his family a home from the vir-
> gin soil of the Great West. . . .* Horace Greeley in
> the New York *Tribune* (1859).

Theodore Judah first visited Washington in 1857 as an engineer imbued with an idealistic plan. When he and Anna
embarked for Panama in July, 1860, he was also a skilled lobbyist. This is the law of Washington's social jungle. As the nation's capital it is, per se, the nation's headquarters for political
tipsters and rumormongers, a sprawl of clerks, subdeputies'
deputies, bureau chiefs, attorneys and careerists engaged in the
everlasting game of guessing election odds, Congress maneuvers and White House moods. Judah was exposed to this during 1857 and again in the critical winter of 1859–60.

By July 1, 1860, four facts were patly obvious to any
Capitol Hill dopester:

   1. As the Republican's first Presidential candidate, John C.
Frémont, in 1856, polled only 500,000 fewer votes than James
C. Buchanan and won 114 electoral seats to Buchanan's 174.

110

2. In 1858, the Republicans won control of the House, thanks to the pro-Abolition Germans, Swedes, Finns and Irish in the north and north central states.

3. The Democratic National Convention at Charleston in April, 1860, split on platform issues. Reconvening at Baltimore on June 18, it stayed split. The Northern Democrats nominated Stephen A. Douglas for President. The next week the Southern Democrats named their own ticket with John D. Breckenridge of Kentucky as Presidential candidate.

4. On May 9 the Constitutional Union party, another "splinter," met at Baltimore and nominated John Bell of Tennessee for the White House race.

The Republican nomination of Abraham Lincoln, in view of the ground swell for Republican platforms, looked like a walk-away.

Several other developments peculiarly meaningful to land speculators and Pacific Railroad lobbyists were building up odds on Capitol Hill during the spring of 1860:

The admission of Kansas, Oregon and Minnesota as free states, plus the creation of Colorado, Nebraska and Nevada as territories, promised stronger political support for a Pacific railroad via a northern, free-soil route.

The spectacular success of the Pony Express' 10-day deliveries brought the Pacific slope 20 travel days closer to the Union.

The Federal policy of giving warrants for free homestead sites to Army and Navy veterans had been lobbied by Horace Greeley and other Republican "liberals" into a campaign to offer a 160-acre homestead in the West to any citizen who would develop it. The Republicans were pledged to this Homestead Act. The Act passed the House and Senate in the spring of 1860, but was vetoed by Buchanan on June 22. It would take Congressional precedence in the 1861–62 sessions.

In 1860, as in 1856, "liberal support by the national government" for the construction of the Pacific Railroad was planked into the Republican platform.

These prospects would cause any middling fair lobbyist to hurry home and "mend fences." And Theodore Judah had, by necessity, become more than a middling fair lobbyist. Obviously the next Presidency would offer the best prospects yet for the enactment of a Pacific railway act. If Lincoln won and the Republicans held their House majority as well, a bill calling for cash loans and land grants to an all-north route might squeak through the Senate, too, and be assured of a White House signature. Then the railroad company with a surveyed route stood the best chance to secure Federal loans, especially in California.

Ted and Anna pursued a planned course that fall and early winter of 1860. Pony Expressmen clattering down the Sierra trail past Lake Tahoe puzzled at the bearded little man stooped over a barometer in the middle of the trail. Wagonmen traveling the Heness Pass road up from the Yuba's headwaters to the Comstock Lode saw the same figure frowning at his barometer there. In the late fall Anna relayed an invitation from Dr. Daniel W. Strong, a druggist at the mining camp of Dutch Flat near the headwaters of Bear River. Midway between Nevada City and Gold Run, and fifty-five miles northeast of Sacramento, Dutch Flat lay on the approach to Emigrant Pass and Donner Pass. Dr. Strong's primary interest was a home-town business boom; it could be instigated by a good wagon road over the Sierra Nevada via Donner.

Judah and Strong rode up the trail to reaffirm the Army's estimate of 6,690-foot elevation at the summit. Judah's excitement grew as he discovered that by tunneling here, and blasting a cliff shelf there, a railroad could be twisted through to Nevada. A quick check of data convinced him. The dream of Central Pacific Railroad had been detailed to Strong; he abandoned his wagon-road scheme for the larger plan. A rough draft of corporate articles for a Central Pacific railroad company was composed in Strong's office. Strong and Judah pledged themselves to stock purchases. Then, while Strong began a solicitation of Dutch Flat friends, Judah hurried back to San Francisco, brought Anna up to date on his three

months' wanderings, and set to work on a promotional brochure called "Central Pacific RailRoad to California."

On November 6, Abraham Lincoln won 180 of the nation's
electoral votes—66 more than Frémont had received in 1856
—against a total of 123 for Breckenridge, Douglas and Bell.
On November 10, Judah's pamphlet was ready for mailing to
potential stockholders. It said, in part: "Confident of the
existence of a practical route across the Sierra Nevada Mountains, nearer and more direct than the proposed line via Made-
line Pass and the headwaters of the Sacramento, I have devoted
the past few months to an exploration of several routes and
passes through Central California, resulting in the discovery
of a practicable route from the city of Sacramento upon the
divide between Bear River and the North Fork of the American, via Illinoistown, Dutch Flat and Summit Valley to the
Truckee River; which gives nearly a direct line to Washoe,
with maximum grades of 100 feet per mile." The Donner Pass
route, he reported, was 150 miles shorter than the Nevada–
Sacramento route used by the Army for the 1853–54 "Surveys
and Explorations."

Dr. Strong wheedled $46,500 worth of stock pledges out
of Dutch Flat neighbors. California law called for stock subscriptions of $1,000 per mile before a railroad could be in-
corporated; the doughty druggist had raised more than a third
of it in his home town. Judah began soliciting San Francisco's
bankers and shippers for the $70,000 still needed. They lis-
tened, asked questions, and declined: The times are too uncertain; Wait awhile and see what happens in Washington;
The United States may be falling apart; There is talk of California secession; What about this General Johnston, anyway?
Would he go along with Senator Wigstaff and the other Texas
"radicals"? "Forget the railroad, young man, until we see
what's going to happen to the nation!"

During January, while Secession flamed from the Sea Isles
to the Mississippi, Judah shifted his campaign to Sacramento
and the Huntington–Hopkins store loft there. Again the facts

point to Judah's astuteness as a lobbyist. He had failed to persuade the financial leaders of San Francisco. In Sacramento he massed his persuasive powers for the Republican leaders of California!

The future Big Four of the Central Pacific-Southern Pacific monopoly were antislavery by heredity and procentral government by conviction. Huntington, Crocker, Hopkins and Stanford had each, with arrogant individualism, pondered the ethical structure of the Wisconsin-spawned Republican Party, brooded over its platform, then judged it more deserving of his citizen responsibilities than the wheezing Whig organization or the evasive, issue-straddling Democrats. At Republican meetings in 1856–57 the four became nodding acquaintances, and unbent a trifle more when they discovered they were former neighbors from upstate New York. Collis Huntington was a manipulator by instinct and by desire. He had ruthlessly traded the $1,000 worth of groceries purchased in New York in 1849 into an 1861 fortune estimated at "more than a million." His political role would always be: the smoke-filled room . . . the back-stairs . . . cash on the table without any receipts or other incriminating evidence. Mark Hopkins was, and would remain, an excellent bookkeeper with a two-dram measure of rustic philosopher. Charles Crocker had moods of extrovertive backslapping but left the speechmaking to lawyer brother Edgar; after the 1857 bid for Sacramento's City Council, Bull, too, channeled his political energies to idea man and cash on the table.

But Leland Stanford, the Albany wood peddler, had become a wealthy merchant with an itching law degree, a hungry ego and an ambitious wife. After five frustrating years as an attorney in New York and Wisconsin he migrated to California in 1852. His brothers had established a mining supply and wholesale grocery in Sacramento, then branched out into the Mother Lode towns. Leland opened another branch at Michigan Bluff, made a lucky investment in a quartz mine, and by 1854 was estimated to be worth $300,000. His dream was to return to

Jane in Albany, reopen his law-office, and settle into the comforts of a mansion on Rose Hill. He sold out and went East. But Albany was too sedate, and Jane wanted to experience life in California. In 1855, Leland brought Jane to Sacramento and re-entered the wholesale grocery business. Consequently, when he embraced Republicanism in 1856 he considered it carefully. Possessed of all the suavity of a lawyer, plus cash, he became the Republican candidate for State Treasurer in 1857 and for Governor in 1861.

By February 10, 1861, the Pony Express dispatches enabled any lobbyist to realize that the two-party system had vanished from the Union's politics. Mississippi, Alabama, Georgia, Louisiana and Texas all followed South Carolina in secession. Coincidentally, a vote for the Republicans became a vote for the Union, while a vote for the Democrats or the splinter parties came perilously close to anti-Union. It followed, then, that the Central Pacific Railroad, even though it built no further than the Nevada line, would become a link in an all-Union transcontinental route. Its fate was tied to the fate of the Republican party. The Republican candidates for the 1861 elections in California would be captives of this same pro-Union and pro-Secession struggle. Votes would be cast for the cause, rather than for the candidates. California's future as a partner in the Uinted States of America hinged on the outcome.

Perhaps the San Francisco bankers had been right; it would be more discreet to "wait awhile and see what happens." But Judah was a Yankee too. His astuteness, however, prevented his adopting this realism. Instead he hammered away, in the store-loft lectures and successive individual interviews, on the opportunity for a wagon road as well as a railroad via Donner. The wagon road built at once, he urged, would yield heavy tolls on the machinery, tools and foodstuffs needed for the Nevada mines; the wagons could haul pay loads of minerals and lumber back on westbound trips.

The rest of Central Pacific's shares were pledged. At the organization meeting of stockholders on April 30—three days before Lincoln's first call for three-year volunteers—Leland Stanford was elected president, Collis P. Huntington vice-president, James Bailey secretary, and Mark Hopkins treasurer. The corporation papers were granted on June 27. Judah had his field crews selected and began running the survey from downtown Sacramento toward Bear River. The job was finished before mid-September, plus barometric reconnaissance of alternate routes via Feather River and Yuba Pass. In his October 1 report Judah estimated construction costs of $12,380,-000 to the Nevada line, and $41,415,000 for the 733 miles to Salt Lake City. He pointed out that the Donner-Humboldt route into Salt Lake was 184 miles shorter than the one surveyed in 1853–1854 for Secretary of War, Jefferson Davis. The Central Pacific board meeting on October 9 approved Judah's report. Then, true to the little engineer's course of political logic, the group nodded toward some Federal plums and passed the following resolution:

> RESOLVED: That Mr. T. D. Judah, the Chief Engineer of this Company, proceed to Washington on the steamer of the 11th Oct. inst. as the accredited agent of the Central Pacific Railroad Company of California, for the purpose of procuring appropriations of land and U.S. Bonds from the Government, to aid in the construction of this road.

Anna had become as deft about packing cases as a Methodist preacher's wife. The luggage was on the pier on the 11th. Her bundle of drawings of Sierra landscapes was heavier. The directors had judged some of them "excellent." Her pen sketches of Donner Lake and Donner Pass were used as illustrations on the Central Pacific's first stock certificates.

Again there is evidence of political strategy in the sailing date. A. A. Sargent was aboard, heading for his first term in Congress. As with Burch two years before, Judah went deftly to work while Anna exuded her charm. Congressman Sargent was a Central Pacific captive before the Pacific mail connection veered east past Cuba and Bermuda to avoid the new

Confederate "ironclads" rumored to be prowling off Albermarle and the Chesapeake.

Washington was digging in for its grimmest winter since the British raid during the War of 1812. Baltimore, still a Secessionist hotbed, threatened to cut off rail and highway connections from the North. A Union army had been beaten again in the Potomac Battle of Ball's Bluff. Winfield Scott finally doddered off to retirement, and was replaced by a strutting midget named George B. McClellan, the boy general who had been one of the lieutenants assigned to Jefferson Davis' "Surveys and Explorations" in 1853.

Matters were desperate on the frontier. Jeff Thompson, the St. Joseph, Missouri, mayor who sponsored the Pony Express, went into a rage because the Lincoln-appointed United States postmaster insisted on flying the Stars and Stripes from the post office roof. Thompson led a mob to the roof, burned the flag, chopped down the flagpole, and galloped off to Lexington, Missouri, to join Sterling Price's Secesh army. His reasons, in analysis, could be traced as much to Missouri back-country hatred for the St. Louis Germans as they could to sympathy for the Confederacy. Virtual hell erupted along the Hannibal & St. Joseph Railroad. St. Joseph was placed under martial law and patrolled by Iowa and Kansas Abolitionist troops from Fort Leavenworth. Cump Sherman, now a colonel, and his Mexican War friend, Colonel U. S. Grant of Galena, were assigned to develop patrol systems for the Hannibal & St. Joseph's bridges. Sterling Price's raiders, after bombing a few bridges and wrecking some trains, succeeded in kidnapping the railroad's president, then sent word he would be shot unless train service was abandoned. Sherman and Grant approved the retaliatory measure of taking the mayor of Hannibal and a few other States' righters into custody and sending back word to Price that there would be another firing squad if anything happened to the president of the Hannibal & St. Joseph. The prisoners were ceremoniously exchanged; the railroad's eight-wheelers growled on, but with armor plate bolted around their boiler bellies and cabs.

Through it all, somehow, the Pony Express held to schedule until Edward Creighton's crews strung the last mile of trans-Rocky telegraph wire up Salt Lake City's Temple Street to Brigham Young's Lion House. Young dictated a message of greeting to the East that closed with the pledge: "Utah has not seceded, but is firm for the Constitution and the laws of our once happy country." Two days later James Gamble's crews rolled the trans-Sierra wires into Salt Lake. Creighton, Gamble and their crew chiefs were guests at the Lion House to hear a telegrapher relay California's message of greeting to Abraham Lincoln:

> "In the temporary absence of the governor of the state, I am requested to send you the first message which will be transmitted over the wires of the line which connects the Pacific with the Atlantic states. The people of California desire to congratulate you upon the completion of the great work. They believe it will be the means of strengthening the attachment which binds both the East and the West to the Union, and they desire in this—the first message across the continent—to express their loyalty to the Union and their determination to stand by its Government on this its day of trial. They regard the government with affection, and will adhere to it under all fortunes.
>
> Stephen J. Field, CHIEF JUSTICE OF CALIFORNIA."

By the time the Judahs reached Washington the new telegraph had tapped the news of Stanford's election as governor. This was sequeled by a sparsely worded message from Huntington saying that if matters looked right for the passage of a railroad act he might come East too. Congress was fretting, Judah sensed, toward the realization that the Union needed morale-building legislation just as much as it needed competent generals. The Arkansas and Texas secessions, coupled with Missouri's semiprivate Civil War, threatened the North's hold on all of the New West. Secret invasions there, coinciding with rebellions by the thousands of pro-South miners in California and Nevada, could realize the Calhoun, Gadsden, Wigstaff and Davis goals of a South and West alliance. Hence there must be legislation that would give Northerners an incentive to fight for the West as well as for the Union. Moreover, the Republican Party was pledged to the Homestead Act and what President Lincoln called "The Union and Pacific Railway Act." A third morale builder shaped up in a bill sponsored by Justin Smith Morrill of Vermont, offering Federal lands scrip to each state and territory for endowment of its College of Agriculture & Mechanics. (This had passed both Houses in 1859, but like the Homestead Act, had been whined at and vetoed by Buchanan.)

Illinois' Logan had swapped "Congressman" for "Colonel" and set off on his destiny as founder of the Grand Army of the Republic and idea man for Memorial Day. But Judah soon had the Pacific Railroad Museum operating in an anteroom. Thomas Durant sniffed the same scent of railroad grants and spent increasing time in Washington too. So did Colonel Silas Seymour, whenever he could wangle leave from Army duties. Colonel Grenville M. Dodge of the 4th Iowa Infantry, recovering from a wound received at the Missouri Battle of Pea Ridge, had recently been elevated to brigadier general and ordered to report to General Halleck in Kentucky. There Dodge's ex-tentmate, Captain Philip Henry Sheridan, told Halleck that Dodge was a genius at building railroads. Dodge was promptly ordered to untwist the havoc wreaked along the Gulf & Mobile Railroad by the Confederates when they retreated—with Albert Sidney Johnston's corpse—from the Shiloh battlefield. Consequently, Dodge followed the cloakroom deals, speeches and committee hearings of the Pacific Railroad Act via grossly delayed mails.

Senators McDougall of California and Harlan of Iowa resurrected the act sponsored in the 1859–60 Congress by Iowa's Samuel R. Curtis (now the "Victor of Pea Ridge"). Judah was named Secretary of the Senate Committee on the act. In the House, "Freshman" Sargent interrupted an afternoon's drone on the State of the Union with a stirring speech for action on,

"Federal aid to the Pacific RailRoad." His bill was referred to committee; Judah was appointed clerk of this committee too.

Through May and June, while McClellan fretted into the Peninsula campaign, Congress readied the three bills that were to be its gift of the New West for both Northern and Pacific Coast morale. A preliminary step was the creation of an independent United States Department of Agriculture, under a commissioner, and the transfer of its experimental gardens, seed testers, agronomists and plant hunters from the jurisdiction of the Patent Office. This May 15th act was followed by enactment on May 20 of the Homestead Act offering a Federal warrant for 160 acres of New West land to any citizen who would erect a sod house or shack on it, plow a few furrows, and make some semblance of residency over a five-year period.

Finally, the Pacific Railway Act reached the floor of the Senate on June 20, won its majority, moved on to the House, and passed easily on the 24th. Next day the armies of McClellan and Lee locked in the grim Seven Days' Battles.

Collis Huntington had reached town via a two weeks' jolt in Ben Holladay's Overland Stage. He huddled with Durant and Judah over the final bill, grumbling at its control clauses. The Federal Government—if it survived—granted the railroad's builders "vacant lands with 10 miles on either side of the lines for five alternate sections per mile—mineral lands excepted." Federal loans to the contractors, not to exceed $50,-000,000, were allocated at: $48,000 per mile on 150 miles of mountain construction; $16,000 per mile on construction to the base of the mountains; and $32,000 per mile for trackage across the desert high plain of Nevada and Utah. The loans would be 30-year Federal bonds with 6 per cent annual interest to be paid to the United States Treasury.

The Act stipulated that the Central Pacific Railroad would build the Pacific Railway east from Sacramento to the California-Nevada border. Senate amendments moved the "eastern terminus of the Union and Pacific Railway" to the 100th meridian line, sixty miles west of Fort Kearney on the Platte. This, the Senators pointed out, would enable St. Louis, Kansas City, St. Joseph, Council Bluffs and Omaha to project numerous connecting roads. Creation of the Union and Pacific Railway as a westbound builder was placed under the jurisdiction of a 158-man board of commissioners. All of these were dutifully named in the Act; Judah, Huntington, Farnam, Ogden and Samuel Curtis were included. But so were Ben Holladay, Louis McLane of Wells, Fargo, and a score of stage-line and rival-route promoters who, quietly unified, could throw monkey wrenches into the complicated agenda for creation of The Union Pacific Railroad & Telegraph Company specified by the Act.

Yet there it was—thirty-one years almost to the month since the Mohawk & Hudson's *De Witt Clinton* had taken one hour and forty-five minutes to pull two stagecoaches from Albany to Schenectady. On July 1, the very day that 1,000 Union youngsters gave their lives at Malvern Hill to end McClellan's rout, Abraham Lincoln signed the Pacific Railway Act. Huntington and Judah sent a telegram of congratulation to Governor Stanford and closed it with the challenge: WE HAVE DRAWN THE ELEPHANT. NOW LET US SEE IF WE CAN HARNESS IT UP.

SECTION **three**

The Promoters

I don't think any man knows exactly what he would do until he is tempted—or any woman. A great many people live honest and virtuous lives that are not entitled to very much credit for it.
—Frederick Low, successor to Leland Stanford as Governor of California, in an interview about Central Pacific's "Associates" (1891)

CHAPTER **10**

THE COMMISSIONERS

> *We shall naturally take up our grand journey at Chi-
> cago. This is just one third of the way across the
> continent, and the beginning of the New West, whose
> spirit is nowhere so proudly rampant, into whose
> growth no other city so intimately enters. The pulse
> of the Pacific beats with electric sympathy on the
> southern shore of Lake Michigan; and if Chicago
> does not hear every blow of the pick in the depths of
> the gold mines of Colorado and Montana, she at least
> has made sure to furnish the pick, and to have a
> claim on the gold it brings to light.... Samuel Bowles,
> The Pacific Railroad—Open (1869).*

National crises seemed to be the most faithful ally of the Pacific Railroad. The Louisiana Purchase and the claims to Oregon Territory evolved the dream about it. The War with
Mexico and the California Gold Rush made it inevitable. The
first Congress during the Civil War pledged a $50,000,000
loan and millions of acres of the Great Desert toward its completion. Now, in the gloomiest week of the Republic's 86
years, hundreds of the Union's most important leaders came
to Chicago to argue the Union Pacific Railroad & Telegraph
Company into being.

The troops of Generals Pope and McDowell were still slink-

125

ing back into Washington from the second Battle of Bull Run. WASHINGTON IS IN DANGER, the Chicago *Tribune*'s correspondent wired on September 1: . . . REALLY IN GREATER DANGER THAN EVER BEFORE. THE CRISIS THROUGH WHICH THE CAPITAL, MARYLAND AND THE COUNTRY ARE PASSING IS EVEN YET UPON US . . . THAT WASHINGTON WILL OR WILL NOT BE TAKEN WE WILL NOT UNDERTAKE TO PROPHESY.

And 400 miles to the north, Minnesota was still in the throes of the Sioux Rebellion. More than 300 settlers had been murdered there, and scores of women and girls enslaved. Every community on the upper Mississippi was under martial law. Confederate agents, the rumors said, were in the Minnesota, Nebraska, and Kansas back countries, urging the tribes to insurrection and promising them, "The Great Plains shall be the red man's forever when our Confederacy wins the war." Iowa, Wisconsin, Michigan and Illinois might be raided.

Nevertheless, Chicago's Bryan Hall was crowded at eleven o'clock on the morning of Tuesday, September 2, 1862, when "the Board of Federal Commissioners for Construction of a Railroad and Telegraph Line from the Missouri River to the Pacific Ocean" opened its sessions. The Pacific Railway Act had named 158 commissioners. More than 75 of them came to Chicago to argue about procedures for a corporation that might take 10—and the gloomier prophesied 50—years to link the Union with its Pacific States.

The project attracted many of the great engineers too. John B. Jervis, now sixty-three years old, rode in with the Pennsylvania delegation. Silas Seymour arrived with the New Yorkers. Henry Farnam, president of the Rock Island, was part of the Illinois delegation.

In all, twenty states and territories had delegates. The largest representation came from New York. Utah, pointedly snubbed by the 1862 Act, did not send an observer.

The convention's attendance and its profound deliberations were extraordinary in view of the task assigned to the commissioners by the 1862 Act. Congress had ruled that the commissioners were to elect a president, secretary and treasurer for the Union Pacific Railroad & Telegraph Company, and then determine where and when the company's $1,000 bonds would be offered for public sale. When $2,000,000 worth of these bonds were sold (10 per cent cash with purchase), the president, secretary and treasurer would supervise an election, by the new stockholders, for a 13-man Board of Directors. Thereupon the President of the United States was to appoint two additional company directors who would act as direct representatives of the Federal Government, so were expressly forbidden to own any of the company's stock. When this election had been fulfilled, the 158 commissioners would automatically pass out of office. Thereafter the obligations of the Act became the responsibility of the stockholders and their directors, under the jurisdiction of the Secretary of the Interior and the half-dozen engineers he would appoint as construction-inspection commissioners.

These details are critical to an understanding of the promoter juggling that took place during the next thirteen months. Since the Pacific Railway Act limited the holdings by any one person to 200 shares of stock, it said—by implication—that for a down-payment of $200,000, an organization of ten or more investors could control the Union Pacific Railroad & Telegraph Company, its Government bonds and its land grants. It is appropriate to report, at this point, that Dr. Thomas C. Durant was not one of the 158 commissioners appointed by the Act, nor is he mentioned in the excellently detailed reports of the convention carried by Chicago newspapers.

While Robert E. Lee's army crossed the Potomac for the Confederacy's first invasion of Maryland, the commissioners created the railroad. William B. Ogden was elected president. The shortcomings of the Act and the necessity for amendments before "capitalists will be glad to take hold of it," themed Ogden's acceptance speech. "This project must be carried through." he said "by even-handed wise consideration and a patriotic course of policy which shall inspire capitalists of the country with confidence. Speculation is as fatal to it as Secession is to the Union. Whoever speculates will damn this project." After citing six technical changes that should be made in the Act—all in the interest of dividends for the investors and an operating fund for the railroad—he turned to the Whitney–Benton theme of Road to India. "Every New York merchant," he prophesied, "will prefer to get his goods in thirty days upon a bank discount rather than to run the risks of a nine-month Cape voyage. This route must command the travel of Europe to India and be the route for the conveyance of goods thence to England. The road will be without competition, with regular rates of tariff, and can easily earn enough to make a profitable compensation. It can be easily built and will cost less than many Eastern roads."

Governor Evans of Colorado assured the delegates that the Pacific Railroad could grade to the 11,400-foot elevation of Berthoud Pass, then "as soon as you get over the Snowy Range you strike a level, well-watered valley all the way to Salt Lake."

Delegate Monell of Nebraska rose to "dispel the Great American Desert Myth for the Eastern capitalists." The South and especially Jefferson Davis were, he charged, perpetrators of the myth:

> Formerly, under the administration when Jeff Davis was Secretary [he said] we had to depend on the South for our information. He said the Pacific Railroad could not pass over this route. Jeff Davis then knew that behind these hills Brigham Young had settled; that Utah was surrounded by a circle of civilization which had passed over those hills. He knew that the whole trade and commerce of Utah passed over them, and in the face of this he sent forth his garbled report.
>
> The railroad is behind the times. While the discussion of this project has been going on, Iowa has built a network of railroads. Although we are poor enough now, if you do not build this road soon, we will build it for you in five or six years. Kansas and Nebraska have sprung from the desert and are pouring their

riches into the bosom of the country. We used to think once, in sailing up our rivers, there was nothing but a desert a few miles beyond the green trees which skirted the river bank. Utah sprang up and now no man can estimate the great tide of travel across those plains. Daily 100 wagon trains pass over them for weeks and weeks. A new-born State [Nevada] has sprung up and the greater part of its mining provision goes over this overland route, which Jeff Davis said could never be constructed.

There is no desert upon that route. In the earlier maps published, which are studied at school, the region of the Platte Valley was laid down as the Great American Desert, and unfit for cultivation. I have traveled on foot from the mouth of the Platte to its forks, a distance of 400 miles, and I can say from actual personal knowledge, that every foot of this land is cultivable. It is a mistaken idea that this is poor land. The valley of the Platte is fertile. *

In the evenings the Pacific Railway commissioners' convention was like any other before or since. The most realistic discussions took place in the hotel bedrooms. Here the alliances for future action were sniffed out, with bourbon and cigars on the commodes and feet on the window sills. Most of the delegates roomed at the Tremont House. The realities of the Pacific Railroad were unveiled in full gloom.

Observe, mused these conversationalists, the advances being made between the Pennsylvanians and Missourians . . . Illinois' brazen courtship of the New Yorkers . . . the eagerness of the Iowans. Power politics was limbering up, and fancy knifework promised. Odds on an alliance of Philadelphia-St. Louis fighting an alliance of New York-Boston-Chicago!

Congress had said the railroad would start at the 100th meridian. And where is the 100th meridian? Way up the Platte Valley—more than 50 miles west of Fort Kearney. Obviously, the musings rumbled on, whoever gets to that 100th meridian first will win the West's trade, plus commissions on everything going through to and from the Orient.

A neat trick could be played. Illinois and New York interests just might try it. The Act had also stated that President

Lincoln had the authority to specify the Pacific Railroad's trackage width. Most of the lines coming into Chicago were 4 feet, 8 inches. But some graduate of the Erie must have built the Missouri Pacific between St. Louis and Kansas City; its rail bed was 5 feet, 6 inches wide. Let some smart fellow get to the White House and influence the thinking there toward a 4-foot, 8-inch width for Union Pacific. Then Missouri Pacific would have to be rerailed and regraded before it could carry through traffic. That just might give a New York-Boston-Chicago combine enough to beat a Philadelphia-St. Louis clique to the 100th meridian and get them a firm grip on that throughway handle. Lincoln was an Illinois man. He'd be reasonable.

There were still the Indians. Why should an Indian believe any white man's treaty, Union or Secesh? Gold rush to Colorado. Silver rush to Nevada. Gold rush to Montana. Just let rumor of gold in the Dacotahs get around. Off they'll go again. The Indians won't stand for any railroad, either. It would ruin their whole setup. No, sir. Union Pacific won't get built until the war's over.

This was the gloom surrounding each mealtime and evening at the Tremont, causing parlor lamps to burn late in the Ogden mansion, drawing engineers and politicians into knots of whispers, nods and back pats along the Bryan Hall vestibules. But the dazzle of Passage to India, an iron link to the Union's Pacific Coast, and real-estate booms across the Great Desert prevailed.

And what clearer harbinger of the West's future was there than Chicago herself? What the railroads had done for Chicago they could do for the West, especially if—as the Nebraskans and Coloradans alleged—the Great American Desert was a myth that had been carefully nourished by Jefferson Davis and the South's leaders.

When the Michigan Southern's ironmen had raced in over the Calumet swamp, Chicago was 18 years old. Despite the ship traffic down Lake Michigan and the hubbub about the

Illinois–Michigan Canal, Chicago had grown to only 30,000 population during those 18 years.

But in 1862, after 11 years as a railroad center, Chicago was sprawled out over muck and meadow to a population of 125,000. It was larger than Nauvoo, Galena, Joliet, Milwaukee, and all its other early rivals combined. It challenged venerable St. Louis as Queen City of the West. The railroads had done that.

Cholera, smallpox, yellow fever, pneumonia and tuberculosis writhed through the tenements; the Chicago River was a cesspool so foul with sludge that the spring runs of whitefish choked to death by the thousands; the cemeteries received so many coffins that they were stacked atop one another and "laid bare by the blowing away of their coverings of sand."

But the Chicago Flyers disgorged four immigrants on Water Street platforms for every one that rode the plumed black coach to a cemetery. Grain elevators and cattle pens barricaded the water front for miles.

On September 4, the Board of Trade gave the commissioners a tugboat tour through the Illinois–Michigan Canal and down the lake front. City engineers were working on a new, deeper channel that would reverse the flow of the Chicago River, thus enabling its sewage to empty west into the Illinois River. That artificial island two miles out in Lake Michigan would house pumps and crews for a tunnel that would bring in comparatively clean drinking water.

The guides pointed out a half-dozen buildings being jacked to the approved city level, 6 feet above the boardwalk. A young contractor named George Pullman, they explained, had undertaken a series of these store- and home-hoisting jobs. The fact should be of interest to the Pacific Railroad gentlemen because young Pullman had turned "muckjacker" in order to earn funds to continue his experiments with railroad sleeping cars. In 1859, he built one for the Chicago & Alton that had real beds down each side of the center aisle. Now he wanted to build a Palace car in which the beds could be hitched up against the wall during the day. But the car would cost $20,-000. Hence he was one of the contractors pioneering the new Chicago. By raising the entire city 6 feet, both allopathic and homeopathic physicians agreed, Chicago could overcome those "noxious swamp vapors" accredited as the source of much of its disease.

Halfway down to the new suburb of Hyde Park the guides pointed to a cottage on a bluff behind the Illinois Central's tracks. This was the summer home built by Stephen A. Douglas. That flower-covered mound near the cottage was The Little Giant's grave. The year before, dying from a complication of typhoid, rheumatism and "infectious throat," Douglas ordered that he be buried there overlooking his Illinois Central's branch line and the city. A fund was being subscribed for a massive brownstone monument at the site.

The commissioners leaned silently against the railing as the tug neared Douglas Bluff. A train of freight cars was backing into a siding below. A platoon of soldiers marched single file down the path beside The Little Giant's grave and deployed out alongside the train, muskets under arms. Then, like a great, gray serpent, a double file of Rebel prisoners stumbled past the mound, ebbed down the embankment, and disappeared into the boxcars. Some hobbled on crutches, empty pants' legs flapping. One stood stock-still at the path's head, screamed, and held out his arms until—after a guard's nod—comrades pushed in, cupped their arms in a cradle, and lifted him to trackside. The Rebs were heading home to be exchanged for Union troops captured in the Peninsula Campaign. The *Tribune* would tell the story in thirteen words tucked at the bottom of one of its city news columns:—"Eleven hundred and eighty-eight prisoners left Camp Douglas yesterday for the South."

Justice, a few of the commissioners reflected, wasn't so blind after all. Douglas had fearlessly argued compromise and popular sovereignty on the slavery issue. But his Kansas-Nebraska Bill and theory of "popular sovereignty" led to the Kansas war, John Brown's raid, and some said the Civil War itself. Now one of the largest prison camps in the Union festered beside his grave and was named for him.

The railroad was changing war too. Generals were sitting up late trying to adapt high iron to all the rules they'd learned at West Point. A war with railroads was a totally new kind of war. A regiment serving in the Mississippi Valley on Tuesday could be marching against Lee in Virginia on Saturday of the same week. Those Rebs might be back behind their own lines within 48 hours. Guns inspected and packed at an Ohio factory today could be firing lead in Tennessee next week. The railroad had changed most of the war strategies used since Alexander the Great, Caesar and Napoleon. Now war was geared to the railroad's 35 miles an hour instead of to the shank's-mare 2 and the cavalry's 8.

If the railroad could build miasmic Chicago into a Queen City and change the ancient rules of war, what could it do to and for the West? The possibilities were staggering.

Next morning the convention reached decisions. Henry V. Poor, editor of the *Railroad Journal*, was elected secretary of the Union Pacific. Thomas W. Olcott, Albany neighbor of John A. Dix and Thomas Durant's friend, was made treasurer. Union Pacific's $1,000 bonds were ordered placed on sale "in all principal cities of the Union" on November 1. President Ogden announced that the commissioners would be free guests of the railroads on the rides home. The convention adjourned with cheers.

Newspapers of late October and November described the bonds' gracious engravings, and carried editorials urging their purchase as "patriotism and faith in the Union's future." One of the first purchases was for five bonds in the name of "Brigham Young, Esq." Samuel Tilden, Henry Farnam, William Ogden and a few other commissioners, made similar investments. But bankers and Wall Street gamblers said No; the war-supply manufacturers would gobble every dollar they could wangle, and pay them interest rates of 30 per cent a year.

The newspapers turned to the greater excitements of war news. The public, when it remembered, shrugged. After all, the Pacific Railroad dream was fifty frustrated years old. By March, 1863, only 150 shares of stock were subscribed, giving the Union Pacific Railroad & Telegraph Company total assets of $15,000.

Dr. Thomas Durant beamed at the figures. Plans were developing delightfully.

CHAPTER 11

HUNTINGTON RULE

> *"The Central Pacific Railroad will be to California
> and the Pacific Coast what the Erie Canal has been
> to New York. The day is not far distant when the
> Pacific will be bound to the Atlantic by iron bands
> that shall consolidate and strengthen the ties of na-
> tionality and advance with giant strides the prosperity
> of our country."* . . . from a speech by Governor Le-
> land Stanford at the ground-breaking ceremony for
> Central Pacific, Sacramento (January 8, 1863).

A showdown between Ted Judah and Collis Huntington was
inevitable. Each was intent on domination. This explains Huntington's decision to come to Washington for the final weeks of
lobbying on the Pacific Railroad Act. It seems to have been
the real reason for their failure to appear at the commissioners'
convention in Chicago.

Since 1855, Ted Judah had carried the Central Pacific Railroad, literally, in his hat. He was its explorer, engineer, surveyor, promoter, bookkeeper, lobbyist, museum director,
purchasing agent and office boy. The question troubling Huntington was whether Judah could now settle into team harness
and concentrate his genius on the task of chief engineer.

Subconsciously, of course, other factors operated. Judah

135

was an aristocrat, born in an Episcopal manse and married into a wealthy New England family; Huntington was a tinker's son, born in a shanty and weaned to a miser's cynicism. Judah was another "little giant" with the little man's usual energy, ego and fox-terrier eagerness; Huntington was a tall introvert, taught by the rowdy frontier to be fox-sly and wolf-ruthless. Judah impoverished himself and probably borrowed funds from Anna and the Pierce family in order to finance promotions for Central Pacific and the lobbies for the Railroad Act; Huntington, during the same years, grubbed a fortune of a million or more out of nuts and bolts, miners' supplies and canned goods.

Logically then, Huntington took his question to Crocker, the Hopkins Brothers and Stanford. The problem worried them too. Even if the line built only as far as Dutch Flat, every hour of Judah's time should focus on right of way, construction of shops, and assembly of locomotives and cars. This was doubly essential if Central Pacific was ever to master the Sierras. And a full-time master trader and lobbyist in New York, Boston and Washington was just as imperative. Huntington was the right man for the multitude of duties back East, provided he could put up with that Washington pussyfooting.

Huntington slouched silently in his chair during the first few anteroom conferences on Capitol Hill. These members of the 37th Congress weren't really satisfied with the Railroad Act, he decided. They were just scared: —liverish about Confederate victory; liverish about California secession. The Act was a kind of nerve tonic, gulped fast and tremblingly.

Huntington maneuvered a chat with Judah around to the subject of rail, locomotive and blasting-powder purchases. Judah implied that, as Chief Engineer, the decisions were his alone to make. Huntington rumbled back at him. Every dollar spent, he insisted, must be invested as cautiously as if it were the Central Pacific's only one. And that might soon be the case. He knew the freight rates, both via Cape Horn and via the Isthmus of Panama. A ton of iron rail delivered around

the Cape cost $17.50 in freight charges and took six months,
New York to Sacramento; the same iron shuttled across the
Isthmus might reach Sacramento in two months, but the freight
cost rocketed to $50 a ton. Delivery charges on a locomotive
via Cape Horn would average $2,300; special handling via the
Isthmus could run to $15,000—almost as much as the manu-
facturer's F.O.B. price.

Hadn't Judah himself estimated construction costs averaging $90,000 a mile for the 140 miles to the Nevada line? The
Government loans—and they were only *loans,* mind you—
were $16,000 for a mile of valley land and $48,000 for a mile
of mountain. In other words, more than two-thirds of that
money must be raised by two methods: shrewd salesmanship
of stocks, and shrewder purchase and routing of supplies.
Judah was chief engineer. Location of the route and perfection
of its operations required all his genius. Shouldn't the haggles
with Pennsylvania ironmongers, New Jersey and Massachusetts
locomotive builders, Delaware explosives makers, New York
shipmasters, be transferred to an old hand? Even more critical
would be the wrangles with Boston, New York and Philadelphia bankers for bond sales and cash loans. Collis Huntington knew these labyrinths. He hoped Judah agreed?

Ted Judah realized that the scowling, hawk-nosed merchant
spoke the truth. He had brooded on the problem ever since
the moment that word came back from the White House that
President Lincoln had signed the Act. The sputter of Lincoln's
pen had transformed Ted Judah from a Galahad with a mission
to—what? He was Central Pacific's founder. But, by contract,
he was now only its chief engineer, subject to the orders of
Stanford and Huntington. He must make a decision. With Stanford as governor of California, and Huntington, the Crockers
and Hopkins all wealthy men willing to invest time and fortunes on the Pacific Railroad, there might never be a greater
opportunity for the Donner Pass route—or for Ted Judah.
How about, he parried, a shopping trip together to New York
and Boston?

The ironmongers in Pennsylvania knew that they held the business end of the whip. The Railroad Act said that all of the Pacific Railroad's supplies must be "Made in the U.S.A." The gunmakers and ironclad builders—each waggling a Washington priority order—would pay premium prices for every ton of iron the foundries could produce during the next year. Five hundred tons of rails a month? On what security? Ted Judah began to argue. Huntington interrupted. He'd always been curious to see an iron foundry; wonderfully important place; could they take a tour through? It worked, and Ted Judah grinned in admiration. Huntington was positively garrulous with questions about ore, the proportions of limestone, the necessity for hardwood charcoal, the possibilities of this newfangled anthracite. Could he come back in a week or two? Perhaps there'd be time to chat a bit more about rails? After all, Congress wanted this railroad built.

Ted Judah began to relax. Huntington shopped the same way Anna went after a silk dress. They toured the Baldwin & Company and Norris & Company works in Philadelphia; Danforth Cook & Company at Paterson, New Jersey; and the William Mason & Company plant at Taunton, Massachusetts, before Huntington would agree to a locomotive purchase.

He grumbled most about the shimmers of brass trim, gold scrollwork and hand painted "scenes along the way" on the engines. These things, he snapped, weren't meant to sit in a parlor. All Central Pacific wanted was a plain locomotive that would climb the Sierras without blowing up. That decoration, the salesman explained, was as subtle as it was lurid. The railroads needed the approval of the ladies. Locomotives were being made stylish from headlight to cab.

The blaze of brass began on the headlight stand and dazzled back through the bell to the valves in the cab. The sides of the headlight were painted with pastoral and mountain scenes. The cab, tastefully enameled a gunmetal black or clove brown, was decorated with garlands of enameled flowers beneath the windows. A vivid scarlet paint was "standard" for drive wheels, with gold-leaf scrollwork on the spokes.

Still grumbling about "the confounded foofaraw," Huntington agreed to the purchase of six locomotives. Two of them, grossing 50 and 47 tons, would be named Atlantic and Pacific. A 46-tonner was to honor Governor Stanford. The work-train engines, weighing only 18 tons each, would be the T. D. Judah and the C. P. Huntington.

Central Pacific's tiny cash reserve was already overpledged. Now there was the grim chore of trying to wheedle short-term loans from the New York and Boston bankers. Then the shopping tour must move on to the toolmakers, the bridge designers, the blasting-powder chemists. Ted Judah announced his decision. He was anxious to get on to Sacramento. Anna was waiting in Greenfield. Why didn't Huntington carry on alone?

The hawk nose twitched. The thin lips arched into a smile. Timely idea, Huntington admitted, because he'd been wondering again about the prospects of that wagon road through the Donner Pass. If Judah could find the time to run a survey, somehow paralleling the railroad route—well, it should bring in cash while the railroad was building. A nice, smooth wagon road from Dutch Flat to the Nevada line would certainly wean toll money away from those Downiesville and Placerville routes.

Judah agreed, but began to fret about it during the sail to Panama. Huntington was too slick. He'd never be able to trust the man, let alone like him. Was he scheming to develop a Donner Road . . . somehow manipulate its profits to his own account . . . and then walk out on Central Pacific?

Enthusiasm tingled back when Dr. Strong and other friends brought him up to date on California's response to the Railroad Act. San Francisco's councilmen were readying a bill for a $600,000 bond issue to be used for the purchase of Central Pacific bonds. Placer County and Sacramento County commissioners proposed similar local measures for a total investment of $550,000. Sacramento's City Council saw no problem in the outright gift of thirty acres of river-front real estate as the site for the railroad's terminal shops, roundhouse and offices.

As for Governor Stanford, his enthusiasms had become downright embarrassing to Republican leaders. Frederick F. Low, Stanford's successor as governor, told the details in 1883 during an interview with H. H. Bancroft. Lobbying by the Crocker Brothers produced a bill in the California Senate that would give Central Pacific $500,000 outright. Once the bill was in committee, Low said, Stanford "went upon the floor of the Senate and cajoled and bullyragged and got this bill through. It was a sort of neck or nothing at that time. The bill itself was of such doubtful constitutionality that people didn't believe it would hold water—that the state under the constitution could not contract a debt of $500,000 without submitting it to the people, and they had no money in the treasury, and if they built this road it would be an obligation to the state. I told Stanford very frankly, I didn't think that thing would stand at all, and he then went to work and whipped it around, pulled very strongly on everybody, and everybody was then very strongly in favor of the Pacific Railroad. They wanted the state to guarantee this $500,000 absolutely, or pay interest on $2,-500,000 bonds of the railroad company."

The bill had still failed to pass, however, when Low won the Republican nomination. "I had a good deal of discussion about it," Low told. "I said I would not sign any such bill as that . . . I would agree if the Legislature chose to pass a bill guaranteeing to pay twenty years interest on $1,500,000 of bonds, but not the principal. That would give them the use of a good deal of money at a time when it was pretty pinching times. And the bill passed in that shape. I signed it and the state has paid that amount.

"In the management of affairs then," he mused on, "Stanford showed more ability than ever before—well, he developed. I thought Stanford a very mediocre man then, but he had dogged persistence, and had faith, which is a great deal in this world."

The governor's obvious faith and open friendship gave Judah the assurance he needed. The Crockers seemed happy in their lobbying. Mark Hopkins remained the impassive bookkeeper. A multitude of engineering problems beckoned. Designs for wharves, storage yards, roundhouse and repair shops on the Sacramento land gift were more important, for the moment, than the location surveys. Crew hiring was his responsibility too. The locomotives would arrive, broken down, in a harumscarum pile of numbered crates. Master mechanics must be lured away from the Sacramento Valley Railroad, steamship lines—anywhere. Carpenters and blacksmiths must be hired, then trained to the peculiar skills of building passenger coaches, boxcars and flats. Designs must be drawn for way stations, freight houses and water tanks.

The blueprints for the Sacramento shops and other buildings filled one wall of Judah's office when Huntington staged home for the late November directors' meeting. The clearest clues to the Huntington-Judah struggle during the next six months come from the biographical letters Anna sent to H. H. Bancroft's researchers in 1891. "Some of the directors," Anna wrote, "could not take it as an overland enterprise, the magnitude of what they had to do. He used to say when he came from the directors' meetings, 'I cannot make these men, some of them, appreciate the elephant they have on their shoulders. They won't do what I want and must do. We shall just as sure have trouble in Congress as the sun rises in the east, if they go on this way. They will not see it as it is. Something must be done. I will not be satisfied before Congress and the world.' "

The directors' meetings began routinely. Judah's official report detailed the Pacific Railroad Act, pointed out its implications and responsibilities, then gave estimates of cash values on the land grants that would be earned as Central Pacific built across the Sierra. A fortune could be earned, he correctly predicted, from the vast stands of redwood and fir. These timbering operations could begin any time, in view of the millions of feet that would be needed for ties, stations, warehouses, water tanks, engine fuel, bridges and tunnel linings. Surplus lumber for sale to home builders, mines, boatyards and farms could, he pointed out, be hauled into Sacramento far more cheaply on the "deadhead" westbound runs of the construction trains than it was then being delivered by the barge tows operating between Oregon and San Francisco.

A glitter came into Huntington's eyes as he questioned Judah on details. Then, abruptly, he asked about the survey for the Donner Pass wagon route. Had it been made? Would it work?

A wall-like ridge, Judah explained, ran all the way to Donner between the Bear and Yuba river systems on the north and the American Valley on the south. Wagon teams could climb the ridge easily, with a minimum of grading. Construction costs shouldn't run over $1,000 a mile, perhaps less. He and Montague had written up full specifications.

Later in the same meeting Huntington introduced a motion that the construction contract for the first thirty-one miles of Central Pacific be awarded to Charles Crocker. The proposal may have been intended as a strategy move to test Judah's voting strength in the board as well as his willingness to go along on the sharp business practices that had become instinctive with Mother Lode merchants. Crocker volunteered to resign from the board if the contract was approved. Judah argued against it. The motion carried.

Through November, and perhaps December, the Crockers, Hopkins, Stanford and Huntington met evenings in one another's homes and argued late. Huntington had an idea; Attorney Edwin Crocker said it was legal and foolproof. In brief, Huntington visualized a holding company that would monopolize all of Central Pacific's contracts, and undertake independent projects such as this Donner Pass wagon road and the retail lumber trade that Judah talked about. Apparently Stanford held out. Yet the facts were frighteningly clear. Huntington had finally wangled rail shipments out of the Pennsylvanians by pledging the personal fortunes of Central Pacific's stockholders. Actually that meant Huntington, the Crockers, Hopkins and Stanford. A scheme like Huntington's offered them security, whatever happened. Thus "the Big Four," as they would be known to history, moved toward creation of The Associates and its sequential Construction & Finance Company. The first venture would be construction of the Donner Pass wagon road as a property of the Associates. Meanwhile, they agreed, they would start buying up the Central Pacific stock of the more timid shareholders.

Stanford was finally willing to go along, with the understanding that his brother, A. P., would be added to the board of directors. Probably decision was also reached to push the appointment of Edwin Crocker as "general agent," as well as attorney, for Central Pacific. Huntington and Hopkins favored the appointment of E. H. Miller, Jr., a former business partner of Hopkins, as secretary of Central Pacific, if and when it became possible to "unload" James Bailey. Thus, with Hopkins as Central Pacific's treasurer, the "arrangements" between the railroad company and the Associates could be handled discreetly.

The ascendancy of The Associates was intimated during the official groundbreaking ceremonies for Central Pacific on January 8, 1863. Governor Stanford was the principal speaker. Five state senators and assemblymen orated too. But Theodore Judah was not listed on the program of speakers. Either gossip was eddying about the marked coolness between Judah and some of the directors, or Judah loyally held to his decision to be the chief engineer, and had passed the hint along to editors that news stories should spotlight on Stanford, Crocker and the politicians.

On President Lincoln's birthday anniversary in 1862, Judah had hired Samuel Skerry Montague away from the Sacramento Valley Railroad and made him an assistant engineer. (After his 1836 tail-gate ride through Troy, Sam Montague had grown up in Rockford, Illinois. In 1852 Peter Dey had hired him as a surveyor's assistant for the Rock Island. He worked with Grenville Dodge for a year before moving over to the Burlington & Missouri as an assistant to Samuel B. Reed. The Pikes Peak gold rush lured him to Denver. In 1860 he joined a wagon train to California and hired out as a location engineer for the Folsom–Marysville extension of the Sacramento Valley Railroad.) Early in 1863, Montague was assigned to handle the location surveys toward Dutch Flat, and soon proved his skills. A few weeks later Judah sent out another young engineer, Lewis M. Clement, a Canadian and former location surveyor on the Welland Canal.

Huntington had returned east to sell bonds, double-check the first shipments of rails and tools, and ferret out the possibilities for a revision of the Railroad Act. His return to Sacramento in midspring marked the renewal of pressures against Judah. On May 13, Judah wrote Dr. Strong that, "I had a blow-out about two weeks ago and freed my mind, so much so that I looked for instant decapitation. I called things by their right name and invited war; but councils of peace prevailed and my head is still on; but my hands are tied, however. We have no meeting of the board nowadays, except the regular monthly meeting . . . but there have been any quantity of private conferences to which I have not been invited."

Charles Crocker was personally supervising the grade gangs on the wagon road from Dutch Flat through Donner Pass. The whisper spread that Central Pacific never did intend to build across the Sierra, but would end at Dutch Flat and serve as a mere feeder line for the wagon road. Newspapers picked up the rumor. San Francisco bankers helped the story gain credence. Home from Union Pacific's commissioners' convention at Chicago, D. O. Mills announced that his bank would "never invest a nickel in that Pacific Railroad." L. L. Robinson and other directors of the Sacramento Valley Road contributed funds to a mail promotion and lobbyist outcry about the "Dutch Flat Scandal." Groups formed in San Francisco and Placer County to fight against local subsidies to the Central Pacific. Both bills were forced into court litigations that delayed their passage for years and eventually yielded almost as much income to attorneys as they did to the railroad.

But Huntington had a new idea. If it worked it would enable him to raise enough money to finance construction as far as Dutch Flat and thus be in a position to collect the Federal bonds and land grants on the first 40 miles. He went first to J. W. Whitney, the state geologist. His question was simple: Where does the western base of the Sierra Nevada begin? Whitney said that the base of the mountains began, geologically, where the brown earth of the valley's flood plain ended and the red podzolic soil of the Sierras began. A little exploration proved that this occurred at Arcade Creek, only 7 miles east of Sacramento.

Huntington beamed. If Department of the Interior scientists and President Lincoln agreed, Central Pacific's Federal subsidy would jump from $16,000 to $48,000 a mile as soon as the embankment reached Arcade Creek—even though the terrain was pancake flat for the next 15 miles. Those 15 miles meant an additional $480,000 worth of Federal subsidy bonds.

Ted Judah took sharp issue. The base of the Sierras, he exploded, began where the Lord had placed the first granite outcroppings—22 miles east at Rocklin. The Associates overruled him. Whitney and other state employees prepared statements for submission to Washington. Huntington carried them East. The Department of the Interior agreed. Abraham Lincoln signed an order moving the base of the Sierra to Arcade Creek. Huntington was able to borrow more money in Boston and New York at the standard wartime rate of 3 per cent interest a month.

Then Mark Hopkins asked Judah for a 10-per-cent down payment on Judah's subscription of Central Pacific stock. There had been verbal agreement at the time of the incorporation that the stock would be awarded to Judah without payment in appreciation for his seven-year struggle to create Central Pacific, and the lobbying through of the Pacific Railway Act. Hopkins, the proper bookkeeper, shrugged. He had nothing about this in writing. He was responsible for company records. The stock could not be listed in Judah's name until the 10-percent cash payment was made.

Similar pressures were being exerted on other Central Pacific stockholders. Some forfeited through nonpayment. Others sold out to the Associates at a fraction of the face values. By early summer of 1863, Judah was contacting friends in New York and Boston about the possibility of buying out the Associates, recapitalizing Central Pacific with Eastern money, and forming a new directorate.

Leland Stanford claimed that Judah remained chief engineer of the road. Huntington, during interviews with H. H. Bancroft's researchers in the 1890's, alleged that Judah was paid $100,000 for his "stocks and interests" in the line. Anna Judah, in her correspondence with Bancroft's staffers, said that her husband "had secured the right and had the power to buy out the men opposed to him and the true interests of the Pacific Railroad at that time. Everything was arranged for a meeting in New York on his arrival . . . gentlemen from New York and Boston who were ready to take their places."

Again, Anna put the dust covers over their furniture and began packing. The couple booked passage on the S. S. *St. Louis,* sailing from San Francisco on October 3. Ted Judah wrote a final letter to Dr. Strong at Dutch Flat:

> I have a feeling of relief in being away from the scenes of contention and strife which it has been my lot to experience for the past year, and to know that the responsibilities of events, so far as regards the Pacific Railroad, do not rest on my shoulders. If the parties who now manage hold the same opinion three months hence that they do now, there will be a radical change in the management of the Pacific Railroad, and it will pass into the hands of men of experience and capital. If they do not, they may hold the reins for awhile, but they will rue the day that they ever embarked on the Pacific Railroad.
>
> If they treat me well, they may expect a similar treatment at my hands. If not, I am able to play my hand.
>
> If I succeed in inducing the parties I expect to see to return

with me to California, I shall likely return the latter part of December.

Heading into Acapulco, the *St. Louis* sighted a dingy Cape Horn schooner sloshing north on a San Francisco course. Judah leaned against the rail and watched her gloomily until she slipped over the horizon. It was the *Herald of the Morning*, carrying the first hundred tons of rail for the Central Pacific. Crocker's crews laid the first rails along Front Street on October 26. In New York City on the same day, Thomas C. Durant and George Francis Train gleefully finished their plans to take over the Union Pacific Railroad & Telegraph Company at the October 29th directors' meeting. Sometime that afternoon, a few blocks away, a ship's doctor helped carry delirious Ted Judah ashore.

CHAPTER **12**

MANHATTAN TRANSFER

> *When they spoke of our national debt, I asked them what right England had to monopolize the entire national debt of the world. I told them that one of these days we would roll up a national debt that would make them ashamed of themselves. . . .* George Francis Train (1863).

It was azalea time, 1863. But this spring the pink Mississippi earth was pocked by caisson wheels slithering the Union's slipknot around Pemberton's 40,000 Secesh troops on the Vicksburg bluffs. Upcountry near the Tennessee line, Brigadier General Grenville Dodge and his staff were experimenting with racial integration. When the order came through from General Grant's headquarters to "report immediately to the White House on an important matter," Dodge groaned.

Although President Lincoln had finally issued the Emancipation Proclamation on January 1, and the thousands of slaves fleeing out of the Confederacy were legally "freemen," organizing them into militia units to police their own jungle camps and help patrol the Atlanta–Vicksburg roads seemed to be quite another matter. Richmond and Atlanta newspapers had already demanded that a price be put on Dodge's head. Had

Kentucky and Tennessee politicians kicked up a rumpus in Washington too?

Automatically, Dodge reviewed his career during the past year to determine just what reply he might give when the dressing-down began. There was ample time for it. Southbound trains had the right of way. Although the cars of his train were a nightmare of maimed men screaming their pain at every brake slam, it sidetracked to let the "Grant Specials" clatter through: tarpaulined siege guns on the flatcars, guards atop the ammunition vans, a full company of militia jammed into each freight car.

Creation of the Negro militia had been forced on him by the war itself, Dodge reflected. No matter how you looked at it, war was a madman's profession. A lifetime ago—at least, the two years seemed that long—the order had come to slug south with Grant down the Mississippi Valley and supervise repairs on the twisted rails, burned bridges and blasted tunnels left by the Secesh.

He had received another assignment to organize a network of spies that would determine the strength of Pemberton's forces around Vicksburg and keep an eye on Joe Johnston's divisions in East Tennessee and Georgia. Finally at Corinth the Negroes began to sidle over the hills, often 100 families in one day. Some brought only their mules and hound-dogs. Some drove oxcarts loaded with children and cabin goods. All of them had heard the rumor that "Mister Lincoln's fixin' to make us free." They squatted in jungles of brush huts and dugouts just inside the Union lines. Then a delegation led by a country preacher came to Dodge and offered to organize patrols to police their camp. It worked. Dodge issued them uniforms. They drilled regularly and kept the peace in their shabby "Freedom Town." After the Emancipation Proclamation there was no holding them. They wanted to enlist and be trained as fighting soldiers for the Union. Grant approved the experiment. And now, Dodge mused, Mr. Lincoln was probably being pressured to dress him down because some Senator was being rabid about "armed Negroes and white womanhood."

If the war would only end. Then he could go back with Peter Dey. Between them they should be able to talk that $2,000,000 stock investment out of the Chicagoans and Iowans so that the Union Pacific Railroad could organize. He fished Dey's last letter out of a pocket and reread it. Back in Council Bluffs from the survey trip to Colorado, Dey had written:

> I learned enough to satisfy myself that no railroad will—at least in our day—cross the mountains south of the Cache la Poudre and probably not south of Cheyenne Pass. I know but little of the position or prospects of the Pacific Railroad Company. Into whose hand the management will fall is a serious question. Mr. Farnam would, if ten years younger, take hold of it. I think as a general rule that there was more confidence felt in him at the railroad convention in Chicago than any other prominent railroad man there. We have finished the road to Brooklyn [the Mississippi & Missouri Railroad to Brooklyn, Iowa] and are slowly laying track toward Grinnell, but when we shall reach that place is all in the future, depending entirely on Thomas Durant and how he feels about it.

Dodge folded the letter carefully and tapped it against the window sill. Perhaps if the politicians were pressuring Lincoln —and it must be a serious charge to have the Commander in Chief order a mere brigadier to the White House—perhaps he'd be asked to resign. In some ways he'd welcome it. Dey would understand and give him his old job. Together they might persuade Farnam to take over, free and clear of Thomas C. Durant.

Nevertheless, his lips were dry and his hands trembled when the orderly at the White House waiting room called his name and opened the door to Lincoln's office. Mr. Lincoln seemed to have aged twenty years since that afternoon on the hotel steps in Council Bluffs. The beard made his face longer and gaunter. His eyes were tired and pouched. But his teeth flared white in a grin as the gangly frame lurched up and swung across the room, hand outstretched. "Need you," he said.

"Need you real bad. I want you to help me decide the commencement point for the Union Pacific Railroad."

Dodge could not restrain a gasp, but stood stiffly at attention until the President was back behind his desk and seated. Seemed to be enough railroad lobbyists around Washington, Mr. Lincoln began, to form a regiment. Each group wanted its hometown named the official terminal for the Union Pacific. Every Nebraska and Iowa village in the Missouri Valley was getting its licks in. He shrugged and smiled. Somehow, it didn't stack up with the extremely poor sale of Union Pacific stock. The Council Bluffs delegation, a week or two before, had included Peter Dey. Dey had quoted Dodge and described his 1856–9 surveys of the Platte Valley route. That had reminded Lincoln of the afternoon at Council Bluffs. So he'd asked the War Department to trace Dodge down and call him in.

Dodge nodded thanks and settled back in his chair. Lincoln reached into a desk drawer, pulled out a roll of maps, then—with droll asides—reviewed the arguments presented by the lobbyists for each community. "I saw," Dodge wrote 30 years later, "that he was very thoroughly posted in the demands of the different places, and I also saw that no other railroad company or place had made any such explorations either east or west of the Missouri River as had we, and that they had no such reliable information."

Sometime during the afternoon Dodge learned about the new decision on track gauge. The official rail gauge for the State of California was 5 feet. Huntington and the Californians had made such an ardent case for it that Lincoln had tentatively approved a 5-foot gauge for the entire Pacific Railroad. Then, the President grimaced, the Chicagoans and New Yorkers had hollered. The New York Central, Michigan Central, Michigan Southern, Lake Shore, Rock Island and Burlington, all used 4′ 8″ gauge. The 5′ gauge, they mourned, would mean adjustable wheel trucks on every through car, or ruinous realignment of roadbeds and enlargement of every bridge and tunnel between Iowa and the Atlantic Coast. Dodge grinned, recalling that the Missouri Pacific was in just as bad a fix with its broad gauge between St. Louis and Kansas City.

Next, the President went on, the Congressmen began groaning too. The official gauge of the Pacific Railroad was about to be changed to 4' 8". So much for that. Now, what should he do about that official commencement point in Iowa? It was a rough assignment for a Council Bluffs homeowner who had devoted five or more years to surveying and talking up the Council Bluffs–Platte Valley throughway. The President, he gathered from the twinkle in his eyes, realized this, and was challenging him as an engineer. Just the same, he couldn't quite believe that this was the real reason for ordering him to Washington.

Mile by mile, Dodge described the shore bluffs, swamps and gradients down the Missouri's midvalley. Sioux City was too far north and Plattesmouth too dangerous during the spring floods. Inevitably, as any engineer would have, he pinpointed Council Bluffs-Omaha as the logical terminal for the Union Pacific. Lincoln said he would think about it, swung his chair around, and asked Dodge's frank opinion about the disappointing sale of Union Pacific bonds.

"The Pacific Railroad is too big for private enterprise," Dodge replied. "The government should build it—or at least amend the Act along the lines indicated by the commissioners' convention." The Government would do everything in its power to encourage private industry, the President said slowly. His next sentences were so carefully couched that Dodge instinctively leaned forward. Something told him that this was the real reason for his trip to the White House.

Perhaps, Mr. Lincoln drawled, Congress might be willing to shift the Federal loans on the Pacific Railroad from a first-mortgage to a second-mortgage category.

This really was it! Such a revision of the Act would enable Union Pacific and Central Pacific to issue first-mortgage bonds. Lincoln was staring at him expectantly. Dodge blurted the question: "May I take the news to New York that the White House would consider such a revision of the Pacific Railroad Act?"

Mr. Lincoln nodded.

The Lincoln–Dodge conversation occurred during the third or fourth week of April. Dodge was in New York the next day, reporting its details to Alcott and Poor. Thomas Durant may have sat in. If not, he heard the story within a few days, began a series of conferences with William Ogden, Cornelius Bushnell and H. S. McComb, then offered to finance a lobby to concentrate on a new Pacific Railroad Act.

At 10 A.M. on July 4, President Lincoln announced the decisive victory over Robert E. Lee's Army of Virginia at Gettysburg. At 10:30 A.M. General Grant wired the White House from Vicksburg, THE ENEMY SURRENDERED THIS MORNING. After twenty-seven desperate months, the Union could grind from defense to offense. The Civil War might thunder on for years and could still end with an independent Confederacy, but now the New West belonged to the Union.

Every banker, broker and industrialist knew the American Routine: War . . . Depression . . . A massive trek into the West by the jobless and dispossessed. Upstate New York, the Ohio Country, Kentucky and Tennessee were the business depression "run-off" after the Revolution. Michigan, Indiana, Illinois, Alabama, Mississippi and Louisiana took up the economic slack after the War of 1812. California, Texas, Western Missouri and Kansas Territory played the same role after the War with Mexico. Nebraska, Colorado, Utah, Montana and the vast Indian heartland of the Dacotah Territory were destined to attract the unemployed and battle-shocked wanderers after the Civil War. The Pacific Railroad would be their throughway.

Grenville Dodge furloughed home to Council Bluffs with malaria soon after the Vicksburg surrender. "I find they are about to organize the Union Pacific," a friend wrote him from New York on August 20. "Durant is determined that it shall be organized as to terminate at Omaha. He asked me this afternoon if you could be induced to leave the Army and take hold. I told him you could. He will write you today upon the subject."

This seems to have been the first indication to Dodge, Dey and the other railroad veterans on the Iowa frontier that Durant was plotting to take over the Union Pacific Railroad & Telegraph Company. Dodge turned down Durant's offer and passed the news along to Dey that the New York manipulator was again demonstrating his skill in intrigue and "double talk."

Durant's next move appeared as a news story in the October 7th issue of the Chicago *Tribune*, under the headline of THE PACIFIC RAILROAD:

OMAHA, NEBRASKA, OCT. 6. The $2,000,000 of stock required by the charter of the Union Pacific Railroad Company, previous to an organization, has been subscribed and paid to the treasurer, and a meeting of the stockholders has been called to convene in the city of New York on the 29th inst. What is still more important to Omaha, the Mississippi & Missouri Railroad has been selected as the commencement of the Pacific route. The western terminus of that Road is on the bank of the Missouri River, opposite this city. A survey for the great Pacific Route, from Omaha west to the Platte Valley, will be commenced in a few days, under the direction of Mr. Dye [Dey, obviously], Chief Engineer of the Mississippi and Missouri Railroad. Lines will also be run from the Missouri River west to the Platte Valley commencing at Bellevue, Plattsmouth and the mouth of the Platte River. The Engineers who are to run these lines are now in this city.

During the 1870's, in an altercation between Council Bluffs and Omaha about the "official eastern terminal" of the Union Pacific, the Supreme Court ruled that President Lincoln's decision fixing the eastern terminal of Union Pacific "on the western boundary of the State of Iowa . . . within the limits of the township of Iowa opposite the town of Omaha in Nebraska" was dated, "November 17, 1863."

The October 7th announcement in the *Tribune* must have

been a Durant handout and part of a typically elaborate plan for "hedging the bet" of the $150,000 to $175,000 he had just invested in order to take over the company.

The Mississippi & Missouri's railhead was still more than 150 miles out of Council Bluffs on October 7. The newspaper report about its selection as "the commencement of the Pacific route" tingled through brokerage offices. The stock began to rise. When it reached 149, Thomas C. Durant sold out. Dodge and others later inferred that Durant's profits in the move were "more than $250,000." He reinvested part of it in the Chicago & Galena and other roads that William Ogden was merging into the Chicago & Northwestern. Subsequently, a second publicity campaign shrilled the Chicago & Northwestern's plan to complete, "the most direct Pacific Railroad connection," via Clinton and Cedar Rapids, Iowa. Its stock, too, rose to 150.

Weeks before October 7, Durant had rigged the plan for his take-over of Union Pacific at the October 29th directors' meeting. The plan was intriguingly simple. By September 1, less than $400,000 worth of Union Pacific bonds had been pledged. The remaining $1,600,000 required before a board of directors could be elected called for a 10-per-cent down payment of $160,000. Durant went to merchants and brokers in New York and Philadelphia with an offer to underwrite this down payment if they would accept the bonds in their names. Later, if they decided that this was a sound investment, they could reimburse him.

Durant confessed the trick during his testimony in 1873 before one of Congress' committees for "investigation of the Pacific Railroad." "Finding it impossible to induce capitalists to engage in the enterprise," he testified, "I succeeded in obtaining subscriptions for the requisite amount only by inducing my friends to subscribe; I advancing the money to pay their first installment of 10 per cent, thereon, giving them the option to retain the stock by returning me my advances, or I would find parties to take the stock off their hands. All of this stock, amounting to three fourths of the whole stock required to be subscribed, was subsequently transferred to me, the parties not choosing, even after the Amendment in 1864, to take any risk in the enterprise."

Again—coincidence. Thomas Durant and Collis Huntington had similar habits and characteristics. Each was a lone wolf, brilliant in economic plotting but ruthless in social relationships. Both were natives of Connecticut. Both, like Judah, Stanford, Crocker, Harte, Dix, Sherman, Montague and Dillon were at the Mohawk–Hudson junction in 1836. Each wrested control of one of the Pacific Railroad companies during the same months of 1863.

During the weeks of the Huntington-inspired showdown between Theodore Judah and The Associates, the ten-year-old partnership between Henry Farnam and Thomas Durant seethed to dissolution. Farnam had supplied most of the funds for the Platte Valley and trans-Rocky surveys made by Peter Dey and Grenville Dodge. Both Dey and Dodge hoped that Farnam would be elected either president or executive director of Union Pacific when construction began. But Durant's juggle of Mississippi & Missouri stock and the rumors about his Union Pacific takeover brought Farnam to a decision he had been pondering for more than a year. He resigned as president of Rock Island and as a Union Pacific commissioner, sold his Chicago home, and booked passage to England for Mrs. Farnam and himself. During the next three years, while Union Pacific writhed through a series of Durant crises, the Farnams toured Europe, Greece and the Holy Land.

Meanwhile, like was attracting like. A partnership between Durant and George Francis Train developed during the summer or early fall of 1863. During the decade since he had roared out of the Liverpool office of his Uncle Enoch's White Diamond Line, Train had become a millionaire who was as deft at writing essays and delivering lectures as he was at gauging market trends.

In England when the Civil War began, Train charmed London bankers into backing construction of a street-railway between Marble Arch and Shepherd's Bush. He ballyhooed the project as "the workers' carriage line," designed small coaches that could be drawn by a team of horses, and set up a schedule of trips every half hour. His "tramcar line" was London's first of the horsecars, cable cars and trolley cars that would enable the world's cities to sprawl out to Suburbia. But it was too radical for the Londoners of 1862. Clerks and factory workers decided it was more manly to walk to and from their jobs. Carriage owners sputtered about the iron tracks and the lumbering vehicles' interference with traffic. Also, Train's temper flared against the British Government's flirtation with the Confederacy, and the construction of Confederate warships at Liverpool shipyards. He delivered a series of lectures criticizing Prime Minister Gladstone on both issues, then plunked boldly for Ireland's freedom. Her Majesty's Government ordered Train out of the country, and one source contends, threw him in jail until sailing time. London's first tramway went into bankruptcy.

But Train had a passion for railroad promotion. In 1863 he bought a few Union Pacific bonds, made Durant's acquaintance, and began suggesting plans for corporations that would control construction contracts and develop Federal land grants as homestead and industry sites. Durant urged Train to explore the idea. He vaguely recalled that some sort of organization for financing railroads had been set up in Pennsylvania. Train nodded. There was a huge one in France, too, called the Crédit Mobilier.

While Durant completed negotiations for a Union Pacific board of directors that would be representative of the states and territories but pliable to any plans he and Train might decide on, Theodore and Anna Judah were sailing toward New York. George Francis Train may have been one of the "Boston gentlemen" who, as Anna wrote in 1891, were waiting to discuss Judah's plan for purchase of the Central Pacific from The Associates. Train's enthusiasm for the Pacific Railroad and his vision of a massive realty promotion across Nebraska, Dacotah and Colorado would have exuded into California and Nevada. However, the probabilities are that Judah was negotiating with some of his old associates on the New England railroads plus banker friends of the Pierce family. The name of Cornelius Vanderbilt consistently appears as Judah's principal prospect in New York. Vanderbilt bought up the New York & Harlem Railroad that year, and began the three-year struggle that gave him control over the New York Central. Statements on record by Vanderbilt's relatives indicate that he distrusted Thomas Durant, so never invested in Union Pacific. Yet by refinancing Central Pacific and focusing his skills on the Pacific Railroad he could have become its tycoon and changed the outcome of the massive race across the Great Desert. But the identity of any of Judah's prospects is guesswork. Anna never identified any of them. Her 1891 letters are the only source of facts about the twenty-three-day trip from San Francisco to New York.

The skies darkened, she told, as their train coughed up the mountain ridge at the Isthmus of Panama. Thunderheads glimmered black and gold above the Caribbean. Ted Judah hurried from the train shed at Aspinwall, purchased an umbrella, and when the deluge broke, gallantly escorted women and children from the train to the steamship wharf. "He could not see them exposed to the rain and not try to do his part and more for women and children who had no one to help them," Anna wrote.

At sea that night Judah complained of a headache and began to shiver. The ship's doctor pronounced it yellow fever —one of the nineteenth century's deadliest plagues. Their stateroom was quarantined. At the New York wharf, sometime on October 26, the ship's doctor helped carry Judah to a carriage. Anna sent the Manhattan Hotel's porter with a message to Dr. F. N. Otis, a family friend. Dr. Otis's examination confirmed the ship's doctor's analysis. Judah was dying of yellow fever. "He has overworked," Otis concluded, "and such men fall victims to such a fever."

A few blocks away on Williams Street, during the same hours, Durant and Ogden were greeting the first delegations of Union Pacific commissioners. Since the company was still under the jurisdiction of William Ogden and the commissioners, Durant's role was that of "friend in the back room." His plan for development of the Union Pacific depended on a majority vote in the board of directors. He must have selected 15 or 20 of the nominees for the board—and run a rehearsal or two on nomination and voting procedures.

John A. Dix was Durant's choice as president of Union Pacific. During the quarter century since his appointment as New York's Secretary of State (and school superintendent) Dix had become one of the most powerful figures in the Republican party. He was one of New York's United States Senators in the 1850's. When the John B. Floyd-Pony Express scandal and South Carolina's secession exposed the methodical looting of Federal funds and Army arsenals by the Southerners in Buchanan's Cabinet, Dix was ordered to Washington as Secretary of the Treasury for the desperate two months before Lincoln's Inaugural. At Congress' insistence he moved into the White House and literally became Buchanan's guardian. The confidence he restored enabled Federal loans that financed Lincoln's program and the creation of Union armies during the spring and summer of 1861.

During the 1850's Dix, too, became a railroad enthusiast. The Erie Railroad elected him president. Durant sought him out while the Mississippi & Missouri was being created, introduced him to Henry Farnam, and persuaded him to act as president of that line. Now Dix, like many Republican leaders, held the rank of major general. His war duties would prevent much attention to Union Pacific matters. But his name should do much for its stock promotions, as well as the "more favorable" Road Act that President Lincoln had suggested to Grenville Dodge.

The October 29th meeting moved smoothly, as per rehearsal. Of the 30 directors elected, 17 were New Yorkers. The total number of shares voted, reported the newspapers, was "2,007 of $1,000 each." On this basis, control of the Union Pacific Railroad & Telegraph Company cost Durant a down payment of $160,700.

The October 30th election of officers was just as routine. Henry V. Poor continued as secretary. John J. Cisco, a New York banker and General Dix's assistant secretary during those grim weeks at the Treasury post, was a logical choice for company treasurer. The election of Dix as president was unanimous. So was Durant's election as vice-president and general manager. Only 16 of the 30 directors were present for the voting, plus the 2 directors representing the Federal Government.

That night, while the new officers drank toasts to "the Road to India" and "the Lifeline of the Union," Anna Judah and Dr. Otis knelt in prayer beside Ted Judah's bed. His face was a livid yellow. His foam-flecked lips opened now and then to mumble phrases about "the road." He died at dawn on November 1.

Again, destiny had readjusted the timetable for the Pacific Railroad. The day after Thomas Durant stole control of the Union Pacific Railroad & Telegraph Company for $160,700, the young genius who had visualized and created the Central Pacific Railroad died in a hotel room a few blocks away. With Judah's death, Huntington rule of Central Pacific and the fantastic future of The Associates was assured.

While a Connecticut Valley train carried Judah's casket toward Greenfield, Massachusetts, President Dix approved General Manager Durant's orders for an elaborate groundbreaking ceremony for the Union Pacific Railroad at Omaha on December 3.

CHAPTER **13**

THE RIG

*The most gigantic and in all respects the most im-
portant thoroughfare ever projected is now fairly
commenced. In a very few years the commerce of
the world will roll across the American continent in
one vast, never ceasing flood. The location of the
road up the Platte Valley and through the South Pass,
where the buffalo ages ago surveyed the route for it,
and where it can be reached from the mining regions
of Colorado and the still richer and more extensive
gold deposits of Idaho, with equal facility, should be
a source of congratulation to the nation and the entire commercial world, who will wait with deep
anxiety the completion of this vast enterprise. . . .*
Editorial, Chicago *Tribune* (December 5, 1863).

The cash balance of Union Pacific on November 1, 1863,
totaled less than $200,000. Omaha was 170 miles up Missouri
River sand bars from the Hannibal & St. Joseph's railhead at
St. Joseph, and 150 miles west of the Mississippi & Missouri's
railhead in Iowa. Every rail, bolt, shovel and keg of blasting
powder needed for construction must be hauled in over one of
these routes. The new owners had enough cash on hand to
finance less than five miles of track.

But Thomas Durant was a gambler. A study of his career
and the web of high-interest loans, mortgage bonds and hold-

ing companies he spun around the captive Union Pacific during 1864 and 1865 leads to the conviction that the saga of the 1866–9 construction was the haphazard aftermath of a stock swindle. Durant, like Huntington and The Associates, invested in the Pacific Railroad with the sole idea of wresting profits from stock manipulations. Somewhere along the way The Associates changed their technique—and built on to become "railroad kings."

Durant's goal never changed. His daring commands admiration. The hazards confronting Union Pacific were far greater than those looming before the Associates. Central Pacific was a California corporation. The Federal land grants and 6-percent loan were pledged for the trackage it was to build over the 140 miles of Judah's Donner Pass route to the California–Nevada border. Since it was a state enterprise and on the other side of the continent, Federal inspections were casual. But Union Pacific was a Federal project and its techniques and efficiency were literally "under the nose" of Congress and the violently partisan press of every Eastern city.

The Indian problem raised a second risk far more ominous to Union Pacific than to Central Pacific. The Spanish and the Forty-Niners had killed off the last vestiges of Indian resistance in central California. The Paiute War of 1861–2 broke the spirit of Nevada's tribes. Charles Crocker later boasted that he kept all the Indians along Central Pacific's right of way pacified by giving the tribal chiefs lifetime passes for free rides in day coaches. But Union Pacific's route aimed at the "sacred lands" of the Cheyenne, Sioux, Arapaho, Shoshone, and other tribes who had mastered the wild horse and bison economy. Inevitably, then, Union Pacific would become involved in the negotiations, and probable bloodshed, of new treaties between these tribes and the Federal Government. A feud already smoldered between the Army and the Department of the Interior's Indian Bureau. Every politician realized that the whisper of a gold or silver "strike" anywhere in Indian country would trigger a "rush" like the "Pikes Peak or Bust" ox trains of 1857, the invasion of the Comstock Lode and Western Nevada in 1859–60, and the push to Montana in 1862–63.

Finally, the Pacific Railroad Act assured Central Pacific of a monopoly on Federal loans and land grants east to the Nevada border, provided it could meet the time requirements. But political pressures forced Union Pacific into bitter competition by defining the 100th meridian as "the official beginning point" of the Pacific Railroad. The first branch line to reach there would win the right to build on toward the California border; and would be in a position to dominate, or take over, the Union Pacific. A revision of the Act could relocate "the commencement point" as easily as it could shift the Federal loans from a first- to a second-mortgage status.

Construction by the competition confronted Durant when his dummy stockholders enabled the October 29th birth of Union Pacific. A week or two before, Samuel Hallett & Company had broken ground for the Union Central Pacific Railroad at Leavenworth, Kansas. Its stockholders included Philadelphia and St. Louis bigwigs; the Union Central Pacific, then, was a realization of the Philadelphia–St. Louis "team-up" predicted during the Federal commissioners' convention in Chicago. Hallett pledged to have rails into Lawrence, Kansas, before January 1, then build on up the Kansas River Valley during 1865, and reach the 100th meridian "before 1866." The firm's circulars to prospective stockholders promised financial support from Colorado; the right of way would follow the Smoky Hill Stage route through Fort Riley to Denver, cross the Rockies via Berthoud Pass, and use "the Great Valley route" into Salt Lake City.

This forced Durant to announce a groundbreaking ceremony for Union Pacific at Omaha. Early in November he sent Herbert M. Hoxie on to Council Bluffs to hire work crews, contact local politicians, and ballyhoo the celebration. A courthouse "fixer" in Des Moines, Hoxie had met Durant during the lobbying for Mississippi & Missouri's Iowa charter. Indications are that Durant kept Hoxie on his personal pay roll as a scout on political developments. Hoxie performed his job well. The "Grand Opening Ceremony" must have gobbled a fourth of the $200,000 in Union Pacific's treasury. The committee on arrangements sent sheaves of telegrams to state governors, Federal officials, bankers and newspaper editors urging each to attend the "gala ceremony and banquet." Companies of Nebraska and Iowa militia hauled cannon out to the Missouri's banks and began firing salutes at noon on December 2. More than 1,000 people followed Nebraska's Governor Saunders up the frozen trail to the spot Durant and Peter Dey finally agreed on, two miles north of Omaha's ferry landing. Peter Dey and Governor Saunders turned the first clods of half-frozen clay. George Francis Train, as principal orator, prophesied that, "Immigration will pour into these valleys. Tens of millions of immigrants will settle in this golden land in twenty years."

New York and Midwest newspapers described the ground-breaking in detail. On December 3, the Chicago *Tribune* printed another beaming Union Pacific Railway editorial, avowing that the project "is in the hands of the largest capitalists and most reliable men in the nation." It closed with a roar at Hallett & Company for attempting to "humbug the people of Chicago, and the Northwest, by any distorted maps and such special addresses as your last circular contains . . . The true policy of Hallett & Company, when they find that the people cannot be wheedled into the belief that they are the Union Pacific Railway, will be to connect their road with the great trunk line at or near Fort Kearney." Thus the Chicago-St. Louis battle to be Queen City of the Pacific Railroad was joined.

The *Tribune*'s promotion of Union Pacific during the next four years was primarily responsible for creation of the "Western trade commissions" sent out to the new railhead communities by Chicago's board of trade. Before 1870 they contracted the bulk of the retail and jobber orders in Nebraska, Wyoming, Colorado, Montana and Utah for Chicago manufacturers. But the *Tribune*'s assumption that "the largest capitalists and most reliable men in the nation" were behind Union Pacific was either wishful thinking or another product of an interview with Durant. The company needed more than $1,000,000 of capital, or credit, to build its first 40 miles of track. The December publicity sold only a few bonds.

On January 1, General Dix signed an order appointing Peter Dey as chief engineer of Union Pacific and Colonel Silas Seymour as consulting engineer. Two weeks later Durant was using his old trick of fanning town feuds as a means of promoting stock sales. It geared with his plan to boost Chicago & Northwestern stock and to postpone Union Pacific construction work until George Francis Train perfected a plan for holding companies.

Grenville Dodge received the first news of Durant's "rig" when his brother Nathan wrote from Council Bluffs during January: "Omaha is in trouble again over the treatment received of Durant and his clique. Orders came yesterday to land all iron at Bellevue, and Omaha people are given to understand that the terminal of the railroad is to be down there." Next came a grumble from Herbert Hoxie: "I just got a dispatch from Durant to ship to Bellevue instead of Omaha, and he says he has ordered freight at Omaha reshipped. This is damn bad."

General Sherman's Corps was advancing on Meridian, Mississippi. Dodge knew this preluded a drive toward Atlanta. He was under orders to organize rail-repair and bridge crews. But he took time to send a telegram of angry protest to Durant. Durant's reply was prompt and stubborn: "My plan will be carried out or the work abandoned. Iron is being shipped from St. Joseph to Bellevue. This is too important an enterprise to be controlled by local interest. The road can be built by the Kansas line, if no other way. No road through Iowa will terminate at Omaha."

The word battle sputtered on. Rumors spread that Mississippi & Missouri planned to by-pass Des Moines and build northwest to a Pacific Railroad terminal 10 to 25 miles north of Omaha. Two weeks later the same gossipers had it "on authority" that "the millionaires are going to pull clear out of Iowa and build from St. Joseph to Fort Kearney." Iowa legislators drew up a bill that would rescind Mississippi & Missouri's charter if it veered from the Peter Dey-Grenville Dodge route through Des Moines to Council Bluffs. Chicagoans, Iowans and Nebraskans sent angry petitions to their Congressmen.

Sometime during the winter, too, a brawling group of Union Central Pacific employees shot Samuel Hallett. He died a few hours later. The St. Louis–Pennsylvania backers spent weeks trying to locate a contractor who would carry on. Before construction got under way again late in the spring of 1864, the corporation had reorganized as, "the Union Pacific, Eastern Division," had abandoned Hallett's plan to build into Denver via the Smoky Hill route, and concentrated on beating Union Pacific to the 100th meridian line in the Platte Valley.

In New York City, Durant, Olcott and Cisco—with casual approval by General Dix—concentrated on lobbying activities for revision of the Pacific Railroad Act. Inevitably they conferred with Collis Huntington. Huntington, in a rare burst of confidence, may have outlined the scheme of The Associates' holding company. This was precisely the type of "rig" Durant wanted for Union Pacific, since it removed all detail accounting for construction and materials' costs from the books of the parent corporation, concealing them from any ambitious politician or embittered stockholder. Both Huntington and Durant were commuting between New York, Washington, and Boston in January and February, 1864. They solicited the same bankers for loans and argued with the same brokers about bond sales.

Moreover, Huntington needed advice. The Associates had named Samuel Montague acting chief engineer of Central Pacific a few days after Theodore Judah's death. But Montague had neither Judah's reputation or experience. Central Pacific needed a consulting engineer with a quotable background of achievement. Judah's death had rekindled the charges about "end of the line at Dutch Flat" and "using Federal funds to build a feeder line for the Donner Pass wagon road." Appointment of an engineer with a sound reputation should help scotch "the Dutch Flat Scandal."

Durant could afford to be gracious. Union Pacific had already hired Horatio Seymour's brother Silas. George Gray, chief engineer of the New York Central, was a likely prospect. Cornelius Vanderbilt was sparring with the Central's owners; Vanderbilt hadn't lost a fight yet. When the Commodore took over New York Central he'd probably put on his own engineering staff. Gray might consider a move to California. Huntington interviewed George Gray, and recommended him to Leland Stanford. Gray sailed for California during the spring of 1864, settled in amiably with Montague and Clement, and decades later succeeded Montague as chief engineer of the Southern Pacific system.

During the conversations about Gray, Huntington may have dropped hints about the Associates' techniques to Durant. If so, they coincided with the discovery that George Francis Train made in Pennsylvania during January or early February. In the early spring of 1859 a group of Pennsylvanians had organized a holding company specifically intended to finance the construction of railroads. It was approved by the State Legislature under the name of the Pennsylvania Fiscal Agency. A board of directors was elected in May, 1863. But no projects were under way when George Francis Train appeared at the Philadelphia office in midwinter, 1864. Train's report to Durant led to a series of meetings.

On March 3, Durant purchased the charter of the Pennsylvania Fiscal Agency. Three weeks later Pennsylvania's Legislature pushed through a special act ruling, "From and after the passage of this act, 'the Pennsylvania Fiscal Agency' shall be named instead thereof 'the Crédit Mobilier of America,' with all the powers, privileges and authorities they had under their former name." Permission was also granted to revise the charter of the company so that an agency "empowered with the authority of the board of directors" could be established in New York City. A railroad bureau could be also established at the "New York agency," the new charter ruled, with "sole management of railroad contracts" under direction of Crédit Mobilier's managers.

The term, "Crédit Mobilier of America" is conceded to have been George Francis Train's brain child. It was remarkably bad judgment as the name for an organization that would seek short- and long-term loans from Boston, Philadelphia and New York bankers. Train had apropriated the name of a joint stock company that had scandalized Europe's bankers for a decade. Founded by the Périer Brothers in Paris in 1852, Crédit Mobilier of France announced its intention to "facilitate the construction of public works and develop internal industry." It launched a promotion campaign for European railroad construction in 1855; and paid some dividends. But the bulk of its investments, banking circles learned, was routed to the accounts of Périer Brothers. Few of the railroads materialized. By 1864, the firm's bankruptcy seemed inevitable—and was. Still, Train borrowed the name and convinced Durant of its merit. Simultaneously, Train financed a second organization to deal in real-estate developments along Union Pacific trackage. He gave this the title of "Crédit Foncier of America." Another "borrowed" foreign firm name.

The initial capital of Crédit Mobilier of America was $1,400,000, invested by Durant, Train, Bushnell, McComb and other Union Pacific directors. Of this, $218,000 was used to repurchase the outstanding shares of the Union Pacific Railroad & Telegraph Company. This not only reimbursed Durant for the $160,000-plus he had invested in the take-over of the railroad from the Federal commissioners, but made him a majority stockholder in Crédit Mobilier; and made Union Pacific a property of Crédit Mobilier—in flagrant violation of the Pacific Railroad Act.

During May and June, Durant joined Bushnell, McComb,

Huntington—and probably Train—in Washington to push through a revision of the 1862 Act.

Huntington was already as much of a Capitol Hill fixture as Ted Judah had been five years before. Matters were looking up for Central Pacific. Its track was approaching Newcastle, 31 miles out of Sacramento. A semidaily schedule of passenger and freight trains operated to railhead. Loans were a bit easier to secure now, especially with the first 40 miles of construction —and more than $1,000,000 worth of Government bonds—in sight. The Associates' prospects would be dazzling if Congress could be persuaded to shift the Federal bonds back to a second-mortgage status and permit the railroad companies to issue their own first-mortgage bonds.

A Massachusetts member of the House committee on the Pacific Railroad was proving an outspoken champion for "more aid to the Pacific Railroad." His name was Oakes Ames. He and his brother Oliver owned Oliver Ames & Sons, the Easton, Massachusetts, factory that produced "Old Colony" shovels, hoes and hand tools. The fine Old Colony shovel was in a hallowed category at California mining camps. Major General Grenville Dodge's engineers and "muckers" whacked Old Colony shovels into the red Georgia clay that spring as they rebuilt bridges and rail lines for Sherman's march toward Atlanta. Lieutenant General Grant's sappers and road builders wielded thousands of others on the artillery roads and entrenchments in Virginia's "Wilderness." The use of Old Colony shovels and tools on the Pacific Railroad would be a wondrous hedge against postwar depression in Easton. Durant and Ames became dinner companions. Eventually Durant extended Ames an invitation to invest in Crédit Mobilier.

Republican "whips" shared President Lincoln's conviction that the 1862 Act should be liberalized. During May, House and Senate sponsors maneuvered the new bill through committees. Yet the Pacific Railway Act of 1864 encountered bitter debate on both floors and passed with a majority of less than two-thirds. But Huntington and Durant won the clause imperative to the success of The Associates and Crédit Mobilier; the Act moved Federal loans back to a second-mortgage status and enabled Central Pacific and Union Pacific to print an issue of first-mortgage bonds. The new Act also doubled Federal land grants to ten sections per mile "within 20 miles on each side of the tracks." (A total of 12,800 acres a mile.) And it liberalized the term "mineral rights" by forfeiting all iron and coal deposits on the grant lands to the railroad companies.

Some of the other clauses drew charges of fraud from the opposition who contended that the Act was rewritten after it had passed the committees and that the final draft was voted "blindly, without awareness of its changes by most members of Congress." The Federal loan bonds were to be paid out by the Secretary of the Interior, ruled one of these clauses, upon completion of each 20 miles of track in the mountain areas; two-thirds of these bonds could be collected by the railroad companies *before* the trackage had been accepted by Federal inspectors. Transportation and telegraph uses by the Federal Government would be paid for at standard rates—one half in cash and one half in credit toward the construction loans. Union Pacific capital stock was shifted from 100,000 thousand-dollar bonds to 1,000,000 hundred-dollar bonds. The president of the United States would appoint, subject to Congressional approval, three inspection commissioners for each road. The number of Federal appointees to Union Pacific's board was increased to five. Both the inspection commissioners and the railroad's government directors would come under the jurisdiction of the Secretary of the Interior of the United States.

Durant later alleged that he spent $437,000 on "expense accounts" during the months of lobbying for the 1864 Act. In 1873, Oakes Ames testified that there was no evidence of such lavishness and charged that "Durant must have put the money in his own pocket." Whatever the truth, Oakes and Oliver Ames were bustling around Boston by September, 1864, soliciting loans for Union Pacific and investments in Crédit Mobilier. During the next six months they sold more than

$400,000 worth of Crédit Mobilier stock to friends and political contacts, and invested another $400,000 of the family fortune in the holding company. By the spring of 1865 they held voting options on more than one-third of this company's stock.

With Crédit Mobilier launched and the Railroad Act revised, Durant was ready to start construction. The new Act stated that all of the branch lines to the 100th meridian must have 100 miles of trackage approved by Federal inspectors not later than June 27, 1866, and must be at the 100th meridian by mid-December; thereafter construction was to proceed at a rate of not less than 100 miles a year. The feud with Omaha, Council Bluffs and Des Moines about the Eastern terminal still sputtered. Peter Dey wrote sardonic letters to Grenville Dodge that labeled Durant as "needing common sense more than anything else." But Dey held on as chief engineer and ran location surveys from Omaha over the bluffs to the Elkhorn Creek-Platte junction.

Formally, on Union Pacific stationery, Durant offered the construction contract for the first 100 miles of Union Pacific to his "advance man"-lobbyist, Herbert Hoxie. Hoxie's reply asked that his contract be extended another 147 miles to the 100th meridian, and wrote, "I will subscribe, or cause to be subscribed, for $500,000 of the stock of your company." The request was formally granted. Hoxie then assigned his contract, at $50,000 per mile, to Crédit Mobilier of America. His fee as dummy in the transaction is estimated to have been $10,000 in Union Pacific first-mortgage bonds.

Dey held his temper, accepted orders from Hoxie, and began building grade. The only work gangs available were river-boat roustabouts and farm youngsters. He had no assurance that Hoxie or Crédit Mobilier could meet pay rolls. A few boxes of shovels and some kegs of blasting powder showed up on steamboats from St. Louis. That was it. Rails and ties, Hoxie said, would "get to rolling" during the winter.

Dey drove the gangs on a dawn-to-dusk schedule, fighting

for embankment mileage before freeze-up. Their grading was atop the bluffs, 15 miles out of Omaha, the morning that Colonel Silas Seymour and Federal Inspector Jesse Williams rode into camp. Seymour carried a letter of introduction from Durant. Seymour and Williams would, the letter said, inspect all grading to date.

The frosts came. So did Seymour's disapproval of Dey's grade. Trackage, he was grieved to report, must run farther south toward Bellevue; a pity that so much of the firm's funds had been used for this "unrealistic" dirt pile. All of it would have to be abandoned, and a fresh start made in the spring.

Early in January, 1865, Peter Dey sent his resignation to Durant. "I am giving up," he wrote Grenville Dodge, "the best position this country has ever offered any man." Like Ted Judah, he had held the position of chief engineer for one year and was forced out by the office politics of a holding-company monopoly.

Silas Seymour settled into an Omaha boardinghouse, as acting chief engineer. The Union Pacific Railroad was still a stock-juggler's mirage, with 247 miles of track to be built during the next 23 months; otherwise the Federal grants would be forfeited.

CHAPTER 14

RED BLOCK

> There is not a tribe of Indians on the great plains or
> in the mountain regions east of Nevada and Idaho
> but which is warring on the whites. The first demand
> of the Indian is that the white man shall not come
> into his country; shall not kill or drive off the game
> upon which his subsistence depends; and shall not
> dispossess him of his lands. How can we promise
> this, with any hope or purpose of fulfilling the obli-
> gation, unless we prohibit immigration and settlement
> west of the Missouri River? . . . . General Pope to the
> United States War Department (1865).

The vision of the Pacific Railroad lured idealists and profound individualists for 50 years. Thomas Benton, Asa Whitney, Brigham Young, Theodore Judah, Collis Huntington and Thomas Durant were cut from other than prototype molds for either "American" or "frontiersman." During the five-year race toward Promontory Point, Dodge, Montague, the Casement Brothers, Reed, and the survey crews, Mormon graders, and heroic Chinese "coolies," would demonstrate similar rare virtues of individualism and initiative. Such an array, playing leading roles in one of the mightiest dramas of the nation's history, demanded a comic *bouffe* relief. This was the character part for Colonel Silas Seymour. He played it with such pomp that, on at least three occasions, he veered the drama toward tragedy.

Across "darkest Nebraska," the Black Hills, Wyoming's desert bowl and the Wasatch canons, Silas Seymour bumbled up to railheads, his umbrella at full balloon, a bedroll puffing up from his saddle like an immense denim bustle. His sparse goatee and gray pompadour completed the make-up of a high-plains Don Quixote. The profundity of his deliberations, like his assaults on technical windmills, paralyzed construction for months at a time.

"Colonel Seymour," Sam Reed wrote to his family from Wyoming, "was outfitted after the following style. First the horse . . . was twin brother to old 'Knockumstiff.' On the . . . saddle . . . was his carbine . . . to be convenient in case of sudden Indian attack; also his poncho, bed, etc., in bulk about a barrel, leaving very little room for the Colonel. When mounted, he would hoist his umbrella and leisurely follow in the wake of the escort or perhaps leading them a few paces. The Pawnee made fun of him from beginning to end."

His convictions were in character too. Silas Seymour had never been able to accept the crosstie as the logical support for T-rails, so still advocated the use of parallel timbers without crossties as the best rail base. Locomotives, he advised the Federal inspectors in 1865, should be "from 28 to 30 tons, with five-foot drivers, cylinders 16 by 24 inches for first-class roads of ordinary grades." In 1903–4 when the Harriman regime modernized Union Pacific's roadbed and equipment, two of the major reroutes ordered were to eliminate 20 miles of the haul over Carbon Summit, between the Laramie River and the Rattlesnake Hills, and then save another 14 miles by rerouting between Omaha and Elkhorn Creek. The shift in the Carbon Summit approach restored the route originally ordered by Grenville Dodge, but changed by Seymour to the longer meander. The Omaha–Elkhorn Creek rerouting restored the grade Peter Dey built during the fall months of 1864, and Seymour ordered abandoned. "Seymour seems to be determined to delay the work as much as possible," Reed complained. "The object apparently is to injure somebody's reputation."

Still, Seymour as "consulting engineer" and "acting chief engineer" suited Durant. Union Pacific needed powerful allies in both major political parties—not only for fund-raising prestige but for those "back-room" conferences that enabled favorable interpretation of the 1864 Act. During 1863–4, Horatio Seymour had served again as New York's governor. After General McClellan's defeat by Lincoln in the 1864 election, Horatio had become a "senior statesman" of the Democratic party and a logical candidate for the Presidency in 1868. He was worthy of discreet cultivation by Union Pacific's hierarchy. And, Durant could have reasoned, there would be no easier path to Horatio's favors than the appointment of plump, pompous Brother Silas as consulting engineer.

Grenville Dodge claimed, in various autobiographical writings, that Durant repeatedly offered him the post of chief engineer during 1863–4–5. Samuel B. Reed claimed that during Christmas week, 1865, Durant offered him the choice of chief engineer or superintendent of construction. But there is no evidence that, even in hours of darkest brooding, Durant considered Seymour for this key post until the showdown struggle with Dodge in the summer of 1868. Instead, Silas Seymour was intended to serve in the dual capacity of a political asset and yes man at "the front office." As brother of the potential Democratic candidate for the Presidency in 1868, Silas was an investment in liaison with the Democratic minority of Congress. As a reactionary, with a broad streak of petulance, he served splendidly as the authority to quote whenever Durant's temper unleashed against engineering or construction executives.

Seymour's rejection of the Omaha–Elkhorn grade, and the subsequent resignation of Peter Dey, was the initial use of the "authority" technique by Durant. It was in pattern with his divide-and-conquer trick for stirring up publicity and stock sales in the Iowa and Nebraska towns. Peter Dey's grumbles about Durant had probably echoed back to New York, possibly via Hoxie. Durant knew that Dey had favored Henry Farnam as president or general manager of Union Pacific, and still favored Council Bluffs-Omaha as Union Pacific's Eastern terminal. This would have been reason enough for Durant's temper to snake toward the conferences that waddled Silas Seymour off to Omaha thoroughly prejudiced against Dey and convinced that the Missouri River bridge should be located at Bellevue.

Seymour's abandonment of the Dey grading set off another volley of protests from Council Bluffs and Omaha. Peter Dey's home town of Iowa City joined them with a petition to the Department of the Interior. A delegation of Federal inspectors reached Omaha in late spring, argued with Seymour, rode along both survey routes, then agreed that Dey's route could be changed "if the Omaha and Elkhorn grades are eliminated." Seymour beamed assent, but held the shovel crews to a route that looped close to the planned west end of Chicago & Northwestern's bridge at Bellevue. His embankment, finally reaching Elkhorn Creek in midsummer, 1865, was 14 miles longer than Dey's and just as steep. The Federal inspectors shrugged and approved it. Tracklaying began in July and ambled west at a pace of not more than 4 miles a month. With Seymour as chief engineer, Union Pacific might reach the 100th meridian sometime in 1870.

However, Seymour had chill reasons for dawdling. Speedy track building would have been impossible in 1865 without a screen of cavalry. Over in the Kansas River Valley, Union Pacific's Eastern Division was being forced to dawdle too. The red block was up. Grenville Dodge and the Galvanized Yankees were out on the high plains trying to end it.

The Sioux Rebellion of 1862–63 had flamed west across the Dacotah, firing the hatred and fears of the tribes on the Great Desert. Throughout the summer of 1864, war parties looted west along the Platte, Kansas and Arkansas valleys. Painted warriors raced ponies around wagon trains in deadly circles; scalping knives dripped blood again. White women and girls who resisted rape were tomahawked; those who didn't were led off to slavery. For weeks the red raiders cut Denver and the Pikes Peak mining towns off from Eastern stage and wagon traffic. Ben Holladay ordered his Overland Stages out of the South Pass country to safer Cheyenne Pass.

Meanwhile, Sherman's army besieged Atlanta. Major General Dodge commanded the 16th Corps that withstood the brunt of Hood's counteroffensive. On August 19, 1864, Dodge received an order to prepare the 16th for another effort to smash through Hood's lines and capture the city. "It was two-thirty when I reached the entrenchments," he recalled, "and my line was so exposed that one could not show himself above the entrenchments without being hit. The boys cautioned me, and said that if I wanted to see the enemy, I could look through a peephole they had made under a log. I put my eye to this peephole and the moment I did so, I was shot in the head. I went down immediately."

The rumor reached Council Bluffs that Dodge was dead. He was unconscious for 48 hours; then was jounced back to a base hospital in Chattanooga on a hammock slung in a freight car. In November, still a semi-invalid, he was assigned to St. Louis to command the Department of the Missouri. Three weeks later the Sand Creek Massacre of 660 Cheyennes sent new waves of hate across the West. Dodge was ordered to Fort Leavenworth. Early in January, 1865, telegraph orders came from U. S. Grant. The Indians, Grant was convinced, would launch attacks throughout Colorado, Nebraska and Kansas. Dodge must beat them to the attacks. That week, from Omaha to Denver, thermometers registered 30 degrees below zero.

The best Army troops then on the high plains were the Secesh veterans nicknamed "the Galvanized Yankees." They had been captured during the Mississippi Valley, Missouri, and Virginia campaigns, or—weary of corn-pone rations and the

Jeff Davis regime—had followed the Negro exodus to the Union lines and surrendered. The War Department offered them a choice between imprisonment in disease-ridden, quagmire camps like Chicago's Camp Douglas, or enlistment in the regiments serving "beyond the Missouri." Thousands chose the West, and thus released Iowa, Colorado and Minnesota troops for Sherman's March to the Sea and Grant's encirclement of Richmond.

Again, during the crescendo of the New West's finale, Southerners would play folk-hero roles of many kinds, but none contributed more to the final conquest than the Galvanized Yankees who kept the Union's life lines open across the plains and mountains during the crucial years of 1865–70.

The Galvanized Yanks out of Forts Leavenworth, Sibley and Kearney followed Dodge in a show of force up the Platte during February. Temperatures averaged from 5 to 10 below. When the Overland Telegraph crackled to life again at Omaha, Edward Creighton, the general manager, notified the War Department. Back came the query: WHERE IS DODGE? Creighton chuckled as he dictated the reply: NOBODY KNOWS WHERE HE IS, BUT EVERYBODY KNOWS WHERE HE'S BEEN. After a few skirmishes, the Sioux, Cheyenne and Arapaho retreated across the Black Hills to the Yellowstone and Powder River valleys. The Pawnee decided to fight on the Union's side. On Dodge's order, Major Frank North recruited the first companies of Pawnee Scouts. They joined his expedition out of Fort Laramie, with glum Jim Bridger as guide, for a reconnaissance in force against the 500 lodges of the Sioux.

Again the wagon trains set out from Atchison, St. Joseph, Leavenworth and Omaha, but with "hired guns" as scouts and night guards. Ben Holladay also posted guards armed with shotguns, as well as revolvers, atop every Overland stage. Storekeepers and wholesale provisioners kept prices Pikes-Peak high. At Denver in late May, 1865, potatoes were $15 a bushel, flour was 15¢ and 20¢ a pound, corn $10 a bushel, beef 40¢ a pound, and ham 45¢ to 50¢ a pound. Along the

Platte, stagecoach stations and Army posts paid $100 a ton for hay and $75 a cord for firewood.

The advent of the Pacific Railroad was a major and direct cause of the Indian rebellions. The Sand Creek Massacre merely hastened the inevitable. The iron horse's crossing of Nebraska and the Black Hills would mean extermination of the bison herds; scores of new towns; an army of land-hungry cattlemen and farmers; and the death of the bison-and-wild-horse economy. From the North Platte to the Big Horns, war chiefs growled the challenge: "Fight for our sacred lands. Stop the white man's Great Iron Trail."

The crisis hurried two politically powerful groups to the stage terminals at Atchison, Kansas. Senators Foster of Connecticut and Doolittle of Wisconsin headed one party. A law student at Norwich University while Grenville Dodge studied there, Lafayette Sabine Foster had been elected Speaker of the United States House of Representatives during the 1850's. Connecticut promoted him to the Senate. The week after Lincoln's assassination the Senate elected him its president pro tem as successor to Andrew Johnson. In effect, then, he was Vice-President, ex officio, of the United States. In May he volunteered to serve on a committee chaired by Doolittle that would "examine the conditions of the Indians" and develop "a more intelligent and effective Indian policy."

An escort of a hundred cavalrymen—most of them Galvanized Yankees—jangled Foster and Doolittle down the Santa Fe Trail for a summerlong schedule of powwows. Within a month Doolittle was convinced that all the trouble was due to "the brutal and cowardly murder of the Cheyennes at Sand Creek; an affair in which the blame was on our side." Foster agreed. They summarily ordered Army commanders in the Arkansas Valley to "halt all operations" against the Indians. Their decision, relayed to Washington, became a factor in the enmity growing between President Johnson and Secretary of War Stanton.

These accusations of "warmongering" involved Grenville

Dodge at Fort Leavenworth. "The Government must understand," Dodge wrote Grant, "that it will have to meet the problem of Indian warfare or abandon the Western country. There are 25,000 Indians on the plains, north and south. We need more troops, not less, for there are 5,000 teams that are trying to cross the plains each month, and it is my understanding that I am to protect this travel at all costs." As though in confirmation, Sioux and Arapaho raiders burned Julesburg, attacked four Army posts, and ambushed a 250-wagon train near Fort Bent.

The second group assembling at Atchison on May 20 would prove more meaningful to the development of the Union Pacific and to the new treaties with the Indians than the Foster-Doolittle tour. The ostensible purpose was, as Samuel Bowles lavished it, "to see the country, to study its resources, to learn its people and their wants, and to acquit ourselves more intelligently thereby, each in our duties to the public." It was, in view of the group's composition, a gem of a purpose; one that should echo pleasantly in the Republican caucus rooms in 1868.

The group's leader was Schuyler Colfax, Speaker of the House of Representatives. Another New Yorker who had migrated to Indiana, Colfax had followed the routine of newspaper editor to Congressman, then won the key post in the House in 1863. It was reasonably certain that Andrew Johnson would not be renominated in 1868. Mr. Colfax acknowledged his interest in inheriting the White House lease. Consequently he was embarking on this transcontinental tour during Congress' recess, not only to familiarize himself with the New West and its problems, but to exude his personality on its voters and perhaps on some campaign funds. Colfax was a strong advocate of the Pacific Railroad and a good friend of Oakes Ames. (If Ames had not already handed Speaker Colfax a small gift packet of Crédit Mobilier stock, he would soon.) Also Colfax was a Methodist and profanely opposed to polygamy. With the War over and the nation refocusing on the New West, he thought some spectacular publicity might be gained by resurrecting those Utah war stories about the Mormon elders' fondness for plural marriages. Editors from Springfield, Chicago and New York were in the party.

The tour was a maharajah's triumph. Ben Holladay provided a spanking new Concord coach. A few hours out of Atchison an eastbound stage passed along the report that 20 soldiers had just been ambushed near Fort Kearney and that another eastbound stage for Leavenworth was "sieved" during a 10-mile running fight with Sioux. General Patrick E. Connor, who had recently threatened to shell the Latter-day Saints' Tabernacle unless Brigham Young obeyed his orders, was the party's guest on the ride to Julesburg. He gave "Mr. Speaker" a wealth of new anecdotes about Utah polygamy and the "despotic rule" of Brigham Young.

Through June and July, Colfax and the editors explored Colorado gold mines, shot bison, elk and antelope, marveled at tales about the mineral and coal deposits in the Rockies, and attended a Brigham Young sermon in Salt Lake City's "bowery" auditorium. (That night Colfax lectured 1,500 Mormons about "the Life of Abraham Lincoln" and got in a few quotable licks against polygamy.) The newspaper dispatches from this hegira excited Easterners about the New West; some of the editors with Colfax turned authors, hence heralded the 1880–1910 era of Western true-adventure books, travel lectures and dime-novels.

A ride up the 50 miles of Central Pacific's trackage during August converted Samuel Bowles, editor-owner of the Springfield, Massachusetts, *Republican,* as a champion of the Pacific Railroad. Reporting it in his dispatch of August 20, he gave warm praise to Ted Judah, but avoided mention of Stanford, Huntington, Crocker or Hopkins. He wrote:

> The Judah, or Dutch Flat, route has got the name and means and is being pushed over the mountains with commendable vigor and rapidity. It is wise for California and the country alike to

sustain it and secure its completion as early as possible . . . the company has used none of the United States bonds or lands granted by Congress in aid of the work. Some two and a half millions in these bonds are now due. The company can issue an equal amount of their own bonds guaranteed by a preceding or first mortgage; but none of these have yet been used. They also have available a million and a half of other bonds on which the State of California pays 7 per cent interest in gold for twenty years. Here are six millions and a half of good securities now on hand for prosecuting the work, beside what is earned as the road progresses, and the power to anticipate the issue of their own first mortgage bonds at the rate of forty eight thousand dollars for a mile of mountains and sixteen thousand dollars for a mile of plain, for one hundred miles in advance of construction.

The work has been done out of about a million of paid-up stock, and subscriptions of the County of Sacramento of three hundred thousands, the county of Placer of two hundred and fifty thousand dollars, and of San Francisco of four hundred thousand dollars, and the profits of that part of the road in running order. Of these sums, nearly half a million is still left, and the road has gone as far as to substantially secure a monopoly of all the business over the mountains, the profits on its completed section will be constantly increasing. Then, besides all this, there are between eighteen and nineteen millions of the twenty millions capital stock of the road, yet unsubscribed for. Sometime, though not at present, this will be paying property; and it may suffice even now for the profits of the contractors.

Thomas Durant's manipulations for Union Pacific and Crédit Mobilier were not proving as successful. During the fall of 1864, Secretary of the Interior Harlan introduced Durant to John Pondir, a New York broker. Pondir agreed to attempt organization of a syndicate of New York banks to raise a short-term—and high-interest—loan. In May, 1865, he delivered $1,000,000 to Union Pacific, with scrip on unearned government bonds—marked down to 90 per cent of par—accepted as collateral. Sometime during the summer Crédit Mobilier took in 35 more stockholders and increased its paid-in capital to $2,000,000. In all, Durant had only about enough to pay for the first 100 miles of track—less than half the distance to the 100th meridian. But he planned boldly. He ordered survey crews to explore the Colorado Rockies and the "Great Valley" into Salt Lake.

A group led by Samuel B. Reed rode straight through to Salt Lake City, held a series of conferences with Brigham Young and other Latter-day Saints leaders, and received assurance of Mormon grading crews and tie-hack gangs if and when construction reached the Wasatch canyons. Then Reed's chainmen signaled east into the Weber and Echo river gorges. The crew under James A. Evans ran a series of lines up the South Platte and the North Platte, then measured possible grades to Berthoud and the other passes behind Denver.

Each group totaled only 15 or 16 men. Their rations were flour, bacon, coffee, beans, hominy and dried fruit plus the game they picked off the job. Work hours lasted from sunup to sundown, six days a week; on Sundays they did the week's wash and repaired equipment. "Our bed," wrote Reed, "consists of Mother Earth and one good buffalo robe, one beaver robe consisting of several skins, for which I paid ten dollars, and my shawl with boots, coats and pants for pillows. Sometimes we sleep in a tent and sometimes out in the open air."

Both crews returned to Omaha in late November, without loss of a man or horse. Between them they had journaled details on 1,254 miles of "continuous instrumental line." Evans shared Peter Dey's 1864 conviction that a standard-gauge railroad could not build over the passes behind Denver unless mile after mile of tunnels were blasted through the cliffs; much of the construction, he reported, would cost more than $100,-000 a mile. Reed was similarly dubious about building Union Pacific's main line into Salt Lake City. The best route ran north of Salt Lake, 50 miles from the Latter-day Saints' capital.

Both engineers passed their data on to Durant. Colorado's promises of "our limitless gold" to Union Pacific were based, of course, on the understanding that the Main Line would follow the South Platte into Denver, cross the Rockies to the

Colorado River headwaters, and twist on to Salt Lake City. Brigham Young's promises of tie-hack and grading crews also anticipated that Salt Lake City would be a division point on Union Pacific, if not the meeting place for Central Pacific and Union Pacific. Both Reed and Evans were veteran engineers. A whisper about their data on the Denver and Salt Lake City terrain could set off howls in Congress that might delay construction for years; or hand the trans-Rockies contract to the Kansas Valley's "Eastern Division" Railroad.

During the same August week that Schuyler Colfax's party rode the Central Pacific to end-of-track, Grenville Dodge left Fort Kearney on a scouting expedition into the Big Horn Mountains. The Crows, Sioux and Arapaho were reported to be rendezvousing there for raids against the Colorado and Nebraska settlements. The prevalence of bison and other game on the great upland ranges south and west of Fort Laramie convinced Dodge that the Indians would fight desperately against white settlements in the area. Then his cavalrymen panned gold dust and a few nuggets from creek beds near Powder River. This news, he knew, would puff to Mother Lode proportions during the gossip sessions in winter quarters at Leavenworth and Kearney. A gold rush into the Sioux "sacred land" might follow. Thus, he mused, the Union Pacific Railroad was confronted both by the Indian "red block" north of Fort Laramie and the mighty barrier of the Central Rockies behind Denver. An ideal solution would be discovery of a pass with an eastern face gradient of 100 feet to the mile, or less— somewhere between Fort Laramie and Denver.

Back at Fort Laramie again by mid-September, he decided to explore south toward Denver. His column reached the foot of Cheyenne Pass on the morning of the 22nd. Dodge ordered the wagon train and most of the cavalry to follow the Denver Trail along the valley floor as far as Crow Creek. Then, with the guide, Leon Pallady, and a dozen troopers, he would attempt to ride south along the Continental Divide's crest from the top of Cheyenne Pass. His patrol was 20 miles south of the Pass in late afternoon when Pallady called out, "Indians down there, and a lot of 'em." A moment's study through field glasses showed 300 or more Crow warriors spread along the slope below them. They had already cut off escape toward the wagon train and main body of cavalry on the valley floor. "They've likely followed us all day," Pallady concluded, "and aim to close in at night."

Dodge ordered dismount, sent the horses across the summit with three guards, deployed the rest of his men behind boulders and lit a signal fire. The Crows circled and began shooting. A band of fifty galloped off toward the top of the ridge, obviously under orders to "Get the horses." As dusk crept up the mountain Dodge and Pallady tossed leaves and pine needles on the fire until it blazed high in the open space before their hole-up. The Crows crept closer, and lost only three warriors in an open-field rush.

A bugle echoed from the valley, trailed by the clatter of a cavalry troop at full gallop. Amazed by the horses' speed up the slope, Dodge jumped to his feet and began shouting. The Crows hesitated, then loped back to their ponies and galloped off. A few minutes later Dodge led his patrol and their rescuers down the ridge. It descended gently to the valley floor at a gradient he estimated to be not more than 90 feet to the mile. Pulling up beside a lone pine tree at its base, Dodge announced, "Boys, I think we've discovered the pass for the Union Pacific." That night he named the top of the pass "Sherman Summit."

It was not coincidence that put Cump Sherman astraddle a nail keg two months later as guest of honor on the "Grand Excursion" of a locomotive and two flatcars to Union Pacific's end-of-track. Accounts vary on the mileage laid by Silas Seymour's crews during the eight work months of 1865. Samuel Reed recalled that the tracks were 45 miles out of Omaha by Christmas Day—an average of 5½ miles a month. Seymour's ineffectiveness, plus the gravity of the Indian situation, convinced Durant that Sherman must be the guest of honor on that flatcar. The appointment of the General's brother Charles as one of Union Pacific's five Federal directors was a minor consideration. Profits for Crédit Mobilier would not be assured until Union Pacific beat the Eastern Division to the 100th meridian and clearly proved its right to assign construction contracts on west. This would mean a pace of more than a mile a day for tracklayers during the 1866 work season. Sam Reed had the leadership to take over as chief of construction. But there were the twin needs of protection from the Indians and a chief engineer who knew the terrain, had the tough executive ability to get along with work gangs and engineers, and was an Indian-fighter to boot. Grenville Dodge was such a man. Sherman and Dodge were staunch friends. Durant wanted Sherman's help in persuading Dodge to leave the Army and finally take over as Union Pacific's chief engineer.

Sherman had accepted the invitation to Omaha because he and Grant were swinging toward the conviction that the Pacific Railroad was "a military necessity." The West seemed destined as a theatre of war for decades and perhaps generations. Ever since the Army's high-plains pioneering by Generals Kearney, Scott and Harney, Army commanders had pursued the stupid course of chasing Indian horsemen with wagonloads of infantry drawn by ox or mule at 2 to 4 miles an hour. Congress had never appropriated funds to police the West with cavalry; it had come closest when it permitted Jeff Davis to experiment with the Camel Corps.

A transcontinental railroad was the solution. Enough troops could be assigned to protect track gangs during the push into Utah. Once trains were running over the Rockies, troops could be transported 500-600 miles overnight. The Pacific Railroad would become the Army's deadliest weapon with which to quell Indian uprisings and protect the massive flow of migrants and goods between the Missouri and the Pacific.

Soon Durant had another strong pair of reasons for urging

Sherman and Grant toward a decision on General Dodge. On February 8, 1866, he wrote the Casements of Painesville, Ohio, "Your proposition to the Union Pacific Railroad Company under date of Feb. 6 in relation to tracklaying is received and has been considered. The Company decides to regard your proposition and this acceptance as the agreement upon the subject."

Dan Casement had stayed home during the Civil War to fulfill the grading and repair contracts he and brother Jack had undertaken in 1859 and 1860. Jack Casement began the war as a major, won his colonelcy by turning the Union rout at the Battle of Cross Lanes in West Virginia, then was brevetted a brigadier general after leading savage assaults against Hood's lines at the Battle of Franklin on November 30, 1864. Home again, he brooded over newspaper accounts about Union Pacific's dawdling, and harangued Dan about making a bid for the 1866 tracklaying contract. Dan demurred until they hit on the notion of building a train that would be a town on wheels complete with bunk cars, tool cars, commissary, blacksmith shop, and a tailpiece of flatcars loaded with rail, spikes, shovels, crowbars and blasting powder. Historically, although the Casements never claimed the credit, this was the invention of the railroad work train. Durant recognized its merits, recalled the Casements' performance on the Michigan Central and Lake Shore railroads, and quickly reached the decision of his February 8th letter.

Spring came. The Casements' town on wheels clanged into being on the Omaha siding. Timber crews crossed flooded fields 100 miles north and south to begin razing every tree usable for crossties and bridge timbers. The nod came from the War Department. Grenville Dodge and Thomas Durant met in St. Joseph, Missouri, on April 24. By dinnertime Major General Dodge was on "prolonged leave of absence" to serve as chief engineer of the Union Pacific Railroad & Telegraph Company at a salary of $10,000 a year, plus a small bundle of Crédit Mobilier stock. (It was felt expedient to make the stock out in Mrs. Dodge's name.)

The next two months would make or break the Union Pacific.

All the Livelong Day

Men of the East! Men at Washington! You have given the toil and even the blood of a million of your brothers and fellows for four years, and spent three thousand million dollars, to rescue one section of the Republic from barbarism and from anarchy; and your triumph makes the cost cheap. Lend now a few thousand of men, and a hundred millions of money, to create a new Republic; to marry to the Nation of the Atlantic an equal if not greater Nation of the Pacific. Anticipate a new sectionalism, a new strife, by a triumph of the arts of Peace, that shall be even prouder and more reaching than the victories of your Arms. Here is payment of your great debt; here is wealth unbounded; here the commerce of the world; here the completion of a Republic that is continental; but you must come and take them with the Locomotive.

—Samuel Bowles, *Across The Continent* (1865)

CHAPTER 15

THE RELAYS

> *When we started, iron was $62. Before we got across the mountains, iron was sold $150 a ton. Locomotives went from $8,000 to as high as $32,500. We paid 2½ per cent insurance in time of peace and in the time of rebellion, we paid 17 per cent insuring the goods around Cape Horn. Many things went up 200 per cent, and I guess many things 300 per cent advance from the time we commenced the road before we got it completed. . . . Collis P. Huntington in* testimony before the Pacific Railway Commission, 1888.

Geographically, the Pacific Railroad began at Omaha and Sacramento. Economically and physically, it began in two offices off lower Broadway in New York City—the shabby hole in the wall occupied by Collis P. Huntington, and the gilt-mirrored suite dominated by Thomas C. Durant. The relay systems evolved there are a significant chapter in the technologic revolution that industrialized the West and veered the United States from an agricultural-rural economy to a factory-urban economy. Construction of the Union Pacific and the Central Pacific was a titanic demonstration of Eli Whitney's assembly-line technique; Huntington and Durant were patrons of technology.

The wrought-iron rail initially specified for each road weighed 50 pounds to the yard. A mile of track, plus side spurs and switches, required 100 tons of rail, approximately 2,500 crossties and 2 or 3 tons of spikes and fishplates (the slotted bars that connect rail ends and permit climatic expansion and contraction of the metal). Grading gangs used wheelbarrows, horse-drawn scrapers, two-wheel dump carts, shovels, axes, crowbars, mattocks and blasting powder. Bridgeworkers required quarry tools and iron rods.

Food stocks of flour, bacon, ham, saleratus, "sweetening," beans, rice and dried fruit were equally essential, since the crews of both lines worked as self-sufficient armies in the wilderness. Locomotives, wheel trucks and switch mechanisms, plus foundry tools for the repair and assembly shops at Omaha and Sacramento, increased the New York purchase and relay task to shipments averaging more than 10,000 tons per month.

Huntington's country-storekeeper skill and boasted miserliness got him through a routine delivery schedule during 1863–5, despite the priority claims of Army and Navy buyers. A few experiences with the surcharge rates via the Isthmus of Panama (four handlings by stevedores as against two on the Cape Horn run) urged him to perfect a purchase and shipment timetable that ran eight months to a year ahead of Crocker's railhead needs. By the time Union Pacific moved into the iron, locomotive, blasting-powder and tools markets in the winter of 1865, the wheedling Yankee had the reputation of being the shrewdest buyer in New York. During the spring of 1866 he outmaneuvered Union Pacific's buyers in the purchase of 66,-000 tons of rail, then blandly teamed with Durant and McComb in a fight against the Pennsylvania and Massachusetts ironmongers who were attempting to form a "trust" that would boost mill prices.

His strategies in securing low delivery costs on the Cape Horn shipments demonstrate the penny-wise philosophy that developed the multimillionaires and "trusts" in American industry from 1880 on. Huntington told the details of one "smart trade" episode to H. H. Bancroft's researchers. After a prowl along the Manhattan and Brooklyn waterfronts, Huntington said, he walked into the ship brokerage offices of E. B. Sutton. "I said, 'Well, I want to get a good ship, a good steady ship —safe. You can go out and run around and give me a list of what you can find.'

"He came in with three or four. He said, 'You can have this one for so much and this one for so much.'

" 'Such a price,' said I, 'is too high. I can't take one of those ships. I am in no hurry,' said I, 'ships are coming in all along.'

"Well, he came back. He went out three times and he came back with twenty-three ships. I got them down whilst talking. 'Well,' said I suddenly, 'I'll take them.'

" 'Take them?' said he, 'take what?'

"Said I, 'I will take those ships if they are A-Number One.'

" 'Well,' said he, 'I can't let you have them. I thought you wanted only one.' Said he, 'I will have to have two or three of them myself.'

"Said I, 'Not those, you won't.'

"Well, those ships took about forty-five thousand tons of rail. Mr. Sutton told me afterward, 'Huntington, you would have had to pay ten dollars a ton at least more if I had known you wanted all those ships.'

"That would have been four hundred and fifty thousand dollars."

Union Pacific's relay problems were as awesome as the 18,000 mile sail around Cape Horn—and more complex. Three delivery routes were available from East Coast iron foundries and locomotive plants to the Nebraska shore. The first required a 3,000-mile sail to New Orleans, a reloading on Mississippi River steamers, and a second reload at St. Louis for the trip up the shallow Missouri. Rail deliveries, via Chicago, involved terminal transfers at Pittsburgh and Fort Wayne via the Pennsylvania route, or at Albany, Buffalo and Cleveland via the Hudson Valley, New York Central and Lake Shore route. From Chicago, materials could be shipped by rail to central Iowa, then transferred to wagon trains for the 150-mile creak to Council Bluffs; or they could be routed via the Chicago, Burlington & Quincy to Quincy, ferried across the Mississippi to the Hannibal & St. Joseph railhead, then loaded on steamboats at St. Joseph for the final haul up "the Big Muddy" to the Nebraska shore. Any of these relays entailed stevedore charges that doubled the freight bills.

The first supplies delivered to Peter Dey used the New Orleans route. Presumably Union Pacific's first locomotive, landed at Omaha on July 8, 1865, took the Chicago–St. Joseph route. Although Durant decided on major use of the Chicago–St. Joseph relay, development of an efficient commissariat and routing system were the achievements of Samuel B. Reed and Crédit Mobilier's "stooge," Herbert Hoxie.

Durant promoted Sam Reed to superintendent of construction during Christmas week, 1865. The Missouri would be frozen tight through February, at least, and churning with spring floods for another month. He and Durant had three months, then, to perfect the "hardware" relay via Chicago and St. Joseph. But timber was an immediate crisis.

Although two or three of the Pennsylvania roads paid heed to Congressman Scranton's arguments and began experimentation with coal firing, all of the locomotives built for Union Pacific before 1870 used chunk-wood fuel. Cottonwood was plentiful in the Platte and Missouri Valleys. It gave a fair flame. Indeed, if worst came to worst, baled hay could be used. (Some of the spur lines in New England and New York fired it during years of farm surplus, and won the nickname of "Hay burners" for their trains.)

But cottonwood logs were too porous for the massive pounding that a crosstie must sustain. With the exception of the stands of swamp cedar used on the Seymour trackage, the hardwood forests nearest Omaha were 400 miles east in Wisconsin and 450 miles northwest in the Rockies' foothills. The Rockies' timber might as well be on the moon as long as the Indian wars were raging. Reed did experiment with a few orders for hardwood ties out of Wisconsin and Michigan. But cartage and stevedore charges brought their costs up to $4.50 (one source claims $10) a tie at the Omaha wharf. Trackage averaged 2,500 ties to the mile. Use of Eastern ties would cost $11,250 a mile, or $2,250,000 for the remaining 200 miles to the 100th meridian.

The alternative was to call in scientists for development of a chemical technique to strengthen, or reconstruct, cottonwood's water-drunk fibers. This method of "transforming farm crops to industrial uses" would create a decade-long flurry across the corn and wheat belts of the West during the 1930's, using the coined name "Chemurgy." Sam Reed introduced the grandsire of chemurgy to the same area in February, 1866, via a behemoth retort called the "Burnetizer." Sometime during the 1850's the English chemist Sir William Burnett, discovered a method for impregnating softwoods with zinc chloride. Dr. Burnett proclaimed that these zinc intrusions gave the softwood fibers the durability of cedar, oak, chestnut, or walnut. Union Pacific's New York office contacted Dr. Burnett, checked the process with local chemists, then ordered castings for an iron cylinder that would be 5 feet in diameter and 75 feet long. The "Burnetizer" began hissing in April. After it was loaded with 250 cottonwood ties, a steam pump sucked out most of the air in the cylinder. Then the chloride of zinc solution was pumped in; the ties soaked in it for three or four hours.

Meanwhile, Reed brought in lumberjacks from Wisconsin and Michigan, contracted with Missouri Valley landowners and launched a timbering operation that razed woodlands for 200 miles along the valley. Next, he bought the steamboat, *Metamora*, rigged it with jackchains and derricks, hooked on barges and used it to haul cottonwood from the stacks the loggers were skidding to bluff edge.

The cedar breaks Dey and Seymour had used for the first 45 miles of track stood in gullies upriver toward Sioux City. A few groves of shagbark hickory and chestnut gloried the creek valleys. There would be enough of these, Reed and the Casements agreed, to use one hardwood tie under each rail joint and three under each spur switch. The rest must be the burnetized cottonwood. The zinc dunking did seem to firm cottonwood up enough to hold a spike; only the spring thaws would reveal whether the wood's lust for moisture had been curbed. (Dr. Burnett's "chemurgy" was literally a washout. During 1870, Union Pacific replaced 300,000 "rotten cottonwood ties" between Elkhorn Creek and Julesburg.)

During January and February, Durant signed contracts for the relay route that would deliver Union Pacific's "hardware." Crédit Mobilier was a Pennsylvania corporation. Pittsburgh was a key supply point for small iron. Business awarded to Pennsylvania carriers might counteract, in political and banking circles, the Philadelphians' support of Eastern Division's route. The contracts were signed with Pennsylvania Central, the Pittsburgh-Fort Wayne & Chicago, the Chicago, Burlington & Quincy, and the Hannibal & St. Joseph.

A fleet of 100 flatcars shuttled supplies over the four roads to wharfside at St. Joseph. Rail came from mills in Pennsylvania, New York and Massachusetts; tools for machine shops at Omaha from Philadelphia. Union Pacific spread its orders for locomotives among a half-dozen firms. The first passenger coaches were built at Fort Wayne. George M. Pullman, eager for publicity as well as for Union Pacific contracts for his Palace Sleeping Car, persuaded Durant to buy the satin-draped Palace car that had carried Abraham Lincoln's body from Washington to Springfield; redecorated and named "the Abraham Lincoln," it became Union Pacific's first club on wheels and was available to directors and Federal inspectors for trips to railhead—and for hunting trips.

Herbert Hoxie was still, according to government records, the official contractor for construction of track to the 100th meridian, the installation of machine shops, the operation of trains, and the location and construction of way stations. It was essential to keep Hoxie "on the premises." After assignment of the contract to Crédit Mobilier, Durant gave him the title of "Superintendent of River Navigation." A month after purchase of the *Metamora,* Durant and Reed bought the river steamers *Colorado* and *Denver.* The three ships, plus scows and the freight ferry operating between Council Bluffs and Omaha, comprised the Railroad Packet Line. Between spring thaw and December freeze-up in 1866, the *Colorado* and *Denver,* plus tows, ferried the bulk of Union Pacific's rail, tools, rolling stock, provisions and track gangs from St. Joseph to Omaha.

Durant's stock-juggled profits were in the bank; he made his peace with Omaha. Reed built warehouses on the waterfront and hired masons to construct Union Pacific's first terminal shop and roundhouse there. During March, Herbert Hoxie transferred downstream to supervise relay operations at St. Joseph, with the new title of "Assistant Superintendent of Construction."

St. Joseph's role as a mere transfer point for supplies to the Pacific Railroad was a subject for bitter brooding in the little city. Only seven years before, Mayor Jeff Thompson had driven Hannibal & St. Joseph's Missouri Express over the ridge to make "St. Joe" the railroad terminal for the West. Sometime during 1859, while plans for the Pony Express were shaping, Jeff Thompson and a few friends formed the St. Joseph & Denver City Railroad and surveyed its route as far as Troy, Kansas. Construction began that fall, with rail and ties ferried across the Missouri, then dragged on to railhead by mule-powered handcars. Townsmen recalled that:

> The builders could go no further without a locomotive. They purchased the smallest engine they could procure and shipped it to St. Joseph, expecting to take it across the river on a ferry boat. After estimating the weight of the engine, and seeing the action of the boat when loaded with heavy wagons, the engineers concluded the ferry was too small.
>
> There were no railroad bridges across the Missouri River, and no railroad on the west side of the river. It was too late in

the fall to get a larger steamboat that could ferry the engine across. If they waited until the river was free of ice in the spring, valuable time would be lost. The only chance was to take it over on the ice when the river froze up. There was a regular highway across the river for loaded wagons every winter.

They graded on the Missouri side down to the river's edge, and up on the Kansas side, got long telegraph poles to use as ties, and had all material ready for a hard freeze. Finally, in January, 1860, the weather became very cold, and the ice was frozen 18 inches thick. They laid the poles on the ice, spiked the rails on, stripped the engine of all weight that could possibly be spared, fired her up and started.

As they approached the ice the engineer jumped off and let the locomotive go across alone. The ice groaned and cracked until we thought it would surely break through. But it held and when it reached the Kansas side another engineer jumped on and ran it up the bank. It was a tremendously exciting quarter hour.

The tiny locomotive's name has been forgotten, but it is significant in the saga of the New West; it was the first locomotive beyond the Missouri.

The Abolitionist-slaver fighting in Kansas halted construction on the St. Joseph & Denver, but the glorious 18 months of the Pony Express kept St. Joseph's hope bright. Then, just before the Pony Express gave way to the Overland Telegraph, a St. Josephan invented the vehicle that would revolutionize the United States Post Office and make the mail a routine essential in the national economy.

William A. Thompson was, like Jeff Thompson and many northwest Missourians, a native Virginian. Sometime in 1860 the Postmaster General transferred him to St. Joe as assistant postmaster. He caught the local enthusiasm for the Pony Express' relays, but frowned over the 2-, 3- and sometimes 4-hour delays caused while "Pony Mail" was being sorted out from local mail at the post office. A railroad car could be built, he concluded, that would enable mail to be sorted en route. Thompson drew up plans for a railcoach fitted out with letter racks and sorting tables. There should be protection, too, against robbers. He specified small, barred windows high up against the roof, and double-thick sliding doors.

The Postmaster General agreed that the idea was worth an experiment. The United States' first railway mail cars were built at the Hannibal & St. Joseph's Hannibal shops in 1862. (One of the mail clerks who worked the run throughout the Civil War was a lanky Englishman whose ambition in life was to operate a good, clean restaurant. His name was Fred Harvey.)

But now, Kansas City and Omaha were the boom towns. When the Mississippi & Missouri, or the Chicago & Northwestern, hammered into Council Bluffs, St. Joe would cease to be even a relay on the Pacific Railroad. Jeff Thompson was a refugee Confederate general in Louisiana. Russell, Majors and Waddell were long bankrupt, with Russell a street peddler in New York, Waddell living with sons downriver, and Majors trying to hire on as a subcontractor to wagon supplies up the Platte for Union Pacific. Even the railway mail car had been copied by Chicago's postmaster, who now blithely proclaimed it his own invention.

And now, out of Omaha, the Casement Brothers were breaking every railroad construction record in the books.

CHAPTER 16

HELL-ON-WHEELS

> *Captain D. B. Clayton, superintendent of laying the track, showed your reporter a specimen of what could be done. He gave his men the hint, and in the space of exactly five minutes, as timed by the watch, they laid down the rails and spiked them for a distance of seven hundred feet. The rails are twenty-eight feet in length. There was fifty rails laid down, of course one on each side of the track. At that rate sixteen miles and a half of track could be laid down in one day. . . . Henry M. Stanley,* My Early Travels and Adventures, *Julesburg, Colorado (September 17, 1867).*

On June 9, 1866, Samuel Reed issued the Construction Train Schedule between Omaha and Columbus, Nebraska, then a trackage distance of 100 miles. When the schedule went into operation, on June 11, railhead was another 3 or 4 miles west of Columbus. During the eight weeks since the Casement Brothers' gargantuan train first creaked onto the line, Union Pacific had added a mile of track a day. It was neither luck nor accident.

Only six years before, along much of the same route, Alexander Majors and Ben Ficklin had set up the 163 relay stations that made the Pony Express possible. Between February 8 and

April 11, 1866, the Casements built a train of 12 to 15 cars that incorporated all of the Pony Express stations' essentials for survival on the Great Desert, plus an assembly-line technique that enabled speedy distribution of ties, rail, spikes, fishplates and bolts. Bunkhouses, kitchens, dining rooms, a blacksmith shop, offices, storerooms, toolhouses and arsenals were built into the cars.

The most comprehensive description of the train, from the millions of words filed by "Correspondents to the Pacific Railroad" between 1866 and 1870, is the April 23, 1869, dispatch sent to Salt Lake City's *Deseret News* by Edward L. Sloan, the brilliant young Irish Latter-day Saint who signed his dispatches with the by-line of "Anon." By that time the train had expanded to 22 cars. He wrote, from the Casements' office car:

> Far in front of the boarding-train may be described the advance of the track-laying forces, a group of some twenty men, armed with picks, shovels, road-gauges, pounders, spike-mauls, etc. They work in sets of two, a man on each side the track; who scientifically bed a tie every fourteen feet. These are called the "joint-tie men." Next come the "fillers" who bed the intervening ties. The "iron-men" follow, ten in number, five stalwart fellows to each rail. With a loud "Away she goes" from the foreman, the two rails, each weighing some 700 pounds, are drawn forward from the truck and, at the word "down" dropped with a precision only acquired by long practice, one at each side, in their place on the ties.
>
> Following the iron-men come the "head spikers" who gauge the width and drive six spikes into each rail. The "back spikers" and "screwers" come next, who finish spiking the rails and screw up the fishplates, heavy iron clamps on each side the rail, thoroughly bolting the joints—a recent excellent invention much superior to the old "chair" splice . . . The spikers are preceded by a set of "spike peddlers," one on each side of the track . . . Next follow the "track liners" who, with crowbars, put the track in perfect line. In rear and directly in front of the huge outfit termed "the boarding cars" are the "back-iron men" who load the rails upon trucks from the side of the grade, where they are thrown from the flatcars upon which they are shipped from the East . . . Water carriers . . . with pail and cup in hand, stand ever near to "cool

the parched tongue" of the feverish tracklayer . . . "Champion Tom" [is] the noble full-blooded American equine who pulls the front truck, in cooperation with the "iron men." [Tom was blind!] . . . practice has made him perfect in his role . . .

The front of Casements' train is a truck laden with such sundries as switch stands, targets . . . timbers for truck repairs, iron rods, steel bars, barrels, boxes . . . straightedges, wrenches . . . cable, rope, cotton waste . . . mattresses and an indefinable lot of dunnage . . . with a blacksmith shop in full blast in rear . . .

In the second car is the feed store and saddler's shop. The third is the carpenter shop and wash-house . . . The fourth is a sleeping apartment for mule-whackers. Fifth, a general sleeping car with bunks for 144 men. Sixth, sitting and dining room for employees. Seventh, long dining room at the tables of which 200 men can be comfortably seated. Eighth, kitchen in front and counting room and telegraph office in rear. Ninth, store car. Tenth through sixteenth, all sleeping cars. Seventeenth and eighteenth, Captain Clayton's cars: the former his kitchen; the latter his parlor . . . Nineteenth, sleeping car. Twentieth, supply car. Twenty-first and twenty-second, water cars.

This immense train had two engines and its "staff" included two conductors, two engineers, two foremen, a wagonmaster, financial manager, storekeeper, a physician and surgeon, and a chief steward with 16 assistants. The civil engineer for the end-of-track had 7 assistants. There was also a telegraph operator and a draughtsman.

The Casement work train not only perfected the standard American system for railroad construction and maintenance, but introduced the assembly line, the sleeping car, the dining car, the lounge car and the portable smithy to the West.

The Casements also bought a herd of Durham Shorthorn and Galloway cattle that ambled alongside the iron trail from Nebraska to Utah, so provided fresh beef all the way. Although millions of cattle and sheep, and even some pig herds (each following a drover-led blind boar), crossed the California-Mormon Trail between 1847 and 1870, all of these were trail drives pushed through during the summer months. But the Casements' "Diamond" herd endured three winters on the

High Plains and pioneered the Cowboy Era that, between 1870 and 1900, transformed the Northern Rockies into a vast cattle domain and provided both the locale and the incidents for the Western-art classics of Frederic Remington and Charles H. Russell and the cowboy prototypes in the books of Theodore Roosevelt, Stanley Vestal, Emerson Hough, Andy Adams, etc.

The majority of the Casements' workmen and foremen were Civil War veterans. The memoirs of Grenville Dodge and the letters of Samuel Reed agreed with Edwin L. Sabin, in *Building The Pacific Railway*, that "Military the work was, in its organization . . . ex-bluecoats and 'Galvanized Yanks' labored with transit, rod, chain, pick and bar and spade and sledge." "Anon" furnished another clue when he referred, in that May 5, 1869, dispatch to the "mud-sill co-laborers." The phrase "mud-sill" is a semantic invention of Georgia and Carolina hillmen, and refers to Southerners raised in log cabins that had puncheon floors and "mud," or adobe, sills.

All of these facts flourish a large question mark against the folklore assumption that "the Irish built the Pacific Railroad." The evidence is that at least two-thirds of Casements' bully-boys, as well as the grading gangs and bridge crews laboring 10 to 200 miles west of them, were "Galvanized Yanks" from the South, Union veterans from the prairie states, Swedes, Danes and "Finlanders" recruited in Chicago, plus 300 to 1,000 Negroes who chose mulewhacker and shovel jobs on Union Pacific as the most exciting way to "Get over the hill and see the elephant."

Most of these crews were familiar with military discipline and at the first thud of an Indian arrow could toss work tools, grab rifles, and go into action as "skirmishers." Consequently, the Casement work train was also a mobile fortress and veteran fighting force invading the red man's Great Desert empire.

This was the epochal assault force that Durant launched when he gambled his personal investments and the future of Crédit Mobilier on the conviction that the Casements' behemoth would beat both "Eastern Division" and the Congressional deadline to the 100th meridian. Overall, then, this work train was as meaningful to the final conquest and mechanization of the West as the steeple-tall, galvanized windmill invented at Beloit, Wisconsin, in 1867 by L. H. Wheeler; the railroad refrigerator car invented in 1868 by William Davis of Detroit; the barbed wire developed by Joseph F. Glidden of Illinois in 1873; and the electric light perfected by ex-train butcher Thomas A. Edison in 1879.

The winning of the West was a victory of technology over topography, climate, and the red man's desperate "last stand." The West's conquerors were—with due respect to the cavalry, the cowboys, the lawmen, et al—the railroad, the steel plow, the windmill, barbed wire, dynamite, and electricity. Through them the Great American Desert and the red man's empire became a gigantic producer of the cereal grains, livestock, citrus fruits, vegetables, metals, coal and petroleum that enabled the United States to weather the industrial depression of the post-Civil War period and grow into a world power. After 1870 the exports from the West provided much of the nation's trade balance in Europe and Asia.

The pace that the Casements established up the Platte Valley ran the railhead past Fort Kearney in late July. Samuel Reed and Grenville Dodge fell into the quickstep. Reed coordinated the advance gangs who dug and blasted a ten-foot roadbed under the direction of location survey engineers, the bridge gangs building wooden spans across the feeder creeks on the Platte's north bank, the tie hacks beavering through every midvalley forest, the relay crews routing hardware supplies via St. Joe, and the mechanics installing car-building and overhaul equipment in the new roundhouse and shops at Omaha.

In mid-August, Grenville Dodge led Silas Seymour, Government Director Jesse Williams and David Van Lennep, a geologist, on a survey exploration to the Rockies' crest, then east via Denver. Van Lennep's assignment was to locate deposits of coal (for the inevitable shift of locomotive fuel from wood to coal), and iron and copper (for mineral-rights' sale to J. Edgar Thomson, Andrew Carnegie and other processors) plus rock formations that would be durable enough for use as track ballast. Williams went along to give government approval to route plans, and quite probably to act as a "friend in court" when it became necessary to announce the fact that Union Pacific intended to by-pass Denver.

The foursome, with a small cavalry escort, relocated the Lone Pine Pass through the Black Hills and sent word back to Evans's survey crew. A plat of the east slope confirmed that Union Pacific could cross to the Wyoming Great Basin and the Continental Divide on a grade of ninety feet to the mile.

The ride south to Denver, enlivened by hunting and a skirmish or two with Indians, established the advisability of a terminal junction for a branch line to Denver on the shore of Crow Creek near the foot of Evans Pass. This was ancient hunting ground for the Cheyenne; any town located there could logically be named for them.

On September 18, Government Inspector Williams hunched on a rock in Berthoud Pass behind Denver, and wrote the editor of his home-town paper, the Fort Wayne, Indiana, *Sentinel:* "The Union Pacific Railroad is under rapid progress. In November next the locomotive is expected to cross the bridge over the North Platte, two hundred and eighty-five miles from Omaha. The opening of this work across the Plains, will soon make the people of the States more familiar with this Rocky Mountain range and its grand scenery; and what is more important, will afford ready access to a new field of enterprise in the work of developing its vast mineral wealth."

Similar letters, written "back home" by the work crews, were turned into front-page stories with the local angle beloved of every editor. The Chicago *Tribune* began carrying a daily report about the length of track laid during the Casement train's previous work day. It was two generations before big-league baseball and the box score, but Union Pacific's track score caused similar betting pools in the saloons and bawdyhouses along Chicago's Clark Street. This in turn stimulated the concern of the madams, pimps and professional gamblers for the "lonesomeness of them poor fellows out there in the wilderness." By September, plans were completed for a "joy and social welfare expedition" of bartenders, monte and faro dealers, madams and "girls" to the winter camp the Casement work train would establish—probably near the junction of the North and South Platte rivers.

The plans being shaped by Thomas Durant and George Francis Train during the same weeks were just as spectacular and similarly impelled by the profit motive. Train rode out beyond railhead in late spring. He exulted at the prairie near the junction of the Platte and Loup rivers, and gave the name "Columbus" to the tiny community. Columbus, Train decided, would be the initial "great city of the West" developed by his Crédit Foncier. He borrowed a survey team from Dodge, laid out home and industry sites along the Platte's north bluff, then hurried East to write newspaper articles and lecture lyceums and church suppers about "Columbus, the new centre of the Union and quite probably the future capital of the U.S.A."

Durant, from June on, worked on plans for a "Grand Excursion" that would boost Union Pacific stock sales and enable a first dividend for the investors in Crédit Mobilier. Construction costs to 100th meridian were totaling more than $12,000,-000. The Federal loans on the 247 miles of track would net only $3,000,000. Now was the time for a master promotion stroke that would put Union Pacific on every newspaper front page in Europe and the United States and break through the passive cynicism of millionaires and bankers. During August, clerks at the New York office labored over hundreds of letters to a select list of the New York, Boston and Philadelphia "elite" and to each member of Congress. They requested the honor of the recipient's company on a two weeks', no-expense journey to the 100th meridian via special train. Departure from New York City was scheduled for the afternoon of October 15.

Herbert Hoxie turned his St. Joseph duties over to an assistant in order to devise an elaborate program of "Western Excitements" for the guests. Durant jittered about the dangers of yellow fever and cholera in the work camps, and hired physicians in Chicago to make an inspection trip to the proposed camp sites for the Grand Excursion.

The Indian attacks feared by Dodge had not materialized. The grim efficiency of the Casement work train made it foolhardy to launch an attack with fewer than 1,000 warriors. Moreover, the War Department had assigned Major North and his Pawnee Scouts to the exclusive task of patrolling Union Pacific's survey route. The simplest object for assault then, in the reasoning of the young braves and subchiefs among the Cheyenne and Sioux, was the locomotive itself. After all, this was the monster that frightened the bison, elk and antelope away from hunting grounds, made a noise like forty-seven devils, and vomited the columns of smoke and flaming cinders that started prairie fires. The halfbreed traders and reservation agents all referred to the monster as "the iron horse."

From June on, parties of young braves circled east behind the work train, each intent on capturing an iron horse. A few efforts were made to lasso locomotive stacks. These succeeded in tilting one or two stacks, but at the price of broken ribs and scarred buttocks. Succeeding raiders decided that a rawhide trip rope would be more effective. Four husky bucks were chosen as anchor men. The medicine man gave them a 40-foot strip of rawhide that he had imbued with powerful magic. Then the party hid behind the sand ridges until a supply train wheezed into sight. When the locomotive was 25 or 50 yards away the anchor men howled their death challenge, leaped to opposite sides of the track, and gripped the rope—taut and waist high—between them. The rest of the raiders concentrated their fire power of arrows and a few muskets at the engineer and firemen. The lead anchor men were catapulted under the engine wheels. This plan, too, was abandoned.

In early August a group of Sioux did succeed in halting a

train near the Plum Creek trestle, 220 miles west of Omaha. They ran off the crew, built a bonfire, and fired every boxcar in the train. Grenville Dodge was still at railhead, readying for the Transcontinental Divide survey with Seymour, Williams and Van Lennep. Dodge's biographer claimed that he led a rescue party of 20 ironmen back 10 miles from the work train. The Sioux fled after a first volley.

Blind Tom hauled the railcar across the 100th meridian on October 5. Down south in the Kansas River Valley, Eastern Division abandoned the race, reorganized as the Kansas Pacific and veered back to Samuel Hallett's route through Fort Riley to Denver. Thus, because of the Casement work train, Chicago became the wholesale, manufacturing and shipping center for Union Pacific's territory and was assured of trade supremacy over St. Louis. The Chicago & Northwestern, now in obvious teamship with Durant and the Crédit Mobilier clique, announced that it would complete trackage into Council Bluffs "before 1867."

On October 17 officials of the Chicago & Northwestern left Omaha on a special train "laden with demijohns, cases, canned meats, fruits and pickles, rolls of buffalo robes and blankets; together with almost any number of breechloading carbines and revolvers." The train sidetracked for hunting expeditions two or three times en route to end-of-track. A wagon train carried the party the remaining 300 miles to Denver for the "Grand Opening" of Chicago & Northwestern's ticket and freight offices over "Union Pacific's Great Connecting Link" to Chicago.

Silas Seymour included a description of this excursion in a dispatch to *The New York Times*. At Durant's suggestion, the portly Consulting Engineer had temporarily become Union Pacific's first public-relations man. The *Times* agreed to publish his dispatches "from the Far West," highlighting the survey trip with Dodge, Williams and Van Lennep and the "Great Union Pacific Railroad Excursion." In February, 1867, D. Van

Nostrand published the series in book form. Union Pacific's stock salesmen distributed thousands of copies to prospective customers.

More than a hundred of the guests invited to the Grand Excursion showed up at trainside on October 15. These included Great Britain's Earl of Arlie, the Marquis Chambrun of Paris, M. O'Dillon Barrot, Secretary of the French Legation and a score of Senators and Congressmen. General S. R. Curtis headed the delegation of Government commissioners. George Francis Train brought his wife Wilhelmina and her French maid.

Durant stood at Jersey City trackside frowning at a telegraph message from Omaha. Sam Reed was delirious with a fever. It might be cholera; the doctors were in consultation at his bedside. He delayed the train until a second wire arrived. The diagnosis was typhoid fever. Durant sighed and gave the nod to take off.

The Grand Excursion routed through Philadelphia and Pittsburgh. At Chicago, on the evening of the 17th, Mayor J. B. Rice and a delegation of the Board of Trade stood at trainside, top hats over breast pockets, to announce that the excursionists were accorded the freedom of the city. Next morning Abraham Lincoln's son Robert, Joseph Medill of the Chicago *Tribune* and George M. Pullman joined the majority of the excursion guests who chose to follow the St. Joseph relay route to Omaha. The Chicago, Burlington & Quincy assembled a half dozen of Pullman's hulking new Palace cars at its Water Street Station. A. J. Vaas and his Great Western Light Guards band came aboard. A caterer was arranging a buffet of "roast antelope, Roman goose and Chinese duck" and a resplendent back bar of champagnes, wine and vintage whiskies in the car assigned to the directors and Government commissioners. In the baggage car the Chicago photographer, J. Carbutt, tallied the boxes and tin trunks holding the equipment needed on his assignment as "official viewist" of the excursion. During the prairie run across Illinois and Missouri, S. R. Wells marched between cars to demonstrate his knowledge of phrenology and wisdom bumps. With tracks cleared for a "highball" run, the Grand Excursion Special clipped a half hour off the record.

The beam on Herbert Hoxie's face was broad. The *Denver* and *Colorado,* each freshly scrubbed to the keel, were at the Railroad Packet Line pier. Another band, flanked by children holding "mineral-oil" torches, swung into a waltz as the train hissed into St. Joseph's Patee House curve.

The "Evening Repast" in the steamers' dining rooms offered "Tenderloin of venison, brazed, a-la-Italian—Bear, brazed, Port Wine Sauce—Mallard Ducks, Teal Ducks, Malaga Wine Sauce—Grouse, larded, Madeira sauce—Quails on toast—Wild Turkey—Rabbit Pot Pie, Boston Style—Prairie Chicken, larded, Tomato Sauce" plus thirty other entrees and cold dishes. Each table had a "pasties" centerpiece of "Pyramid of Sponge Candy, Pyramid of Rock Candy—Gothic Style, Ornamented Fruit Cake with Nougat Vase" or a "Pyramid of Macaroons." At eleven o'clock, Hoxie took a torch to the *Denver*'s prow and wagged it above his head. Up and down the Missouri's shore his stevedores set off festoons of rockets, sky bombs and Roman candles. The bands, each clustered on a hurricane deck, swung into a grand march. The steamers cast off, chuffed their own cottonwood-chunk fireworks into the moonlight, and churned upstream.

That night, too, Vice-President Perry H. Smith of Chicago & Northwestern ushered the rest of the excursion's guests into sleepers for the "Great Connecting Link" railhead. The group reached Council Bluffs on the morning of the 22nd, soon after the *Colorado* and *Denver* whistled up to the Omaha landing. Hoxie's former domain, the ancient steamboat *Elkhorn,* was still the only transriver ferry. Perry Smith, as eager for publicity gimmicks as Durant, led his group into the *Elkhorn*'s salon and initiated each, with a "brandy libation," into the "Ancient and Honorable Order of the Elkhorn Club." Its "bucks" elected officers, set up a schedule for "morning exercises and ablutions in the Platte," and announced exclusive hunting parties for "the week in the Western Wilderness."

Durant excused himself after the pierhead greetings to hurry Dr. Alexander, the excursion's physician, to Sam Reed's sickroom. Dr. Alexander confirmed the diagnosis of typhoid and announced that the sturdy engineer had passed the crisis.

That afternoon stagecoaches carried the party up the clay ruts on an inspection trip to the Union Pacific's shops and roundhouse and the burnetizer machine. At the Grand Ball in the Hernden House that evening, peppery General Philip St. George Cooke—who had commanded the Mormon Battalion on its 1846–7 march to the Pacific—and all his staff for the Army's Department of the Missouri marched in in full dress.

The rail journey to the 100th meridian began on the morning of Tuesday, October 23. The nine-car train, drawn by two locomotives draped in bunting, contained one of the Hannibal & St. Joseph mail cars—redecorated as a bar on wheels— a cooking car, a baggage-and-supply car, four coaches newly built at the Omaha shops, the "Abraham Lincoln" car—reserved for the use of Durant's personal party—and a new Directors' car. Senators, Congressmen and Federal commissioners were assigned to the plush chairs of the Directors' car at the rear of the train so that they might have "a satisfactory view" of trackage, bridges and way stations. As the train chuffed up the Missouri–Elkhorn Ridge, a dozen waiters relayed tray luncheons down the aisles. The conductor was under orders to hold the run to twenty miles an hour with five-minute inspection stops at the Papillon and Elkhorn bridges and the Fremont and North Bend stations.

At sunset, the train reached the tent city that George Francis Train's crews had erected alongside the Columbus station. Its street was dominated by a mammoth dining tent. The sleeping tents, each labeled with name tags, were outfitted with sweet-grass mattresses, bison robes and homespun blankets. Durant's instructions called for an after-dinner Indian war dance by a troupe of Major North's Pawnee. The Major held the rest of the Scouts in an up-track camp, under orders to have their war paint on by 4 A.M. At 5 A.M. on the 24th, the Major led them in a false "dawn raid" through the tent city. There were no late sleepers. The train headed west again at nine.

The trip operated on the same leisurely schedule, with a two-hour halt at the Loup Fork Bridge for a sham battle between one of North's Pawnee companies, dressed in the war costumes they had worn for the morning's "raid," and a second company dressed as Sioux. Superb actors, the Pawnee charged headlong at their "enemies," shot blank cartridges and barbless arrows, heeled ponies into collision and jabbed spears at one another so viciously that the ladies of the excursion fled back to the cars. (In 1880, "Buffalo Bill" Cody hired the Pawnee Scouts for his "Great Wild West Show." Their mock battle, first produced for the Grand Excursion to the 100th meridian, became a favorite of audiences throughout the United States and Europe.)

The train reached the 100th meridian in late afternoon. The Casements had erected a wooden arch and sign across the track at the spot. But there had been six months of crackdown, with "General Jack" jogging up and down at the head of the line on his black stallion, his tongue-lashings almost as biting as the blacksnake whip curled across his saddle, his eyes scowling after every needless work gesture. Tracklaying moved as flawlessly as the pistons of a locomotive; railhead, moving west at an average pace of 1½ miles a day, was now 40 miles up the Platte. The 100th meridian stop, then, served only a publicity highlight, permitting "Viewist" Carbutt to set up his camera and photograph successive groups of Government officials and guests posed in front of the wooden arch.

The western terminal of the trip, designated Camp No. 2, was across the Platte from Fort McPherson, 279 miles west of Omaha. The tent layout was similar to George Francis Train's creation at Columbus, plus a barbershop, a telegraph office and a newspaper tent where compositors and printers were working on the first edition of the *Railway Pioneer,* a newspaper being published daily for the excursionists. Troops commanded by Colonel J. K. Mizner patrolled the grounds. North's Pawnee went out on scout that night; there were reports from upriver that bands of Cheyenne or Sioux were in the area. Nevertheless, the first issue of *Railway Pioneer* carried the announcement that, "Gentlemen wishing to go on a buffalo or antelope hunt will please report to Captain Hollins at headquarters. Captain H., with an experienced hunter, will accompany the party. Buffalo are said to be in abundance on the Republican, and Antelope nearer camp. The party will be absent about four days. Horses and ponies will be provided."

On the 25th, the train chuffed another 10 miles to end-of-track. The tiemen, ironmen, screwers and spikers put on an exhibition. Ladies were permitted to feed sugar lumps to Blind Tom. The work train was host for a rollicking frontier luncheon of baked beans, fried steak, jellied buffalo tongue and sand-cherry pie topped by (New England's choice) a dollop of pan gravy.

Camp No. 2 folded tents on the 27th. Most of the party returned to Chicago for a banquet and interminable speeches at the Opera House. Durant produced his last "Western Excitements" in a two-hour stop near Kearney to inspect a prairie-dog village; and a second stop at dusk to view the 20 mile front of a prairie fire he had ordered to be set off, "an hour after the Excursion leaves Kearney."

A second special train, trailing in from Omaha, was placed at the disposal of General J. H. Simpson, General Samuel R. Curtis and Major M. W. White, the three Government commissioners, for use in their track inspections. The trio stayed on the prairie for another month. On Christmas Eve, General Simpson wrote the editor of The Washington, D.C. *Chronicle* from the new city of North Platte: "All along the road, where the Company has established its stations, settlements are springing up rapidly; and here at this point whence I write, North Platte Station, *where three weeks ago there was nothing* are already some twenty buildings, including a brick engine round-house, calculated for forty engines . . . a water tank of beautiful proportions . . . a frame depot . . . a large frame hotel nearly finished, to cost about $18,000; a long, spacious movable building, belonging to General Casement and his brother, Daniel Casement, the great tracklayers of the continent, calculated for a store, eating-house and for storage purposes; together with sundry other buildings."

The "sundry other buildings," so delicately circumvented in the General's description, were also "movable." Like the Casements' commissary warehouse, they had arrived via boxcar from Chicago as "prefabs." All were one story, oblong, and with canvas tent extensions. A few arrived complete with mahogany bars, back mirrors and bottled goods. Others were accompanied by cases of roulette wheels, faro tables, cartons of loaded dice, and several sets of carefully nicked playing cards.

A third type of building had a satin-draped front parlor —with a bar in one corner. A mineral-oil lamp with red bull's-eye shade sat in one of the windows. Out from the parlor ran a dim corridor with curtained cubicles five feet wide on each side. Each cubicle contained a straw mattress, a rocking chair, a commode, and a young woman.

These saloons, faro joints and cribhouses were investments by some of the derby set along Chicago's Clark Street. Jack Casement ordered them off railroad property. The newcomers smirked, built at the edge of right of way, and began snugging in for the winter. They were under orders to "stay with the work train" and leech every dollar they could from the crews. Jack Casement himself, growling his worries to Dodge and Reed, gave the settlement the name of "Hell on Wheels." It would cause more trouble, he prophesied, than the Indians.

The week after Christmas, leaving North Platte settled in for the winter, Simpson, Curtis and White rode back to Omaha. For General Curtis the past five weeks had been the proudest of his life. As an Iowa Congressman, he had labored for passage of a Pacific Railroad Act from 1855 on. He encouraged Ted Judah to open the Pacific Railway Museum. The Pacific Railroad Act of 1862, based largely on his 1860 bill, passed the House only a few weeks after the Union Army he commanded defeated Van Doren's Confederates at Pea Ridge. In the summer of 1863 he had to dab his eyes and swallow before starting his acceptance speech as chairman pro tem of the Union Pacific commissioners convention at Chicago. Now he had seen almost 300 miles of Pacific Railroad glimmering up the Platte, and every inch of it enthusiastically acceptable to his fellow commissioners. The old gentleman sighed as he followed Simpson and White into the carriage at the Omaha Depot, then staggered and slumped to the floor. The doctors pronounced him dead of a heart attack. He was still smiling.

In New York that week, Durant purred over the hillocks of press clippings and correspondence that the Grand Excursion had generated. Sidney Dillon and Oakes Ames were due in that afternoon for a conference. The time was ripe to launch a public offering of Union Pacific's first-mortgage bonds.

In Omaha, Sam Reed sat up in bed, scowling over his backlog of correspondence and work sheets. One letter puzzled him. He reread it. New York was routing out a new type of explosive known as "Patent Blasting Oil." It was a veritable hell broth, according to reports; sometimes the stuff exploded for no apparent reason. The bridge engineers wanted to try it out. Best to take it up the line by special train, "and SLOW."

CHAPTER 17

CHAPTER **17**

PATENT BLASTING OIL

The frightful experience of the people of San Francisco in Nitro-glycerine has caused them to make that article contraband of trade. The agts. have managed to smuggle some of it into the interior. . . . Some parties, including the Rail Road people, are talking about manufacturing it on the ground and using it. . . . Letter to E. I. du Pont de Nemours & Company, Wilmington, Delaware, from Rodmond Gibbons & Company, San Francisco (January 30, 1867).

A typically drowsy Sunday morning introduced November 5, 1865, to New York City's Greenwich Village. The overnight steamers from Boston and Baltimore blew their whistles, slapped eddies along the North River piers, and set off the routine cussing of longshoremen while they wheeled Northern Spy apples, Maine potatoes, Gloucester codfish and Chincoteague oysters down cargo ramps. Along Greenwich Street early churchgoers took to the gutters to avoid the drunks sprawled snoring on the sidewalks.

In his cubbyhole off the lobby, the porter of the Wyoming Hotel reached for his broom, stumbled against a box, winced and gave it a kick that slithered it against the wall. The box, black with shoe-polish stain, was about two feet long and a

216

foot high. A guest had left it in the checkroom early in the summer, but seemed to have forgotten about it. The porter had taken to using it as a footrest for guests who stopped by for a shoeshine.

He reached again for the broom, sniffed, and turned. A trail of orange-red smoke was eddying across the floor. It had a gunpowder odor, but smelled greasier and somehow sourer. The smoke was jetting from the box like steam out of a petcock. He scooped it up, scurried across the lobby, and heaved it into the center of Greenwich Street. As it hit, a great flame gushed to the rooftops. The roar left him stone deaf, staring numbly at the cobblestone slivers quivering in his arms and chest and the blood oozing down his hands. The center of Greenwich Street was a slimy yellow hole, its mud still boiling. Across the street, sunlight filtered into jagged new holes in house fronts.

Hours later, at a hospital, the porter told detectives all he could remember about the box. The owner's name had been scrawled on it—a German name, something like "Bohrs" or "Bahrs." Whoever he was, he had acted like a gentleman, given a two-bits tip, and said he would call for the box as soon as he "closed a business deal." The vicious power and the rotten-orange smell eddying from the hole identified the box's contents as the nitroglycerine compound called "Patent Blasting Oil." It was its second appearance on the Atlantic seaboard. Five months before, a Colonel Otto Burstenbinder had brought the first batch in from Hamburg, Germany and demonstrated its potency to a group of engineers and gunpowder salesmen by blowing impressive holes in a cliff of the lower Palisades. Manufactured in Sweden by a chemist named Alfred Nobel and his German partner, Dr. C. E. Bandmann, Patent Blasting Oil was a mixture of gunpowder and the nitroglycerin discovered about 1846 by the Italian chemist, Ascanio Sobrero.

Liquid nitroglycerin was so sensitive to heat, or even to a tiny impact, that no explosives factory would produce it until in 1863 the Nobel family developed this method of mixing it with gunpowder. One batch had wrecked the family factory near Stockholm, killing Alfred Nobel's younger brother and four others. But miners and highway engineers in central Europe were using Patent Blasting Oil on "hard-rock" jobs.

New York police decided that the mysterious "Bohrs" or "Bahrs" brought the box of Patent Blasting Oil to America with the intention of becoming a salesman-demonstrator. He was never traced, but the publicity he produced via the Greenwich Street explosion brought inquiries from New England quarrymen, Pennsylvania miners, and finally from the Union Pacific Railroad.

Soon after Grenville Dodge signed on as chief engineer and the Casements' work train began clanging the great iron trail, Durant's commissary opened negotiations with Nobel for test shipments of Patent Blasting Oil that could be tried out by the crews who would be blasting bridge foundations in the Platte Valley.

Meanwhile, Nobel–Bandmann explored the most obvious markets in the United States—the hard-rock borings into the Mother Lode of northeastern California and the Comstock Lode of western Nevada. Dr. Bandmann's brother Julius headed the San Francisco wholesalers—Bandmann, Neilson & Company. The firm became the Pacific Coast agent for Patent Blasting Oil, and received its first shipments via Cape Horn about the time of the Greenwich Street explosion. Some of the Virginia City and Grass Valley mine shafts were a mile deep and used hundreds of kegs of blasting powder each week. Central Pacific Railroad was in the market, too, blowing more than a hundred kegs a day for rock cuts and tunnels in the Sierra. Any explosive of high potency, however temperamental, was worth an experiment.

The steamer *European* docked at Aspinwall on the Panama Isthmus on April 2, 1866, and began unloading freight for California. Next morning the longshoremen dragged a heavy case assigned to Bandmann, Neilson & Company over to a loading net, tossed a few bundles atop it, and signaled to the winchman. As the net lifted, both the *European* and the pier vanished in an orange flame. Chunks of burning wood and charred flesh thumped on tin roofs half a mile away. Port officials estimated a total of sixty dead and a $1,000,000 loss. The Bandmann, Neilson case had contained seventy boxes of Patent Blasting Oil.

The gory details still rated follow-up stories in San Francisco newspapers on April 16. That noon hour the granite warehouse of Wells, Fargo & Company on Montgomery Street burst with a volcanic roar, belching a searing flame and acrid cloud; firemen found fourteen dead and a score of maimed in the ruins. Wells, Fargo officials admitted that a shipment of Patent Blasting Oil had been carted to the rear platform of the warehouse for delivery to Bandmann, Neilson. The City Council passed a law that forbade transportation of the mixture within the city limits.

The New York City, Panama, and San Francisco explosions, occurring over a six months' period and echoed by angry newspaper editorials, stepped up Nobel's research for a blending agent that would make nitroglycerin less volatile. He finally discovered such a mixture, late in 1866, by saturating diatomaceous earth with nitroglycerin. He prepared the mixture in paper-covered sticks, like oversized Chinese firecrackers, and named it Dynamite. But dynamite was too late for the Pacific Railroad.

By the summer of 1866, Central Pacific's need for explosives was creating a market shortage, even though two or three firms in the Bay Area manufactured both sodium-nitrate and potassium-nitrate types of blasting powder. As California agent for E. I. du Pont de Nemours, Rodmond Gibbons kept a close watch on developments and relayed the local trade gossip to Wilmington. On May 18, 1866, he reported: "The R. R. Co. is consuming 175 to 200 kegs per day and they have been getting powder at times from Parker and us, as we have reason to believe when the Cal. Co. could not keep them fully supplied." Just one month later he admitted that "instead of trying to sell Blasting Powder we are obliged to husband stock, to protect the mining interest. If we & Parker chose to do so, we could dispose of our entire stock to the Rail Road Co.'s Agt. & leave the miners in the lurch."

During June, Gibbons opened negotiations with an agent of the Associates for 15,000 kegs of niter powder at $3.75 a keg and a comparable order of "soda powder," all to be shipped in iron kegs (so that moisture would not be absorbed during the six months' sail around Cape Horn). He wrote Wilmington:

> The R.R. Co. have *eleven thousand* Chinamen now employed grading and tunneling through the mountains, and are consuming 300 kegs per day. As nearly as we can learn, it will require *two years* for them to get through with the heavy grading. The controllers of the R. R. Co. belong to that *smart* class of men who are inherent sharpers & who always take a roundabout means to attain their ends in preference to a straightforward course. They buy the 15,000 kegs through a broker instead of coming to us direct. Most of their powder they use in *bank blasting,* say from 15 to 25 kegs at a time, so the soda powder will answer their purpose, provided the packages are secured against the ingress of air. The R. R. men seem to believe that there is not enough powder made in the U.S. to supply their wants and have been encouraging shipments from England. The sale we have made will put a stop to English importations.

But, again, Huntington, Crocker, Stanford and Hopkins were "shopping around." The bid for du Pont powder seems to have been a gesture to bring the California companies into line with lower prices. A few weeks later Gibbons sent his agent John Skinker up the Bay to sales-talk Charles Crocker into a purchase of du Pont gunpowders. Skinker wrote the following report of his interview:

> Crocker had just returned to town from Stockton, and I called at his home at 7½ o'clock, and had a long talk with him. He informed me he had a contract with the California Powder Co. to take from them 2500 kegs per month, for which he paid them $2.75 nett, but he could consume even more than that amount. I finally offered him 5 to 7 thousand kegs at $2.60. He then made

me the offer of $2.25 for it, which of course I declined. He stated he could give no more for it, as he was satisfied imported powder was weakened or lost much of its strength by the voyage to San Francisco, and he was satisfied a keg of California Powder would do ⅓ more work than any imported powder brought here. I tried to convince him otherwise, but he insisted it was so, and said all his workmen were of the same opinion, although they were at first prejudiced against our domestic Powder. He said Hopkins & Huntington were of the same opinion as myself, as to the superiority of DuPonts & Hazzard Powder over the California make, and he thought I could make them a sale of it. I then made a search for Mr. Hopkins but could not find him at home or elsewhere.

Crocker's zestful defense of local industry was hokum. On October 29 the ship *Templar* delivered 4,000 kegs of blasting powder at Central Pacific's wharves. The *Templar* was out of Boston, where the Federal arsenal had been auctioning off gunpowder made "surplus" by Lee's surrender the year before. Similar auctions were under way at the Army arsenals in Watervliet, New York, and St. Louis. Central Pacific and Union Pacific bid in lots at all three places and got some of it for $1.50 a keg. (Testifying before the Senate's Pacific Railway Commission in the 1880's, Collis Huntington sniffed his disgust of "wartime profiteers," and said that blasting powder "went up to $15 a keg." But 90 per cent of Central Pacific's blasting operations occurred during 1866-7-8.)

Although shrewd shopping and the purchase of War Department surpluses helped the Associates hold down Pacific Coast gunpowder prices, they served even better as a method for concealing the railroad's upcountry manufacture of nitroglycerin. Gibbons finally heard the rumor in late January, 1867, and wrote du Pont that "some parties, including the Rail Road people, are *talking* about manufacturing it on the ground and using it . . ." By March he had enough confirmation to report, "The Rail Road Co. are experimenting with *Nitroglycerin* & the directors say they intend to make use of it largely." In June, he relayed the story that "one of the foremen on the line of the R.R. works has recently fallen a victim to Nitroglycerin. He was 'sounding' for a new blast, and struck some of the material that remained unexploded in the former blast & exploding under his blow, it killed him."

What actually happened in the high Sierra and Wyoming gorges as a result of America's first massive use of nitroglycerin is another great-iron-trail mystery. Both Central Pacific and Union Pacific manufactured it in log-cabin factories deep in the wilderness. Then the deadly "stuff" was carried pack-a-back, or by mule cart, up the mountains to the bridge gangs and tunnelmen. Chinese and Galvanized Yank laborers learned to fire it by trial-and-error methods that maimed or killed hundreds of them. Some of the rock cuts and tunnels still used by Union Pacific and Southern Pacific across Wyoming, Utah, Nevada and California are monuments to the unknown dead of nitro's terror reign across the vanishing "Desert."

Neither Central Pacific nor Union Pacific records indicate that any contractual agreement was made with Nobel-Bandmann. The formula for nitro was known to many chemists. Union Pacific built its first nitro plant outside of Julesburg during the summer of 1867. But it trailed Central Pacific by six months. The Gibbons letters to du Pont indicate that Crocker had his plant operating by January or February, 1867. He hired James Howden, a chemist who had recently emigrated to San Francisco from England, and built a log-and-stone factory for him on a lake near the west end of Donner Pass, far back from the wagon road and right of way. Freighters delivered the retorts of glycerin, nitric acid, and other ingredients that Howden needed. A crew of Chinese laborers—and no one ever told how often it was necessary to replace them—carried out Howden's orders for mixing batches of nitro as it was needed at railhead and at the tunnels. Within a few months, reports told, Howden was "drinking to excess" and the Chinese did the blending alone.

But Chinese heroism was commonplace all across the Sierra that winter. Locomotives crossed the Sierra crest on log rollers, hauled by 500-man teams. Thousands slept in ice caves, cut off from provisions for weeks at a time. Others worked from dawn to dusk suspended in wicker baskets that swayed a thousand feet above a river's rapids. The phrase, "Not a Chinaman's Chance," became an American simile because of the heroism of the coolies in the high Sierra during the winter of 1866–7.

CHAPTER **18**

NOT A CHINAMAN'S CHANCE!

> *We have seen it urged against the Chinese that they are bound fast in the swaddling clothes of superstition, from which they show no disposition to emancipate themselves. But who can expect them to do otherwise under the treatment which they receive? The very name of Christianity must be disgusting to them with such examples of its fruits before them, as they are too often compelled to experience. Cling to their heathenism? They would be little less than idiots not to do so under the circumstances. Men may prate to them about American civilization, free and enlightened institutions, the spirit of progress and advanced Christianity until doomsday, but they will fail to respect or attach any value to these high-sounding phrases and professions while they are treated like wild beasts. . . . An editorial, "Chinese Labor in the West," Deseret News, Salt Lake City (May 26, 1869).*

American mores dictated that a "foreigner's" road to liberty and the pursuit of happiness must struggle through ditches, slums, and sweatshops. For the Palatines, Huguenots, Scotch, and indentured servants of the eighteenth century, and the Germans, Scotch–Irish and Irish of the nineteenth century, the process averaged 25 years. But the bias confronting non-

224

Europeans was gigantic. The Negro did not gain acknowledgement of constitutional freedom until 250 years after Dutch traders landed the first shipload of slaves in Virginia. The Chinaman, socially ostracized by the nickname of "coolie," became the Pacific Coast's substitute for the Indian and Negro slave. Construction of the Central Pacific Railroad was his cross and his crown.

The 1849 gold rush drew thousands of Chinese to California. They were segregated to separate communities and separate jobs. Their shacktowns soon assumed the status of Europe's ghettos. The Irish migrants to California became their most vehement baiters—and for an obvious reason. The Irish immigrant had been the bogtrotter and shantytown work horse of the East Coast's industrial development since 1820. He had dug the canals, cleaned the outhouses, groomed the horses, and served as the butt of newspaper jokes and humorist-lectures. The California gold-rush country provided the Irishman with the first American locale where he was accepted as an "Anglo-Saxon equal." He responded exuberantly and, as a group, became the most despotic of all in bullying the non-whites.

The Chinese adapted so deftly to the white Californian's pace that the importation of male Chinese cooks, house boys, gardeners, and laundrymen was a thriving San Francisco business by 1855. British traders in Canton and other treaty ports profited from the operation. The word "coolie" was a British export out of India, with an original Hindu meaning of "porter" or "native unskilled laborer." On the eve of the Civil War, newspapers estimated that 42,000 Chinese labored in northern California. The majority were wiry sons of Yellow Sea fishermen, city laborers, or two-acre farmers. They averaged 120 pounds in weight; few were taller than 4' 10". Their transportation across the Pacific, in ships as ancient and filthy as the Atlantic's "middle-passage" slavers, was contracted on a system similar to the "indentured-servant" technique of New England, Virginia, and Georgia during the seventeenth century. Chinese trading companies, organized by the socio-political "tongs," provided passage and food. In California the trading companies' agents located jobs and usually collected the salaries. The San Francisco *Call,* Sacramento *Union* and other newspapers which campaigned about the problem of "Chinese Human Traffic" during the 1860's contended that most of the Chinese workers in the state received only $4 to $8 a month, and that the bulk of their wages went to "the companies" in repayment for trans-Pacific passage.

This was only partially true. The Californians' segregation forced the Chinese into tight fraternal groups. The companies acted as insurance firms, bankers, marriage brokers, and concubine purveyors. California laws denied citizenship rights to the Chinese, limited their immigration to "male workers," and specifically barred Chinese testimony in any court. But every Chinaman in the state was forced to pay a Personal Tax, a Hospital Tax, a $2 contribution to the School Fund, and a Property Tax. The Chinese who worked the "tailings" and abandoned placer and hydraulic mines on the Mother Lode paid a Permission Tax of $4 per head, plus an annual Water Tax. The San Francisco *Call* on March 30, 1867, estimated that the state of California and its local governments levied taxes of "more than $2,000,000" on its 65,000-70,000 Chinese residents during 1866.

Economically, then, the white Californian had little reason to side with Secesh in the Civil War or fight to defend the "South's institution" of slavery. Slaveholding entailed expensive responsibilities; a sound, mature slave brought $1,000 on the Georgia and Louisiana auction blocks. The owner was responsible for the health, food, shelter, and creature comforts of his slave investments. But coolie labor in California involved little responsibility beyond the payment of $1 per day per employee to the companies. The Chinese provided their own "keep" and housing. They worked diligently from dawn to dusk, seven days a week. They could be fired from a job "on the instant" and employer responsibility would end then and there. When a Chinese worker died the companies shipped his remains home to China and another "Ah Kee" or "Lee" or "Chung" stepped deferentially into the job. Slavery could not have survived the Chinese labor competition in California. The California Legislature did pass a law in 1858 forbidding further importations of Chinese. But its only penalty was a $400–$600 fine against the captain of the ship—a modest tax on the profit from a cargo of 100 to 500 seasick Celestials crammed into an aft hold. It was rarely enforced.

The Stanfords and Crockers, in common with prosperous California families, employed Chinese house boys and cooks. "As a class they are quiet, peaceable, patient, industrious and economical." Leland Stanford wrote President Johnson in his October, 1865, report on Central Pacific's progress. Both Stanford and Crocker turned to the Chinese companies when new mining booms at Eureka, Elko and Virginia City created a crisis in Central Pacific's work camps.

In June, 1865, Central Pacific's railhead was at Clipper Gap, 43 miles out of Sacramento. Ahead lay the grim job of blasting the roadbed up the cliffs of the Bear River gorge in order to reach the ridge rising to Donner Lake and the Sierra's crest. White labor had been used in every phase of the construction. But when news of new Nevada silver strikes spread, "signing up with the C. P." became the favorite method for free transportation to railhead; a week's work would stake the 100-mile walk on to Nevada. For every 1,000 white workmen signed up in the Bay towns that spring, 100 stayed on the job longer than a week; the other 900 went "over the hill."

"Hire some Chinese," Crocker ordered. Construction Superintendent J. H. Strobridge bristled; Chinese might make good house boys and gardeners, but they were too puny for railroad work. Stanford backed Crocker. Strobridge grumped agreement to try out a gang of fifty. His foremen reported angry mutterings about working "alongside the Chinamen." Strobridge promised that the Asiatics would be organized as separate crews. A little work spurt by the whites, he hinted, could show up the "coolies" and end this crazy Crocker–Stanford idea.

The Chinese marched through the white camps like a weird procession of midgets, blue cotton pants flopping, dishpan-shaped hats shadowing grave faces, delicate hands hidden in billowing sleeves. The white crews catcalled, and went boastfully to work.

The first night's reports were disturbing. The Chinese shovelmen took smaller bites in a bank, and their barrowmen trundled lighter loads to the fill, but they worked methodically, without gossip breaks or time out for smokes. Two or three times a day a youngster plodded among them carrying two kegs slung over a shoulder at each end of a bamboo pole. The barrels held hot tea. Each workman sipped a cupful, then literally bounced back to the job. By dusk, the coolies' right of way was longer and smoother than any white crew's.

Then another strange heathen ritual occurred. As the "coolie" gang trooped into camp, every man jack shed his work clothes and stepped naked into line behind the sleeping tents. There the cooks had set out rows of whisky kegs—one for each man. They filled these with warm water, and stacked piles of towels and clean clothes beyond. The gang sloshed, soaped, rinsed, dabbed themselves with flower water, and slithered into the clean clothes. The rule was obvious: no bath, no dinner. Thereafter, none of them seemed the least bit tired. They sat beside their campfires late, humming songs or chirping like angry orioles around a fan-tan game.

Next day the whites stepped up the speed, cut down work breaks and voluntarily halved their lunch hour. The Chinese pecked methodically on, and by week's end had built the longest stretch of grade of any gang on the line. Grudgingly, Strobridge gave the word: "Send up more coolies."

By the time Schuyler Colfax, Samuel Bowles, and Elbert Richardson arrived at railhead in August coolie gangs were commonplace. The white laborers demanded a $2-a-day minimum, plus board. But the Chinese companies smiled agreement to $35 a month for a workman, then accepted responsibility for providing cooks and mess facilities if Central Pacific would pay for such supplies as "dried oysters, cuttlefish and bamboo sprouts, sweet rice crackers, salted cabbage, vermicelli, Chinese bacon, dried abalone, tea, rice, pork and poultry." Crocker's brother Clark was a partner in the San Francisco firm of Sisson, Wallace & Company that took Central Pacific's contract to import the foodstuffs.

In his annual report for 1865 Samuel Montague admitted that "the Chinese experiment has proved eminently successful," and added, "they are faithful and industrious and under proper supervision soon became skillful in the performance of their duty. Many of them are becoming expert in drilling, blasting, and other departments of rock work." The Chinese mastery of "rock work" was the cruelest blow of all to the white man's ego. Trackhead held at Colfax, 55 miles from Sacramento, for the winter of 1865–6. Surveys had confirmed the route to Dutch Flat—which wound up the precipice face of the American River gorge for 12 miles—as the most logical, even though it meant blasting into ledges rising a plumb quarter mile above the river bed. There were no trails; not even a goat path. In at least two places retaining walls would have to be built across gullies 100 to 300 feet wide. The white gangs had nicknamed the giant cliff "Cape Horn." Work on it was a challenge for steeplejacks, ex-sailors, anyone who could dangle over that blue-black gulf hour after hour in a bos'n's-chair to hand-chip holes, tamp in the blasting-powder, fix and light the fuses before shouting, "Haul away-y-y-y!"

A Chinese foreman clogged up to Strobridge one summer day in 1865, bobbed his hat, and awaited permission to speak. Men of China, he explained, were skilled at work like the big job on Cape Horn. Their ancestors had built fortresses in the Yangtze gorges, carved and laid the stones for the Great Wall. Could a Chinese crew be permitted to work on Cape Horn? If so, could reeds be sent up from San Francisco so that baskets might be woven?

The white crews sneered disbelief. At night the Chinese camp wove baskets like the ones their ancestors had used for high work since the Han Dynasty. The baskets were waist high and round. The eyelets woven into the top were located in the proper position of the Four Winds, and painted with symbols intended to repel the evil eye. Ropes ran from the eyelets to a central cable. Each basket would have a hauling crew at the precipice top.

As for gunpowder, little instruction was necessary. Gunpowder was a Chinese invention. Every boy set off firecrackers on New Year's and feast days and knew the latent dangers that could transform a handful of the gritty gray dust into a lightning bolt.

All through the fall and winter of 1865–6 the wicker baskets bobbed like tiny gray kites against the skyline, the hand drills chattered a tom-tom beat, the powder blasts puffed flame. By spring the little men could walk four abreast up Cape Horn's face. That summer the Leland Stanford, the Collis P. Huntington, and the Theodore D. Judah engines chuffed pompously after them. Here and there in a foam-flecked back eddy of the American River floated the remnants of a wicker basket, the waterlogged top of a conical hat. Central Pacific did not keep record of coolie casualties.

After 1865, estimates indicate that an average of 15,000 Chinese a year landed in Pacific Coast ports. Ship captains and the companies obeyed the rule that only "male laborers" should be brought to San Francisco. But Chinese sex urges were as strong, and less inhibited than the white man's. Hundreds of "singsong" girls, and a few contract wives were smuggled in, most of them via Vancouver or the port villages on the Olympia Peninsula. In 1867 the San Francisco *Call* wrote indignant editorials about "Chinese Merchants of Chinese Prostitutes," and the Grass Valley *Union* ran a series of alleged interviews with "Hi Ke," who was paying $550 in gold for each prostitute he imported. The price, contended Hi Ke, should not be over $200, because most of the girls died from consumption or mountain fevers. Even if they did survive a winter, the "upkeep is very high."

The Chinese also insisted on joss houses and priests to serve them. This "heathenish, idolatrous" practice shocked the Irish as much as the Methodists. But business was business; joss houses and Buddhist shrines appeared at the Central Pacific work camps. Huntington had fought whisky peddling to the white crews, but the Chinese work camps usually had a supply of opium, a rack of pipes and "yen she gow" scraper tools. After an eighty-hour week dangling over a cliff edge or hauling rock out of a tunnel mouth, their crew bosses reasoned, a man deserved his own kind of recreation. Crocker and Strobridge never asked questions. Possibly neither Huntington nor Stanford ever learned about the sickly sweet smoke and smiling "drunks" in the bunks on Saturday nights.

East from Colfax, Judah's gradients climbed 4,550 feet on the 42-mile line to Sierra Summit, a 7,042-foot elevation mark beside Donner Lake. The entire Sierra crossing called for 15 tunnels, 10 on the west slope and 5 on the east. The longest —1,659 feet—would bore through the summit itself. Hundreds of gullies and ravines must be filled, and at least eight long trestles built. Specifications called for redwood and spruce construction on all trestles, with spans 38 to 60 feet high and from 350 to 500 feet long. The "power" available was two-wheel dump carts, wheelbarrows, axes, ropes, nitroglycerin, blasting powder, mules and Chinese.

Crocker sent 500 Chinese up the stage road with the engineers in the spring of 1866 to begin the bores on the Summit Tunnel. Montague decided to start the work from four faces: the east and west portals, plus a center shaft that would enable horizontal digs in each direction. The rock was so hard that blasting powder merely shot back out of the holes, with minor chipping of the surrounding rock. The pace averaged only 7 or 8 inches a day until the nitroglycerin factory went into production near Donner Lake. Even then the laterals weren't finished until December.

Union Pacific heard the story of the difficulties at Summit Tunnel and began to spread gossip along Wall Street that the job would hold up Central Pacific for years, thus assuring Union Pacific all of the trackage across Utah and Nevada to the California line. Two East Coast inventors launched another rumor that caused a series of angry letters between Stanford and Huntington. J. J. Couch of Philadelphia had invented a steam-driven power drill about 1849; J. W. Fowle, a Boston inventor, improved on it. Manufacture and promotion of the Couch-Fowle drill began soon after the end of the Civil War. Huntington sent a description to Stanford with the suggestion that it might be just the thing to speed work on the Sierra tunnels. The drill could deliver a blow a second—five times as fast as a prime hammerman.

Stanford was enthusiastic and sent the correspondence up the line to Crocker. Crocker rode over to Strobridge's office car and went through the Couch–Fowle folders with him. Strobridge sighed and shook his head. It had taken wagon teams six weeks to haul one donkey engine to the Summit bore. The wheezy monster, nicknamed "the Black Goose," was the only steam-power machine between Dutch Flat and Virginia City. It was being used to pull buckets of blasted rock out of the central shaft. Using a steam hammer up there meant switching power off that hoist every time the hammer cut in. It wouldn't do.

Crocker grunted agreement and relayed the decision to Stanford. Stanford argued. Crocker stood by Strobridge's decision. The story leaked out. Durant sent a brochure to bankers and stockbrokers boasting that "Union Pacific's engineers have modern ideas and are using the latest and best labor-saving devices to expedite speedy, accurate construction." Silas Seymour, writing the *New York Times'* series, slyly inserted the dig that while Union Pacific intended to reach Salt Lake City in 1869, "Leland Stanford, Esq. confidently anticipates that [Central Pacific] will be able to reach Salt Lake City during 1870."

Stanford might have made such a cautious estimate in a letter to Washington. But Crocker, Strobridge and Montague were building the railroad. And there wasn't a word in their rule book about delaying construction down the Sierra's east-slope canyons until the Summit Tunnel was finished. Strobridge might not want to fiddle around with that new-fangled trip-hammer way up there 75 miles from Nowhere, but dragging 2 or 3 locomotives, 25 flat cars, and 20 miles of rail up the stage road was another matter. Central Pacific would be in Nevada by '68.

Through the late summer and fall of 1866, Montague's surveyors staked out a right of way from Summit Tunnel's east portal down the Sierra's wall to the Nevada border. Up from Dutch Flat the Chinese laid redwood ties and iron along the ridge into Cisco, only 12 miles from Summit Tunnel's west portal. On November 24 the first trains wheezed into the new Cisco Station. They were loaded with rail, ties and chair irons, and had two engines to the train. Waiting for them were every logger rig, box wagon and cart Strobridge could muster. An army of Chinese stood beside mounds of rope and tie chains. All that night the gangs loaded rail on the logging wagons, chain-passed the kegs of spikes and cases of tools into carts, then finally inched three of the locomotives off the tracks and atop skid sleds.

The procession toward Summit started on the morning of the 25th. Carts carrying nitroglycerin and blasting powder went first, with orders to keep at least a mile ahead. The wagon train followed, trailed by the logging wagons loaded with rail. At the rear, hundreds of Chinese tugged alongside the mule teams to skid the three locomotives across the Sierra.

Two weeks before the locomotives were inched into Donner Pass, snowdrifts spumed ten feet above the road banks. Strobridge called off all work on the trestles between Cisco and Summit and ordered every Chinaman uphill to dig out the wagon road, spell the tow gangs on the locomotives, and keep a cart path open between Summit Tunnel's portals and the rock dumps.

The great log skids, swabbed with lard, carried the locomotives over the Summit sometime in January. Ahead of them, more than a thousand Chinese had cut a right of way 200 feet wide down the mountainsides as far as Truckee Canyon. "These are not Yankee forests," Assistant Engineer Clement reported to Crocker. "The trees are four, six, eight feet in diameter." The tiny lumbermen, swathed in padded-cotton gowns and fur caps, felled the giant redwood and spruce, sawed the trunks into 15-foot lengths, slithered them off the right of way, blew out the stumps, and hacked the frozen earth into a semblance of roadbed.

But the blizzards won. From late January through April the crews between Donner Lake and Truckee lived and worked like arctic moles. The tunnelmen stayed in their rock bores and saw daylight only when they were ordered to poke through new airholes and smoke vents. On down the east slope, deep into Truckee Canyon, work camps were buried to the stovepipes. "In many cases," the engineers wrote, "the road between camp and work was through snow tunnels, some of them 200 feet long. The construction of retaining work in the canyons carried on through the winter. A great dome was excavated in the snow, where the wall was to be built, and the wall stones were lowered through the shaft in the snow to the men working inside the dome . . . There were many snowslides. In some cases entire camps were carried away and the bodies of the men not found until the following spring."

It must be assumed that scores, and possibly hundreds, of Chinese froze to death or were killed in avalanches that winter between Cisco and Truckee. Fatalities were numerous, too, from the nitroglycerin blasts in the tunnels. Sometime during the spring of 1867, Strobridge went to Summit to inspect progress on the tunnel. A delayed nitro blast hurled rock slivers into one eye and left him half blind for life. Crocker allegedly gave the order to "bury all that damned stuff." If he did, it wasn't obeyed. Nitro blasts thundered in tunnels and rock cuts, and finally pulverized the frozen earth all the way to Promontory Point.

When spring did come to the East Slope the survivors dug out the 10- and 15-foot layers of wet snow and ice covering the right of way. Up toward Summit from Cisco hacked a new army of their countrymen, just shipped in from San Francisco. By the time the lupine blossomed across the slopes, 12,000 Chinese labored on the Sierra's crest.

The yellow man had proven his superiority at hard labor. He had endured scorching heat and howling blizzards in the canyons and worked stolidly month after month in ice caves and tunnels. Every gully trestle, blasted cliff and tunnel from Colfax to Truckee was a headstone for his unknown dead. The locomotives and flatcars snorting freight down the East Slope and the bores rumbling toward union beneath Summit earned him the right to become a California folk hero.

But in San Francisco on March 6, 1867, a raucous mass meeting in the American Theatre launched the Anti-Coolie Labor Association. Mobs of men and women howled through the streets, pelting Chinese with rocks and filth. All that spring the drunks and young "toughs" found their sport by setting fire to Chinese laundries and cigar factories, emptying chamber pots on the doorsteps along Grant Avenue, and howling indecencies at Confucian funeral processions. The phrase began to echo in newspaper editorials, sermons and street talk: "Not a Chinaman's Chance."

There were 100,000 Chinese in California that year. The Pacific Mail Steamship Company had just announced a routine schedule between San Francisco and Hong Kong. The young journalist Henry George studied the city's outburst of hate and fear and puzzled about the future. "What will happen," he wrote in his journal, "when the Pacific Railroad is finished, and Chinese labor is loosed upon the rest of America?"

Crocker and Strobridge weren't sociologists. They ordered

more Chinese up the line. The telegraph reported that Union Pacific was on the move again, clanging iron at a two-mile-a-day clip. Then Union Pacific's deadliest summer succeeded Central Pacific's deadliest winter.

CHAPTER **19**

IN DARKEST NEBRASKA

*At night new aspects are presented in this city of
premature growth. Watch-fires gleam over the sea-
like expanse of ground outside the city, while inside
soldiers, herdsmen, teamsters, women, railroad men
are dancing, singing or gambling. I verily believe that
there are men here who would murder a fellow creature for five dollars. Nay, there are men who have
already done it, and who stalk abroad in daylight un-
whipped of justice. Not a day passes but a dead body
is found somewhere in the vicinity with pockets
rifled of their contents. . . . Henry M. Stanley at
Julesburg (August, 1867).*

West of Iowa, spring was the time when winter and summer
fought their annual duel. The river ice turned gray, exploded
into massive stilettos, then eddied across the flatlands on yellow
foam. The buffalo wallows became lakes. A sultry, sun-
speckled morning could prelude an afternoon of arsenic-tinged
cloud banks that swelled to dragon shapes and ushered in a
half hour's deathlike silence before the inferno of tornado
columns. By the time winter withdrew, still snarling, to the
Rockies' crests, summer had daubed its greens from the
Missouri to the Black Hills. Nebraska's spring of 1867 was no
exception.

"Only one train came in after [us]," Samuel Reed wrote from Omaha on March 25. "A severe storm commenced at North Platte, blockading the road as it progressed eastward. Twenty-four hours after its commencement, the storm had traversed the entire length of our road [and blocked the railroad] as far east as Marshalltown. The Missouri River is still fast frozen. I have six locomotives on the east side of the river and would not hesitate to cross them on the ice if we needed their services on this side."

Three weeks later he was in Omaha again with a dismal report of havoc along the line. "Fifty thousand dollars," he wrote on April 18, "will not repair the damage done by the flood. The ice broke first at Loup Fork. The bridge sustained the immense pressure and caused the ice to flow out on both sides cutting away the embankment about one mile on each side . . . Between North Platte and Kearney the water flowed from the Platte in a stream about a half mile wide, cutting the road its entire width . . . taking off iron, ties and embankment. At Prairie Creek the bridge was carried downstream. East of Shell Creek there are from four to six miles with nothing but ties and iron left. At Elkhorn River, about half a mile of track is gone. . . ."

North Platte was ready for the emergency. The hillocks of rails, ties and hardware had grown through the winter. Alongside them were stacked more than 15,000 tons of freight waiting transport to Army posts and the new frontier towns in Idaho and Montana. "Encamped in the immediate vicinity of this town," a newspaper reported during May, "are 1,236 waggons, divided into trains of 27 waggons, each train officered by 29 men and a superintendent. There are Mormon emigrants bound to Utah, settlers for far Idaho, and pilgrims to mountainous Montana . . . The prairie around seems turned into a canvas city."

The Casement work train split itself into two sections. One half rumbled east to repair flood damage. The second half followed the ironmen up the north shore of the South Platte toward the Cheyenne–Sioux hunting grounds and Lone Pine Pass. During November and December, Dodge and Evans had made a final effort to locate a 2-per-cent grade through the Rockies behind Denver. On the basis of their report Union Pacific would by-pass the Pikes Peak region, cross the Black Hills via the Lone Pine Pass, then build a branch line south to Denver from its Crow Creek Crossing. There was no reason to hold grade gangs, bridge teams and supply wagons off that Lodgepole Creek route veering north out of Julesburg; Denverites were already cursing the Union Pacific and cheering the Kansas Pacific's dig across Smoky Hill.

This year, too, the Casements needed a long work season. Their new contract with Durant might be as catastrophic to their bank balance as a massive Indian raid. The agreement the general manager had forced on them read:

We the undersigned propose to lay and fill the track of the Union Pacific R.R. [the word "Co" was written, then inked out] during the next year according to the instructions and subject to the acceptance of the Chief Engineer and as fast as required (not to exceed three miles per day) for Nine Hundred Dollars per mile and upon the following terms and conditions—The Railroad Company to furnish all the materials for the track at or west of the new base of supplies three hundred miles west of Omaha, or at the most convenient point for transferring in that vicinity—Also to furnish all the locomotives cars wood and water necessary to be used in hauling and distributing the track materials west of said new base—To transport free of charge all men and supplies needed to carry on the work. And to pay us for all delays of more than one day caused by want of motive power track materials or any default of neglect of the company. The track to be laid in a workmanlike manner and filled with materials from the side of the road. The track to be accepted upon the completion of every twenty miles and an approximate estimate made by the Engineer in charge of the work and paid monthly.

We will furnish all engine and trainmen, also oil waste and tallow for all trains in our employ—We will receive track material within one hundred feet of the track—Will make no extra charge of cutting or filling in beveling ties which does not exceed six inches or for putting in all the necessary frogs and switches and will place the labor of all our men at the disposal of the company during the time of all delays for which they are charged and we will charge only the amount of our expenses—All trains in our employ to be subject to regulation by the company and under the general control of the superintendent of the company. We will at option of the company, on ten days notice reduce our gang of track layers to a force sufficient to lay one half mile per day.

J. S. & D. T. CASEMENT

The details of the Casement contract dictated by Durant in November, 1866, reflected a new crisis that was developing in Union Pacific. The Casements' construction feat during 1866 won the race to the 100th meridian and assured a profitable future for Crédit Mobilier. Yet Durant greedily held the Casements' 1867 fee to "$900 a mile." Although the Casements deducted an average of $1 per employee a day for board and bunk, crew wages and supply costs brought their overhead to $700 or more a day, without consideration for "acts of God" or the constant threat of Indian raids. The work train would operate at a loss if construction slowed even to three-quarters of a mile a day.

Worse than that, the Casements would have no legal recourse if anything did happen. The Hoxie Contract, held by Crédit Mobilier, was fulfilled when the rails reached the 100th meridian. The 35 miles into North Platte were laid without a master-contract assignment by Union Pacific; and this situation still existed. The Casements, grading crews, bridge builders and surveyors were pushing west toward the Sioux–Cheyenne heartland on Durant's say-so alone. And it was touch and go whether his waspish orders would continue. His temper flare-ups and stockmarket trickery had generated a power struggle within Union Pacific. The railroad was building without the approval of its directors.

The headquarters' crisis traced back, as the more observant bankers suspected it would, to the election of General Dix as

Union Pacific's president. Durant had selected Dix as a figure-head. And he was one. The old gentleman's interests were in national politics; he consistently referred decisions on Union Pacific matters to Durant. Thus, to the grading gangs as well as to Wall Street, Thomas C. Durant was "Mr. Union Pacific." His curtness and lone-wolf maneuvers were becoming as dis-tasteful to the Ames Brothers as they were to Sam Reed and Peter Dey, and eventually to Grenville Dodge.

In October, 1866, the White House appointed General Dix United States Ambassador to Napoleon III's court. At the Union Pacific board meeting, just before the Grand Excursion to the 100th meridian, Dix resigned. Oliver Ames and Sidney Dillon were elected to the board that afternoon. During the thirty years since he had bought newspapers from young Bull Crocker at the Troy Station and had given orders to engineer's assistant Ted Judah, Sidney Dillon had made a fortune as a railroad construction contractor. Oakes Ames persuaded him to buy stock in Crédit Mobilier, then sponsored his election to the Union Pacific directorate.

Dillon shared the Ames Brothers' growing distrust of Du-rant. So, it developed, did other directors. Oliver Ames was elected president of Union Pacific in November. Through the winter Dillon and the Ameses quietly bought up shares of Crédit Mobilier and solicited voting options from stockholders known to dislike or fear Durant. By spring they had a majority. At the May 18, 1867, meeting of Crédit Mobilier, Durant was voted off its board of directors.

Durant's stockholdings were too large and his knowledge of construction details too intimate to remove him as executive vice-president and general manager of Union Pacific. More-over, the Ameses and Dillon feared he might spill the whole story of Crédit Mobilier to the White House or—worse still—to the Democrats. The power struggle centered on a master contract to succeed the Hoxie contract. Durant had been nego-tiating with L. B. Boomer, a Chicago bridge builder and Un-ion Pacific subcontractor, to take over as Crédit Mobilier's dummy on the 150 miles west of the 100th meridian. The Ames Brothers-Dillon group refused to accept Boomer and countered first with a 58-mile extension of the Hoxie contract, then with a bid for a 268-mile contract to John M. S. Williams. Durant obtained court injunctions against both bids on the ground that their estimated costs were "too high." The feud was carried on through summer and fall while Durant continued his steely rule over the railroad's personnel.

Financially, the Crédit Mobilier plum was ripening. The publicity created by the Grand Excursion, plus assiduous salesmanship in New York and Boston, marketed more than $10,-000,000 worth of first-mortgage bonds. This, plus loans on the Federal bonds, enabled payments to the iron mills, relay railroads and locomotive works, and restored credit at Omaha and Council Bluffs banks for the weekly pay rolls.

Fully aware of the crisis at headquarters, Sam Reed, the Casements and Grenville Dodge struggled west toward deadlier crises with the Indians and the rowdies of Hell on Wheels. The Cheyenne and Sioux broke winter camp near Fort Larned, Kansas, in April, massacred at stage stations and ranches along the Smoky Hill and Santa Fe trails, then rode north toward the Platte.

Dodge's survey crews waded through the Platte's floods, under orders to make the location survey west to Lone Pine Pass. One crew, headed by L. L. Hills, reached the base of Lone Pine Pass in early April and began to stake east toward Crow Creek. They were six miles from the Creek when 100 Cheyennes ambushed them. Hills died in the first assault. An axman took command. The party fought off another screaming charge, holed up until dark, then fought its way back to North Platte. Cheyennes yanked out the right-of-way stakes, raided wagon trains, and chased bridge crews away from the Lodgepole and Crow Crossings. WE NEED 5,000 SOLDIERS EAST OF THE MOUNTAINS AND NORTH OF THE PLATTE, Dodge wired to General Sherman.

"I regard this road as the solution of Indian affairs and of the Mormon question, and I will help you all I can," Sherman replied. General Grant backed him with a message that took a blunt sideswipe at Durant by pledging, "every protection . . . both to secure the rapid completion of the road and to avoid pretexts on the parts of the builders to secure further assistance of the government."

But Congress was weary of war and jittery about the national debt. Assurance by Secretary of the Interior Browning that the Indian problem could be settled with conferences and another set of treaties had convinced Capitol Hill committees. Consequently the War Department didn't have enough budget to recruit 500 cavalrymen—let alone 5,000—for the Platte. The entire command at Fort Kearney consisted of 12 infantrymen and a band of musicians. Fort McPherson, 120 miles up the Platte, held one company of cavalry, one battery of artillery, and a squad of infantry. Fort Sedgwick, across the South Platte from Julesburg, held 6 companies of infantry, one company of cavalry and a squad of artillery. These three posts, with a total of less than 200 mounted men and 600 foot soldiers, were the only army forces available between Omaha and Denver.

Grading crews and bridge builders had to be strung out over the 250 miles to the Crow Creek Crossing. The Casements' gangs were pounding rail toward Julesburg at an average of two miles a day. Dodge and Jack Casement reached a decision, rounded up a troop of war veterans, and started upcountry. At each grade camp and bridge foundation they organized crews into gun squads, rehearsed them in deploying techniques, then selected sites for the construction of timber-lined dugouts that could be used as emergency forts. Every gang was ordered to keep rifles stacked within one-minute reach, and to post lookouts atop each embankment.

But this system could not work for the surveying teams. They were out front and on their own, very much as the Mountain Men had been a half century before them. Percy Browne's crew was across the Black Hills on May 12, running elevations fifty-five miles west of Fort Sanders (near present Medicine Bow, Wyoming). Dodge had obtained a detail of cavalry from Fort McPherson to guard them. A war party of more than 100 Sioux sprang an ambush on the afternoon of the 12th. The surveyors and cavalry detail held them off and holed up for the night. The Sioux charged again at dawn. Browne led the survivors back to railhead for more ammunition.

During the last week of May, Dodge escorted three Federal commissioners beyond railhead to a grading camp. The morning was bright and peaceful. At noon the gangs unhitched their teams and headed down the bank for lunch buckets. Dodge and the commissioners lolled chatting beside the dump carts. A fusillade roared across the slope, echoed by a chorus of war whoops. A column of Sioux charged down the right of way. A half-dozen braves veered howling among the horse and mule herds and stampeded them; the others fired mockingly between the workmen and their stacked arms. With the teams in stampede, the warriors fired another volley and raced back over the ridge. At railhead that night the commissioners sent a long telegram demanding MORE CAVALRY PROTECTION FOR THE RAILROAD. Sherman ordered three companies up the Platte from Fort Leavenworth, Kansas.

The Indian raids throughout Western Kansas and the upper Platte, the mounting feud between the War Department and the Interior's Indian agents, and the spectacular rush of Union Pacific's railhead toward the Black Hills, promised "Wild West" headlines to newspaper and magazine editors from Chicago east. British, French, German and Scandanavian editors were also interested. British investments in the India and China trade were concerned about progress on the Pacific Railroad; French capitalists had large investments in the canal Ferdinand de Lesseps was dredging at Suez; and there were hundreds of thousands of Germans and Scandinavians in Wisconsin, Illinois, Minnesota and Missouri. From June on,

North Platte and Casements' railhead were hosts to "special writers" and correspondents stabbing questions, scribbling notes in a dozen languages, and driving the telegraph operators frantic with night dispatches and "urgent" bulletins.

No one in this press corps was more alert or ambitious than the twenty-five-year-old Galvanized Yank named Henry Morton Stanley. Born in Wales, he had suffered through a childhood that could have been a prototype for David Copperfield. After a series of Dickensian and dime-novel adventures which embraced New Orleans, the Civil War, Denver, Smyrna and Constantinople, he joined the staff of the St. Louis *Missouri Democrat* as a "Far West" correspondent and obtained "stringer" assignments from several Eastern dailies. He was with the Hancock-Custer expedition to the Kiowa and Southern Cheyenne at Fort Larned, Kansas, in April, 1867, shipped up the Missouri to Omaha, and reached North Platte in late May. The abandon of the new city shocked even his worldliness: "Every gambler in the Union seems to have steered his course for North Platte," he reported, "and every known game under the sun is played here. The days of Pikes Peak and California are revived. Every house is a saloon and every saloon is a gambling den. Revolvers are in great requisition . . . On account of the immense freighting done in Idaho, Montana, Utah, Dakota and Colorado, hundreds of bull-whackers walk about, and turn the one street into a perfect Babel. Old gamblers who revelled in the glorious days of 'flush times' in the gold districts declare that this town outstrips all yet."

The Casements' train was forty miles upriver. Some of the ironmen rollicked back to North Platte for Saturday night brawls. There were fistfights, a few knifings, and now and then a body or two to fish out of the river. Sunday night brought the routine roundup: the foremen moved from saloon to saloon in squads, blackjacks at wrists and guns ready; work as usual at Monday's sunup. But North Platte was already downcountry—a has-been town. The bullwhackers would be on the plains by mid-June. And they'd never come back. Railhead in 1868 would be out West somewhere. The real problem was Julesburg. That was to be the next division terminal. From September until snowfall, wagon trains would roll in there from the high country, their crews' pockets heavy with six months' pay. Julesburg promised to be really bloody.

The "redskin terror" soon beckoned Stanley, with space rates that could net him ninety dollars a week. He joined the escort of Major General C. C. Augur, commander of the Department of the Platte, on an inspection trip of the ranches and stage stations burned since April. Augur told Stanley about the new Washington ruling that, "No escort shall be provided for Wells, Fargo & Company's coach east of Fort Sedgwick [Julesburg]. All passengers and freight must be sent to the end-of-track from whence sufficient escort shall be provided for all coaches westward . . . Major North will divide his command [Pawnee Scouts] into small detachments to scour the bluffs immediately contiguous to the Platte." He also verified that General Sherman had just wired Governor A. C. Hunt of Colorado: RAISE A REGIMENT OF 500 MEN AND HAVE THEM READY IN CASE I CALL FOR THEM.

The Sioux and Cheyenne extended the General's trip by chasing Wells, Fargo stages across the unpatrolled twenty miles between Julesburg and railhead on June 1, 2, 4 and 5; four passengers and three Wells, Fargo employees were killed in the running fights. Then the Reverend W. A. Fuller, an Episcopal missionary, provided the week's best escape story by jumping off a stage roof into the Platte and swimming under water to a clump of hazelbush. (The miracle was that the Platte was deep enough for the feat.) The Sioux killed the driver and guard and ran off the horses. Reverend Fuller stayed in the hazelbush until dark before heading back to Julesburg.

Two Lodgepole Creek ranchers, out chasing mules that the Indians had stolen, found a white woman's scalp but no mules. At dusk on June 12 a band of 125 Sioux jumped a wagon train at O'Fallon's Bluffs, ten miles west of North Platte. The train was loaded with supplies for Fort Phil Kearny on the besieged Bozeman Trail. Again the raiders' first move was to stampede the 250 mules. The herdsmen had been surrounded and the animals were scattering when the bullwhackers sortied out from their wagon circle, ripped off a few volleys, and ended the fight; they claimed 9 Indian dead, and one animal lost from the train.

The work train entered Julesburg during the last week of June, paused while the crews laid spur tracks to the foundation stakes for the roundhouse and depot, then sidetracked for the freight trains bringing up the portable warehouse and supplies from North Platte. The saloonkeepers, madams and gamblers shipped up their prefabs too. Hell on Wheels rebuilt in a cottonwood grove along the South Platte and was ready to roar again by Saturday afternoon.

Generals Dodge and Casement stalked down the dirt street, scowling at the flamboyant signs. A madam tapped a silver dollar against a windowpane. A Chicago "dandy" strutted past. A "dance-and-drink" girl slithered out of a saloon tent, kicked her satin skirt waist high, and shrilled, "Raht oveh heah, dahlin's." They shook their heads, pushed past her to the bar, and ordered beers.

Dodge pulled out a telegram just in from Washington. It was signed by Grant himself. Jack Casement read it. General John A. Rawlins—Grant's neighbor from Galena, Illinois, and now his chief of staff—had contracted tuberculosis. His physician had ordered him to the mountains for a few months. Grant was sending him to Julesburg with an escort of two companies of cavalry under Colonel Mizner. General Grant would be deeply grateful, the telegram went on, if Dodge could be Rawlins' host and guide in the mountains. Officially, General Rawlins was under orders to determine sites for new Army posts along Union Pacific's right of way. The itinerary would of course be at General Dodge's discretion.

Jack Casement lifted his mug in silent salute and winked. General Rawlins plus two troops of cavalry meant that Dodge could conduct a survey in force clear through to Salt Lake City. And in the process the War Department would gain a far clearer picture of the task confronting Union Pacific.

But—Casement frowned as he handed the telegram back— what would Dodge do about Congress? Council Bluffs had elected him its Congressman last November while he was tramping around Berthold Pass with Evans in a blizzard. The scrap between President Johnson and the radical Republicans was getting ugly. "When," he rumbled, "d'you think you'll find time to go to Washington, Mr. Congressman?"

"October—perhaps November," Dodge said, and sighed. "I didn't ask for the job. Matter of fact, I forgot about it until Evans and I got back to North Platte and saw the stack of telegrams congratulating me on the election. I'm sorry for John Rawlins, but his trip's a godsend for us."

General Augur returned to Julesburg that weekend to await General Rawlins. Sam Reed was in town, too, and wrote his family about the "tour of the gaslights" made by Augur and his staff with the Casements and Dodge as guides. "The first place we visited," Sam wrote, "was a dance house where a fresh importation of strumpets had been received. Such profanity, vulgarity and indecency as was heard and seen there would disgust a more hardened person than I. The next place visited was a gambling hell where all games of chance were being played. Men excited with drink and play were recklessly staking their last dollar on the turn of a card or the throw of a dice. Women were cajoling and coaxing the tipsy men to stake their money on various games; the pockets were shrewdly picked by the fallen women of the more sober of the crowd."

Henry Stanley went along too. He assured the *Missouri Democrat*'s readers that martial law was "the only sure preventative of these murderous scenes" since "the civil law is as yet too new to be an impediment to the unwashed canaille, and it certainly offers no terrors to the women who travel about undressed in the light of day.

"These women," he went on, "are expensive articles, and

come in for a large share of the money wasted. In broad daylight they may be seen gliding through the streets in Black Crook dresses, carrying fancy derringers slung to their waists, with which tools they are dangerously expert. Should they get into a fuss, Western chivalry will not allow them to be abused by any man whom they may have robbed."

Western chivalry must have influenced Stanley's copy. Any strumpet aspiring to a "large share of the money wasted" on her would have landed in the Platte with her throat slit. All of Julesburg's bawds worked on commission to saloon operators or cribhouse madams, who in turn were "staked" by liquor wholesalers and sporting-house syndicates in Chicago and St. Louis. Like their sisters of the trade on North Clark and Fifth Streets, the Julesburg girls operated under the brass-check or sales-receipt system. They earned commissions from bartenders for the drinks they "pushed" on male companions, and received a receipt from the madam for each cash-in-advance trip to a "crib." If they lured a man out behind the tents to a stick-up, it was all in the night's work; another commission job. Pickpockets and gunmen were organized on a kick-back system too; most of them were on pay rolls of the saloons, cribhouses and gambling halls as "spielers," dealers or bar boys.

Prostitution was a taboo subject in the public press of 1867. The Julesburg descriptions that Stanley sent to the *Missouri Democrat* were daring. He held back one of the most deadly implications of all. Evidence indicates that many, perhaps more than half, of Hell on Wheels' women were avid distributors of gonorrhea, syphilis and Phthirius Pubis, the crab louse. The probabilities are that they infected 25 to 50 per cent of Union Pacific's gangs.

Health laws were unknown. The prophylactic had not been invented. Members of the American Medical Association gave little professional attention to the prevalence of venereal disease until Dr. Marion J. Sims of Alabama, the association's 1876 president, devoted his inaugural address to "syphilis— one of the most fatal diseases we have in this country." The only medical group concerned with venereal disease in 1867 was the United States Army Medical Corps. Their records show that almost one-fourth of the total Army personnel were treated for it that year. The total "mean strength" of the Army in 1867 was 47,233 men. Of the 10,153 treated, 5,873 had syphilis and 4,280 had gonorrhea. (Of these, 8,236 were whites and 1,917 Negroes—an infection rate of 204.96 per 1,000 for the whites and 271.91 for the Negroes.)

Since the 1867 outbreak is the highest ratio of venereal infection reported in the entire history of the Army Medical Corps, the cribhouses and camp followers west of the Mississippi must have played a major role in the flare-up. Coincidentally, the only other comparable aggregations of men in barracks in the United States that year were the work gangs of Union Pacific and Central Pacific. The Central Pacific's Chinese maintained their own "sporting houses" and assumedly did a better job of health supervision. Army statistics suggest that the infection rate among Union Pacific's crews was at least as high as it was in the Army.

Both Casement and Dodge were familiar with the bulletins on "Venereal Disease" issued by the Army's Sanitary Commission in 1862, and the recommendation that, "the practices of the Belgian Army be followed: (1) Report the woman who gave the infection and remove her from the community; (2) Impose a penalty for failure to report an infection at once; and (3) Get all infected personnel out of quarters and into a hospital." The Army cures then prescribed for gonorrhea included: sulphate of zinc solutions, "alkaline mixes, cubebs, injections of a weak solution of nitrate of silver every two hours, and Epsom salts." The only known treatment for syphilis was to daub the chancres with mercury ointments.

Control of "v.d." as well as a taste of martial law for Hell on Wheels were obvious motives for the raid Casement and Dodge planned. Dodge verified that there was such a raid. It must have occurred in early July. General Rawlins' cavalcade reached Julesburg on June 28. The itinerary Dodge worked out called for a Fourth of July celebration at the next division point on the Crow Creek Crossing, and the townsite's christening as "Cheyenne." West over Lone Pine Pass and Sherman Summit, then, the Rawlins-Dodge expedition would follow the survey lines across the desert to the Wasatch passes and Great Salt Lake Valley.

With Rawlins and Dodge jogging up Lodgepole Creek, the Casements and Sam Reed picked a squad of their brawniest ironmen, loaded them into a boxcar, and steamed back to Julesburg. More than a thousand prostitutes, gamblers, bartenders, pimps and shills were readying Hell on Wheels for "big money" over the Fourth. At least 3,000 graders and wagonmen were coming in from the camps. The ironmen deployed out from the Casement warehouse at dusk, guns cocked. A squad of reserves stayed near the boxcar, under orders to "come on the double" if the gunfire got rambunctious. The Sunday night roundups at North Platte had familiarized the Casements with the worst toughs and the filthiest bawds. Months later Jack Casement allegedly told Dodge, "The worst ones went out to the edge of town . . . to the cemetery." The raid that night was a foretaste of the Vigilante hangings and gun battles that would torture every town founded along the Union Pacific through its birth of civil government in 1868–9. The ironmen stalked in, shot down the toughs who pulled guns, marched "the worst ones" out to the cottonwood grove and hung them. It is equally logical that Casement and Reed had a list of girls known to be infected and that they imposed the Army's rule No. 1 for "v.d. control" and shipped them back to Omaha.

Hell on Wheels operated over the Fourth, but with the ironmen on patrol, the "dips" and "grifters" at heel, and fighting restricted to the gouges and groinkicks between graders and wagonmen.

Julesburg stayed on the simmer for another three months while the work train laid iron up the Lodgepole's valley toward Nebraska's west border. There probably was, as Henry

Stanley indicated, an average of a murder a night during August and September. The wagon trains were rumbling back from Montana and Colorado; the town swarmed with bullwhackers, guards and prospectors "coming out" with pokefuls of gold. But the railroad gangs fared reasonably well on their play nights, with the ironmen on patrol.

The Casement cleanup of Julesburg was still prime gossip along the iron trail when a band of Cheyenne engineered the Indians' most spectacular train wreck. The warriors, led by Chief Turkey Foot, knew that Fort Kearney was all but abandoned and that the cavalry guard supplied to General Rawlins had reduced the complement at Fort McPherson to one or two troops. Moreover, there was great prestige to be gained by capturing an iron horse. During the evening of August 6, Turkey Foot's braves piled ties atop the track a few miles west of Plum Creek, shinnied up the telegraph poles, hacked off a hundred feet of the iron wire and used it to crimp the ties to the rails. Then they squatted behind the bank and waited.

The first vehicle to arrive was a handcar carrying a repair crew out to locate the break in the telegraph line. The Cheyennes fired. William Thompson, the crew chief, went down and was scalped. But in the chase after the rest of the crew, the warrior who had attacked him dropped the scalp. Thompson was still conscious. Just then a freight train's headlight shone downriver. The Cheyenne gave up the chase and again hid behind the embankment. Thompson slithered over to his scalp, picked it up, staggered erect and began running east toward the Plum Creek Station.

The pile of ties and the derailed handcar careened the freight locomotive down the bank. The fireman burned to death in the gush of flame from the firebox. The engineer was thrown free, but the Cheyenne scalped him and threw him back into the blazing locomotive. The conductor and brakemen heard the firing and war whoops, scrambled out of the caboose, and sprinted east. They flagged down a following train, then stood guard on the cowcatcher and tender while it backed into Plum Creek, picked up the station crew there and retreated to Elm Creek.

Omaha rounded up soldiers and railroaders and rushed out a trainload armed for a major battle. Soon after the train arrived, Thompson stumbled in, still gripping his bloody scalp. A physician promised him that the scalp could be grafted back on his skull, and put it to soak in a bucket of cold water while a locomotive and caboose raced Thompson back to the Omaha hospital. (The grafting didn't take. Thompson lived to be a grandfather—in a black skullcap. His scalp, still afloat in a jar of alcohol, was on exhibit at the Omaha Museum for decades.)

The train Turkey Foot and his Cheyennes derailed had contained a carload of millinery supplies and a carload of whisky, both en route to Julesburg. The Cheyennes built a bonfire, got roaring drunk, decked themselves with ribbons, flowered bonnets and strips of silk and held the giddiest hoedown ever whooped on the Platte. Next morning, when they sighted the relief train and its soldiers, they rode off; the remains of the fireman and engineer fitted into two boxes, 30 by 12 inches.

On August 9, North's Pawnee Scouts caught up with 100 of the Cheyennes near Plum Creek Ranch. They killed 15, and captured 2 braves, one squaw and a thirteen-year-old boy. The Platte Valley seethed with rumors for weeks. Omaha itself prepared for a siege, but Turkey Foot's raid was the last foray of the year in Nebraska.

Sometime in October the work train eased across the Lodgepole Creek bridge and began the climb out of Nebraska. When the Casements pulled out of Omaha in April, 1866, Nebraska had been a territory with a half-dozen communities along the Missouri River bluffs, a few ranches clustered near the Platte Valley forts, and a population little changed from the 28,000 listed in the 1860 census. Now, less than eighteen months later, a score of towns stood along the 464 miles of the Great Iron Trail. Nebraska became a state over President Johnson's veto on March 1, 1867. The 1870 census would reveal a population of 123,000.

George Francis Train's roseate vision for Columbus had already burst. Nebraskans voted the little prairie town of Lancaster, fifty miles west of the Missouri, as their State Capital, and changed its name to Lincoln. Durant's hauteur and Train's boisterousness met head-on sometime during the year; Union Pacific severed relations with Crédit Foncier and created its own, Town Lots Division. "Train said he was sacrificed by the railroad men," Sam Reed wrote home, "and cursed long and loud."

Forty-three miles ahead of the work train as it crossed the state line, the tent city of Cheyenne was already bustling toward a 10,000 population as the acknowledged capital of the new Territory of Wyoming.

CHAPTER **20**

THIS SACRED LAND

> *Achan! Achan! Achan! Father! Father! Father! Listen well. Your young men have gone on the path, and have destroyed the fine timber and the green grass, and have burnt up the country. Father, your young men have gone on the road, and have killed my game and my buffalo. They did not kill them to eat; they left them to rot where they fell. Father, were I to go to your country to kill your cattle, what would you say? . . . Father, you talk about farming, I don't want to hear it; I was raised on buffalo and I love it. Since I was born I was raised like your chiefs, to be strong, to move my camps when necessary, to roam over the prairie at will. Take pity upon us; I am tired of talking. . . .* Chief Bear's Tooth of the Crows during Treaty Council, Fort Laramie (November 12, 1867).

The Rawlins-Dodge ride from railhead to Salt Lake City during the summer of 1867 heralded the end of the red man's 150-year-old horse and bison economy. The 650-mile expanse of the Continental Divide and the bleak high plains between Julesburg and the Great Salt Lake Valley were the doorway to the last huge area of primitive wilderness left in the United States. Opening that doorway meant doomsday for the land of the Cheyenne, Sioux, Crow, Arapaho, Blackfeet, Kiowa,

255

and all the northland tribes as surely as the farmers' push up the Mohawk Valley in the 1760's presaged the end of the Iroquois' empire, and the wagons creaking into the Great Smokies after 1800 omened the Cherokees' loss of their homeland.

The briefing conferences between Generals Rawlins, Grant, Sherman and Congressional committeemen during May and June revealed the Federal plan to create a fortified throughway between the Platte and Utah. Generals Rawlins and Augur were to determine the site for a new Army base at the foot of the Black Hills in the vicinity of Union Pacific's Crow Creek Crossing. Rawlins, in conference with Dodge and the Army commanders who would join the expedition en route, would select sites for other forts along Union Pacific's route across the high-plains basin and the Continental Divide. Fortunately the construction of Fort William P. Sanders in 1866 as guardian of the western approaches to Cheyenne Pass now seemed to be in line with Union Pacific's route from Sherman Summit into the Great Basin. General Dodge had already indicated that a division point might be established on the Laramie River near Fort Sanders.

Congress, complained the War Department's executives, would probably continue its moans about "balancing the budget"; the Army might be slashed back to a personnel of 25,000—less than 5 per cent of its 1865 strength. But by building new forts now, an armed corridor could be created along Union Pacific that would not only guarantee a speedy throughway between the East and the Pacific slope, but would provide supply bases for future Indian wars. Eventually, then, Fort Laramie and the other "Great Desert" posts along the old Mormon-Oregon route through South Pass could be abandoned. The railroad, coordinated with the telegraph, would enable troops to rush overnight from the Missouri Valley or Utah to any sector of the Indian frontier, equipped with horses, forage wagons and the new Gatling guns. The plan was a momentous step toward mechanizing the Army.

Equally ominous to the red man's economy were the implications of this armed corridor. Ranches and towns would
follow the high iron as avidly as they had in the rush across
Nebraska. The gun, ax, saw and steel-snouted plough—and
now the windmill and barbed wire—were the frontiersman's
pitiless confederates. Thousands of gold prospectors were already in the South Pass area and hundreds of miles north along
Powder River's Bozeman Trail. The army of lumberjacks
that Union Pacific must send out to cut hardwood for its ties,
bridge timbers, stations and fuel, would launch a forest razing
as devastating as the ones that had crashed up and down the
Appalachians and across the Great Lakes bluffs since 1800.
Now, too, the coal, iron and copper deposits located by geologist Van Lennep and others could be exploited; each would
create a wasteland of trash and deadly smelter fumes.

The Union Pacific corridor would inevitably widen as a result of these spasms of industrial development. This would dis-
tort the botanical balance that perpetuated the bison and
big-game herds. So the red man's economy was doomed. He
must choose, again, between all-out war or adaptation to the
white man's sedentary routine of farming and ranching. The
Doolittle-Henderson committee had won White House and
Congressional approval for a series of treaty conferences with
the plains Indians. These were to be convened during late
summer and fall. Generals Sherman and Harney would lead
the Army's delegation. The Sioux would be ordered to settle
on reservations in the Cheyenne and White River country of
the Dacotah, just north of Nebraska's northwest border. The
Cheyenne would be ordered south to the Arkansas River Valley in southern Colorado and Kansas. Peace or war, the decision meant that Union Pacific's corridor would open a strip
for town, ranch, lumberman and miner exploitation 100, and
perhaps 300, miles wide, between the Platte and Utah.

Rawlins briefed Dodge on these prospects during the two-
day jog up Lodgepole Creek and over the ridge to Crow Creek.
Dodge suggested that the Crow Creek division point might

make an excellent site for the Army's Black Hills base. Troops stationed there could protect both the Denver Road and the Lone Pine Pass and would also be in position to rush relief forces up the Bozeman Trail to Forts Laramie, Fetterman, Phil Kearny and Reno.

When they reached the Crow Creek Crossing they found that the Army would soon have a city to guard too. Newspapers had announced the location; the New York office touted its real-estate opportunities. Scores of wagons were parked on the bluff, some beside half-built cabins. The tent offices of real-estate agents fluttered hand-lettered signs offering, CHOICE LOTS NEAR THE PACIFIC RAILROAD. The red-and-black covers of rouge-et-noir tables gleamed in a half-dozen saloons. A madam in a starched purple dress lolled on a campstool in front of a tent "crib."

Plans were set for a big Fourth-of-July celebration, these first settlers announced. They'd even lugged in fireworks plus an anvil for the big shoot. If General Rawlins would make the principal address of the festivities, perhaps General Dodge would do the honors of christening the city? The generals agreed.

Augur and Rawlins led a cavalry patrol up and down the creek bluffs, stared west toward the mountains, and finally agreed on the site for Fort D. A. Russell. Dodge went into conference with Jacob Blickensderfer and Silas Seymour. Blickensderfer, a competent civil engineer, was the White House appointee to determine the point where the Rocky Mountains' eastern base began. Collis Huntington's hoodwink of President Lincoln and the Interior's topographers when he persuaded them to move the base of the Sierras fifteen miles west had become a cloakroom classic in Congress. For once the radical Republicans and Andrew Johnson were in agreement. This time Washington would double-check the spot where Union Pacific's loans made the jump from $12,000 to $75,000 a mile.

Such a massive decision demanded, of course, the presence

of the consulting engineer, Silas Seymour. Moreover, Dodge and Durant were beginning to exchange caustic notes. Durant was convinced that his chief engineer had switched allegiance to Oliver Ames. (Typically, Durant overlooked the fact that Ames was now president of Union Pacific.) Thus Colonel Seymour and umbrella had been ordered to join the Rawlins-Blickensderfer party. It was also fitting, Seymour urbanely announced, that the consulting engineer acquaint himself with all the problems of the route into Salt Lake and thus be in a position to answer directors' questions at the board meetings in October.

Another column of settlers' wagons clattered in during the morning of July 4. General Rawlins delivered a commendable speech about the significance of Independence Day and the glorious promise of the New West. Dodge followed him with a talk that formally christened the community as Cheyenne. The cheers were punctuated by a successful firing of the anvil. Thereafter the saloons took over, and except for the evening's fireworks display and the line of customers outside the crib tent, dominated the rest of Cheyenne's birthday.

General Rawlins obeyed physician's orders and retired early. He rose at dawn, ordered his horse, and cantered off for a prebreakfast run. The horse strode up a ridge. Across the plain stretched the pink clay embankment for the railroad. A grading gang was already at work, their shovels a silver shimmer in the sunrise. The General sighed and lolled back in his saddle.

A fusillade of rifle shots cracked. A shovel flung high up the bank, turned lazily and shivered back to earth. The man who had thrown it pitched face down to the ground. The fusillade echoed again. More graders fell; the rest ran toward their wagons. Down a draw plunged a column of Indians, rifles and knives glinting, heels gripping the ponies' ribs like hawk talons. The charge screamed among the wagons, crossed the embankment, and vanished in a gully. The silence swirled back.

Rawlins raced back to camp, roused his cavalry, and led

them out to the grade crew. There were five dead and as many wounded. The foreman had recognized the raiders' war paint. They were Cheyennes. This was their christening party for their namesake city.

The expedition based on Cheyenne for another two weeks while Dodge checked Evans' stake-out over Sherman Summit (Evans' job so pleased him that he ordered the name of the pass changed from "Lone Pine" to "Evans" on company maps). The Black Hills crossing took another week. Seymour drawled questions about the grade, insisted on a cavalry escort for his prowls after "a more suitable route," and spent an entire day frowning over details of the bridge that—135 feet above the high-water line and 650 feet long—would span Dale Creek.

General John Gibbons was waiting at Fort Sanders. He reported that Red Cloud, the Sioux chief believed responsible for the Fetterman Massacre the previous December was on the warpath again, boasting that he would destroy Forts Phil Kearny and Reno and close the Bozeman Trail. That same evening the telegraph relayed the news that Percy T. Browne's body lay at a Wells, Fargo stage station a day's ride west.

Dodge rode out with a cavalry squad next morning, assigned the squad to guard the rest of Browne's party in the location survey toward the Great Basin, and brought Browne's body back to Sanders. He wrote a detailed report of the surveyor's gallant last stand to Oliver Ames: Browne's re-equipped crew had ridden west again in June to continue the stake-out from the spot where the Sioux had jumped them on May 12–13. At noon on July 23, near the Medicine Bow River, a column of 300 Sioux warriors attacked. The crew fought off the first charge and managed to retire to a hilltop. There they waited until the howling warrior wave broke the hillcrest, then brought down the lead horses and kept pouring lead into the pile-up that followed. The rest of the Sioux rode out of range and deployed for a siege. In midafternoon a sniper shot Browne in the chest. Browne told the crew to light a campfire at dusk and prop him beside it, then make a dash for the Wells, Fargo station twelve miles south. But just before sunset the Sioux reassembled, fired a volley, and galloped north. The crew rigged a litter from their rifles and cartridge belts, lowered Browne on it, and carried him to the stage station. He died an hour after they arrived. Finishing the report to Ames, Dodge pledged, "We will push this road to Salt Lake in another year or surrender my own scalp to the Indians."

The reason for the Sioux's failure to starve out the Browne crew became obvious within two weeks. During July, Red Cloud sent word to all Sioux bands ordering them in for a campaign against Forts Phil Kearny and Reno and the wagon traffic along the Bozeman Trail. On August 2 more than 3,000 of his warriors attacked Captain James W. Powell and 32 men on Big Piney Creek. Years later Red Cloud admitted that Powell's marksmen unhorsed more than 1,000 Sioux during the Wagon Box Battle that afternoon and crippled his campaign. Dodge and Rawlins assumed that the troop that attacked Browne's crew were en route to join Red Cloud at the rendezvous in the Big Horn and could not delay another day for a "coup" on Browne's gallant eleven.

The Dodge-Rawlins cavalcade took a month to explore from Fort Sanders to the Salt Lake valley. Rawlins decided on another fort location atop the bluffs on the west bank of the Platte's North Fork. A few miles west he knelt to drink from an ice-cold spring gushing out of a rock, pronounced it the best water he had ever tasted, and enthused about the setting. Dodge estimated the mileage from the west base of the Black Hills and decided the spot was about right for another work-train division point. He named the site Rawlins' Spring, and inked it in on his work map.

A few days later on the Red Desert they met the Charles Bates survey team, intact but out of water. Rawlins ordered a barrel of water, some provisions and his latest copy of *Leslie's Illustrated Weekly* transferred to the Bates wagons. That night in the joint camp Bates repeated the gossip he had heard about

Central Pacific from the Mormons in the Green River Valley. Crocker's Chinese, they said, were still hammering away on that Summit tunnel. There were supposed to be 15,000 of them, all told. Work trains were running through Truckee Canyon; railhead should be at the Nevada border before winter. But the Summit and several of the east-slope tunnels would not be finished before snowfall. It looked as though Cisco would be Central Pacific's railhead for another winter.

At Green River, Seymour paraded up and down the bluffs for a day, frowning at every rock ledge as a possible better site for the bridge than the one Sam Reed had selected three years before (and Dodge had approved a year ago). At Fort Bridger the party waited for two days in the hope that Jim Bridger would ride in from his hunting trip. At Weber Valley, Rawlins received his introduction to Mormon life when a boy ran into the living room of the home they were visiting, bobbed a greeting, and blurted, "I just come over fer pop's slippers. Mom says he's gonna stay with us this week."

On August 30 an escort waited at the mouth of Weber Canyon to lead the way to Camp Douglas, the hilltop fort behind Salt Lake City. The grooms were still unsaddling late that afternoon when Brigham Young and wife, Amelia Folsom, drove up to the officer's clubhouse. Amelia had grown up in Council Bluffs; Dodge recalled her as one of the pigtail crowd who had gawked around the Missouri & Mississippi survey camp. Young was on his ebullient best behavior. The officers were invited to the Beehive House for dinner next day and an "evening's concert" of harpsichord and harp with a violin solo by Young himself. The entire cavalcade was extended the "freedom of the city," including passes to the theatre and reserved pews in the Tabernacle on Sunday morning.

The rare honor of the invitation to Beehive House went beyond the fact that Rawlins was the Army's Chief of Staff. Schuyler Colfax had not rated an invitation in 1865 (nor did he again in 1869). The Mormons needed new industries and cash. The migrations of converts from the British Isles and

Australia had been almost too successful. The Church could supply graders, wagonmen, blasters and tie hacks for Union Pacific's right of way from the Green River west to Nevada. And the same forests that had supplied the poles for the Pacific Telegraph could furnish excellent cedar ties and hardwood bridge piers.

Thus the rococo, velvet-draped "Long Hall" on the second floor of Beehive House experienced another historic conference. Dodge was on a spot. Sam Reed's surveys indicated that Union Pacific would add more than a hundred miles to its route by looping into Salt Lake City. The best gradient ran down the canyon of Echo Creek to its junction with the Weber River, then followed the Weber into Great Salt Lake's valley, near the foot of Bear River Bay. From there, the cheapest and shortest rail route west arched north around the head of Great Salt Lake in the tracks of the Bartleson-Bidwell pioneers. And Salt Lake City was at the foot of the lake. The logical solution would be to build a branch line down to the city, similar to the Cheyenne-Denver branch. Dodge couldn't reveal this to Brigham Young, any more than he could make loose promises about subcontracts from Crédit Mobilier.

But the evening was delightful. Young's children trooped to the head of the stairs and curtsied. The dinner was pure New England, right down to the damask tablecloth and captains' chairs. The ladies played both religious and popular duets. Young proved to be a fine fiddler.

In conferences the next day Young was urbane. He verified Charles Bates's gossip about Central Pacific. Crocker was boasting that his coolies would build a mile of track a day across the Nevada Desert after April or May, 1868—a sprint that should bring them into Salt Lake City by the summer of 1869. Young smiled, then leaned back in his chair. Didn't Union Pacific, he asked, want its own throughways to the Pacific? The Latter-day Saints Church would support two such routes. One would cut southwest across Utah and Nevada and cross the Sierra to Los Angeles or San Diego. The second would run northwest, from somewhere around Green River, to follow either the Snake River or the Mormon Wagon Road through Idaho to Portland and Seattle. If the generals wished to explore either of these possibilities the Church would be pleased to furnish guides and arrange facilities.

Dodge declined on the trip southwest, but would be pleased for any aid in examining the terrain between the Green River and the Snake. Union Pacific's directors were eager, he knew, for terminal facilities on the Pacific. The Oregon route should be of particular interest. He promised, too, to deliver to Ames and Durant, in person, the Latter-day Saints' proposition on subcontracting.

The expedition rode due north through Ogden and Brigham City, explored the desert west toward the Promontory Range, then took the Mormon Road into Idaho. The terrain convinced Dodge that Brigham's plan was sound. A line could be built from Green River to the Snake's Valley, then looped northwest to the middle valley of the Columbia. He wrote a detailed report for Oliver Ames. During the ride East he reached another decision. Percy Browne had been his choice as location engineer for the Utah Division. Now Jacob Blickensderfer was displaying competence and capacity for leadership. Dodge asked him to sign on for the job and Blickensderfer accepted.

General Rawlins had decided that modernization of Jim Bridger's fort on the east base of the Bear River Divide plus the site on the North Platte River would provide adequate protection for the Union Pacific's throughway to the Wasatch. Fort Halleck, established in 1862 to protect the Oregon-Mormon Trail approach to South Pass, was only ten miles north of the right of way planned over the Laramie Plains. His recommendations were approved in Washington. The chain of forts that protected Union Pacific across the Continental Divide were: Russell at Cheyenne, Sanders at Laramie, Halleck near Medicine Bow, Fred Steele just east of Rawlin's Spring and Bridger on the Wasatch approach.

The news at Fort Sanders caused Dodge to hurry on to Washington. The 40th Congress had convened its second session in July, in anticipation of the radical Republicans' drive to impeach President Johnson. Only the week before, General Sherman had been ordered to leave the Indian Treaty discussions at North Platte and return to Washington to testify about the struggle between Johnson and Secretary of War Stanton.

Rows of Cheyenne and Sioux sat on the embankment at railhead, gravely kibitzing the ironmen. Jack Casement pointed out one of them as Turkey Foot, the chief who had directed the freight-train wreck and massacre near Plum Creek the previous August; he had ridden in with Pawnee Killer, Spotted Tail, Standing Elk and other war chiefs to demand that "work stop on these roads" and that the red man be allowed to live "in old ways."

In reply, on September 20, General Sherman had announced the Federal edict of Sioux reservations in the Dacotah and Cheyenne reservations in the Arkansas Valley. "Our people East," he warned the council circle, "hardly think of what you call 'war' here, but if they make up their minds to fight you, they will come out as thick as a herd of buffalo, and if you continue fighting you will all be killed. We advise you for the best. We now offer you this: choose your own homes and live like white men, and we will help you all you want. We are doing more for you than we do for white men coming from over the sea. This Commission is not only a Peace Commission, but it is a War Commission also. We will be kind to you if you keep the peace, but if you won't listen to reason, we are ordered to make war upon you in a different manner from what we have done before."

Pawnee Killer and several Cheyenne chiefs stalked out of the tent, emerged from their lodges an hour later "with their faces painted a fiery red," and galloped off toward Julesburg. The telegraph warned station agents and railhead. North's Pawnee Scouts went on 24-hour patrol. But nothing happened. Possibly, Casement concluded, Pawnee Killer and his renegades were off in the hills "sulking it out." They had until November 1 to make up their minds. Then the commissioners would return to North Platte for the decision on "reservation or war." Dodge hurried on to Washington to be sworn in as the most delinquent member of the 40th Congress.

The procession that rode out of Cheyenne toward Fort Laramie in early November was guarded by two companies of cavalry and a battery of Gatling guns. Cramped into the two wagons were generals, Senators, Indian commissioners and a bevy of newspaper correspondents.

Red Cloud sent down a refusal to bring in his Sioux, since the 600-mile ride would interfere with their fall hunting and meat curing. He would, he said, "come in" during 1868 if the Great Father showed a willingness to give up the forts on the Bozeman Trail. The ritual of calumet smokes, handshakes and orations were repetitious of the North Platte and Medicine Lodge councils. The Federal commissioners offered a reservation for each tribe, a government annuity of $15 per capita each year, courses in sedentary agriculture by the Indian agents plus gifts of trade goods and "guns and ammunition for hunting." Their alternative was war, with Congressional committees already pledged to increase the Army's budget for recruitment of another 4,000 soldiers if the tribes demurred.

The Crow lodges had dragged 400 miles down from the Yellowstone. The chiefs knew that they might lose half their horses and some of their women and children on the bleak trip home, especially if they had to face the wrath of Red Cloud's warriors too. Chief Bear's Tooth, "tall in stature and very deliberately got up," gave the mighty plea that began: "Achan! Achan! Father! Father! Father! Listen well. Call your young men back from the Big Horn." In essence it thundered the fears of Turkey Foot and Pawnee Killer at North Platte—of Santana, Ten Bears and others at Medicine Lodge: "Keep our country pure and clean. Preserve the old ways."

But the Crows signed the treaty. And Pawnee Killer, Turkey Foot and the Cheyenne renegades were waiting at North Platte a week later. "To secure the present generation as faithful friends," they pleaded, "do not send any more wagons up to the Powder River country. Send no more young men here. Recall your soldiers from our country, and then we shall be happy, as we have been in times long ago." The commissioners agreed that the Bozeman Trail would be discussed during the 1868 conference with Red Cloud at Fort Laramie. They hoped it would be possible for the white man's greatest fighter, General Grant, to attend. The Brule, Oglalla and Cheyenne shrugged and signed. This would assure them the gifts of trade goods and ammunition; beyond that no white man's treaty was worth much.

The commissioners' train rolled off to Omaha. At least, they agreed, they had secured the Indians' pledge—whatever it was worth—for Union Pacific's throughway across Wyoming. If Red Cloud held his warriors in check until next summer's treaty council at Fort Laramie, the Casements should have railhead across the Laramie plains and halfway to Wasatch. Julesburg was a ghost-town litter of abandoned shacks and refuse heaps.

A group of merchants held evening meetings in the Casement warehouse office at Cheyenne to consider elections for a civil government—or for a Vigilante committee as a bloody prelude. Ten miles west the work train spewed iron and ties for the assault on Evans Pass. The weather was holding. Another three weeks and head-of-track could be at Sherman Summit.

In New York, Silas Seymour was finishing a series of conferences with Thomas Durant. He carefully folded the drawing he had just made of the Evans Pass escarpment, purred his sympathy for "the necessity of such an unfortunate delay," and waddled off to the Engineers' Club. Durant began to dictate a telegram to Jack Casement.

The track gleamed halfway up the pass toward Sherman Summit. There was snow in the air. But chances were excellent that railhead would be on the Summit before the blizzards came. The telegraph key in the Casements' office began to clatter. The operator reached for a sheet of copy paper; started copying. The blood drained from his face. He threw the pencil across the office and gritted out "Goddam!" Durant was ordering all work stopped on Evans Pass and trackage abandoned. Colonel Seymour had decided that the Evans gradients were wrong. Details on the new route were being mailed.

SECTION **five**

The Race

We surely live in a very fast age;
We've traveled by ox-team, and then took the
stage
But when such conveyance is all done away
We'll travel in steam cars upon the railway!!
Hurrah! Hurrah! for the railroad's begun!
Three cheers for our contractor, his name's
Brigham Young.
Hurrah! Hurrah! We're honest and true
For if we stick to it, its bound to go through. . . .
—The "Canon Song" of the Mormon Graders,
James Crane, Sugar House, Utah. (First reported
by Anon. from "The Head of Echo," July 31,
1868, and published in the *Deseret News*.)

CHAPTER 21

THE SKY LINES

> *These mountains are underlaid with gold, silver, iron, copper and coal. The timber ranges will develop an immense lumber trade, and the millions upon millions of acres of government land being brought into the market and rendered feasible for settlement will bring to the government more money than all the bonds amount to; and this land and these minerals never would have brought this government one cent if it were not for the building of these roads. The inaccessibility and the trouble and cost of developing the country through which they run would have cost ten times more under any other circumstances— These railroads, when completed, will build up an interest right in the center of that heretofore great unknown country, an empire that shall add to our wealth, population, capital, and greatness, from a source we never expected, and by no other means could we ever obtain. . . .* Grenville M. Dodge, speech to United States House of Representatives (March 25, 1868).

January 8, 1868, was the fifth anniversary of the Central Pacific's groundbreaking ceremony at Sacramento. During a half decade the Associates had built 146 miles of track—an average of 29.2 miles a year. The cost had been about $20,-000,000 "in cash and convertible paper," or about $14,000,-

000 in gold. The death toll of Chinese coolies exceeded 500; was probably closer to 1,000.

Union Pacific, Seymour-frustrated a few miles west of Cheyenne, was 520 miles out of the Omaha Depot on January 8, four years and one month after its December, 1863, ground-breaking. (The Casement work train had averaged 24⅔ miles of track a month since April, 1866.) The actual construction costs were in the neighborhood of $25,000,000, but book-keeper juggles of $10,000,000 of paper profits to Crédit Mobilier brought the "official" cost total to $35,000,000. Union Pacific's death toll totaled fewer than 25 with another 100-150 murdered in the brawls at Hell on Wheels.

On January 8, 1868, Promontory Point, Utah, was a desert plateau on the California Trail route around the north end of the Great Salt Lake. But that day Central Pacific's eastern-most railhead at Verde California, Nevada, was 557 miles from Promontory Point; and the Casement work train, at the foot of Evans Pass, was 550 miles from Promontory.

Central Pacific was snowbound. The Sierra blizzards were as devastating as they had been in 1867. Again thousands of coolies lived in shacks and ice caves down the east slope, working 12-hour days on foundations and timber for the 37 miles of snow sheds. These vast, peak-roofed wooden tunnels, Crocker and Montague belatedly realized, were the rail-road's only hope of maintaining winterlong traffic across the mountains. Some of the sheds required protective masonry walls, 50 feet uphill, to fend off avalanches and spring floods. These walls were built via the snow-cave system developed in 1867; the Chinese masons worked in eerie caverns gouged into the snow banks. Blasting crews and timbermen continued work on tunnels down the east slope. The 7 miles of grade between the bores tilted 116 feet to the mile; Crocker decided not to lay rail on this stretch until the tunnels were finished.

Union Pacific's winter at Cheyenne brought blizzards, gun-fights, hangings by the Vigilantes, a period of martial law, and an all-out argument between Silas Seymour, James Evans and the Federal commissioners. They were simultaneous. Evans refused to give in to the Seymour-Durant edict on changing the grade up to Sherman Summit. Dodge backed Evans and briefed the Federal commissioners before they left for Washington for a midwinter inspection. The Evans grade, with two-thirds of its track laid, rose 90 feet to the mile; no curve exceeded six degrees. The route specifications sent out by Seymour and Durant in December reduced the grade to 80 feet a mile, but called for so many sharp curves that twice as much motive power would be needed to haul a train over the Black Hills. The commissioners snowshoed up and down the slopes and finally approved the Evans grade. Thus all Seymour achieved was to halt tracklaying on the east slope of the pass for the winter, thereby accommodating the vice and gun play that dominated Cheyenne between December and April.

The town had lustier transients that winter than North Platte and Julesburg had ever seen. Through it stomped thousands of lumberjacks headed for the Black Hills' forests. Many were shanty-boy veterans out of Wisconsin and Michigan, and scores were plug-uglies on the lam from East Coast police.

In toto these tie hacks were the fulfillment of the fears voiced by Bear's Tooth, Turkey Foot and Pawnee Killer at the fall peace councils. Their job was to raze the forests of the Black Hills. James W. Davis, a brother-in-law of George Francis Train, went on Union Pacific's board in 1864, and was appointed to the committee on contracts. In December, 1867, Davis & Associates subcontracted with Crédit Mobilier to deliver a million ties, plus bridge, water-tank and station timbers to grade sidings across Wyoming; their contract rate for a finished tie was 69¢ to 90¢, depending on the haulage distance.

The gangs brawled in Cheyenne for a week or two, then sledged out to a dozen river valleys. From January on, the crash of falling trees echoed up the Big and Little Laramies, the Black Fork, Bear and Green. Spring floods would tumble the logs down to the booms being built near trackage. In February, ox teams began to haul portable sawmills over the mountains. Tie Siding, Dale Creek, Fort Steele, Piedmont and Green River became the big timber-storage depots for the tie hacks' handiwork.

A countertemptation for a winter in the lumber camps was the rush to the new gold fields of the South Pass region, 200 miles northwest in the Wind River Mountains. The best route to them ran north up the Bozeman Trail from Cheyenne, then west through South Pass, to the Sweetwater River Valley. In repetition of the California, Montana and Arizona "rushes," the Sweetwater Mines began as placer pannings along the creeks, expanded to high-pressure hydraulic washdowns of dirt banks, and within a year or two blasted on to the routine of hard-rock tunneling. Union Pacific's railhead winter at Cheyenne coincided with the Sweetwater's placer phase. Graders and teamsters who didn't return East for the winter layoff had the opportunities of a gold rush a mere two weeks away. Hundreds took the trip and assisted in the births of Atlantic City, South Pass City and Pacific Springs. A few found gold. Come April the Union Pacific's grading jobs were waiting 100 miles down Big Sandy Creek and Green River.

A third and more clannish profession explored Cheyenne that winter. Dr. Van Lennep, the geologist, discovered coal in the ridges 60 miles north of Fort Sanders. New York headquarters ordered Sam Reed to hire Cornish and Welsh miners and route them out there for test diggings. The chunk wood secured in trimming the Black Hills timber would fuel Union Pacific locomotives for years. But coal-burning grates were already on order. After 1871, trains would make smoother, faster runs over the Rockies because of coal's thermal superiority. The acrid black smoke would become a symbol of the United States' railroad saga, just as cinder walks, slag fill and cinder block would become standard materials for home and business-block construction across the West. During February the miners sledged over the mountains, blasted into the black rock, and founded Carbon—Wyoming's first coal town.

Each division point established by the Casements' work train became the new east terminal of stage lines and freight wagons. Cheyenne was the winter base for stages and bull-whackers. By January the young city had business blocks that, at first glance, were substantial brick and marble. But close examination revealed them to be the factory twins of Hell on Wheels. The "bricks" and "marble" were hand-tinted wood stamped out in prefab sections by Chicago mills, then shipped to railhead with do-it-yourself instruction sheets.

Building the civil government was a more difficult task. The thousands of mules, horses and oxen in the Union Pacific and freighter corrals were as tempting to some white men as they were to the Indians. Gangs organized to steal them and then smuggle them off to the Sweetwater and Denver auctions. Scores of pickpockets and gunmen rode in from Chicago and St. Louis to prey on the patrons of Hell on Wheels. The 200 girls employed by the brothels were now politely identified as "the Nymphs du Grade." Their madams hired burly Negroes or downcountry plug-uglies as bouncers; they were dexterous with blackjacks, sheath knives, rabbit punches and groin kicks. Madams and girls carried derringer-type or tiny Smith & Wesson .22 revolvers, known as "whore specials," tucked into garters or worn as belt ornaments in beaded leather holsters.

In addition to these threats to law and order, arrivals who couldn't afford Chicago prefabs, or even tents, dug caverns into the banks of Crow Creek, hung blankets over the entrances, and moved in. Some of these places were commodious enough to house livestock too. At least one was a hideout for stolen horses and mules held there until rebranding scars healed.

Thievery, shootings and claim jumping became so routine that a delegation of merchants and railroaders rode out to Fort Russell for a conference with Colonel J. D. Stevenson. A few days later wagonloads of soldiers surrounded Hell on Wheels. Bayonets fixed, the infantry herded every barkeep, shill, dealer, madam and floozy onto the prairie. Colonel

Stevenson lectured them from horseback. Cheyenne, he roared, would become Union Pacific property when the Department of the Interior turned over the land deeds to the Union Pacific. In the interim the city remained Federal property and could go under martial law whenever the fancy seized him. And it seized him now. Until further notice troops would patrol Hell on Wheels. If any fights broke out they were under orders to shoot first and ask questions later.

Martial law ended after a mayor and city officials were elected, a police force appointed, and a one-room slab-sided cabin converted into a city jail. The bosses at Hell on Wheels smirked and streaked back to the Julesburg and North Platte routine. The jail became a hobo flophouse. Mayor Luke Murrin added 25¢ to each fine he imposed, "to cover the expense of stimulants necessary to efficient administration of justice," then ordered a $10 fine for participants in any gunplay within the city limits "whether they hit their target or not." By February a secret Citizens' Committee was meeting nights at the Casement warehouse. They made their first public appearance the night after Charles Martin's murder trial.

Martin and a faro dealer named Andy Harris had accumulated enough cash, via alley stick-ups and nicked cards, to buy a dance hall. Then they argued. Martin drew first and put five bullets into Harris. The police department escorted Martin to jail. His trial came up at the March session of the United States District Court; the jury freed him. Martin went back to his roominghouse, bathed and shaved, put on his best duds and set out for a night in Hell town. He was on his third or fourth drink when a man strolled in, tapped him on the shoulder, and said, "Fellows out there want to see you."

A moment later Martin screamed from the alley. Some of his cronies rushed to the door. A squad of men in black eyemasks was backing away, revolvers trained on the door. Martin, a rope around his gullet and hands pinioned, moaned in their midst. "Better get back inside," a voice growled. The next morning a wagonman found Martin's body dangling from a tree limb at the east end of Main Street. An hour later police found a note under the jail door announcing that the corpse of "Morgan the mule thief" was also available a mile up Crow Creek.

The Citizens' Committee operated for another six months and hung at least twelve men. A score more were horsewhipped out of town with threats that they would be shot on sight if they ever returned. The Committee backed the plea by Cheyenne churches that brothels and saloons be closed between 10 A.M. and 2 P.M. on Sundays; Mayor Murrin proclaimed it a new city ordinance. By the summer of 1868, with Hell on Wheels across the Black Hills, the police department resumed as Justice's sole escort. The black masks were burned or tucked away in desk drawers for emergency reference. No speculations were voiced, at least in public, about the Committee's membership. The Casements, Sam Reed, and probably Durant, knew who were involved. Colonel Stevenson maintained an official hands-off policy throughout. Evidence suggests that the Committee was organized by Union Pacific's Town Lots Division, with the approval of Colonel Stevenson.

Successive Vigilante committees in Union Pacific's new towns paralleled the appearance and matched the techniques of the South's Ku Klux Klan. Legh Freeman became their noisiest Wyoming advocate. Freeman's volatile presence in Cheyenne during part of the 1867–8 winter is a matter of record, since he moved the equipment for his weekly newspaper, the *Frontier Index,* from Julesburg to Laramie sometime between October, 1867, and March, 1868. As a vicious and thoroughly un-Galvanized Southerner, Freeman was a logical idea man and lieutenant for Cheyenne's Vigilantes. Moreover, there must have been substantiation for the charge of "King of the Vigilantes" later howled against him at Bryan and Bear River City.

A native of Virginia or Georgia, Freeman fought for one of the Secesh armies, migrated to Nebraska during 1866, and signed on as a telegraph operator at Fort Kearney. There he discovered a newspaper press abandoned in a warehouse and evolved a plan for a railroad newspaper that could cash in on the advertising of the merchants of Hell on Wheels. Yellow journalism, a generation ahead, was pallid compared to the vituperations Freeman flaunted in the news columns of the *Frontier Index*. From Fort Kearney to Bear City his editorial page carried a standing masthead slogan that read:

THE MOTTO OF THIS COLUMN
ONLY WHITE MEN TO BE NATURALIZED IN THE UNITED STATES. THE RACES AND SEXES IN THEIR RESPECTIVE SPHERES AS GOD ALMIGHTY CREATED THEM

(The most complete file of this "newspaper on wheels" is owned by the Bancroft Library on the Berkeley Campus of the University of California, but the first issue at Bancroft is datelined "Fort Sanders, Dakota Territory," on March 6, 1868. The Union Pacific Historical Museum at Omaha owns one copy of *Frontier Index* datelined "Julesburg, Nebraska" during July, 1867.)

Somehow the *Frontier Index* got its printing presses across the Black Hills during February. By April 21, the paper had moved another three miles north to publish a first edition at "Laramie City, Dakota Territory." Freeman may have put out several editions in Cheyenne. In any case, the Ku Klux Klan technique of the Vigilante committees coupled with Freeman's vicious editorial campaigns across Nebraska, Wyoming, Utah and Montana between 1867 and 1884 mark him as a logical—and typical—organizer of this form of lynch law.

Jacob Blickensderfer and the Utah Division surveyors had crossed the Black Hills during the first week of February, staged into Fort Bridger, and pushed on into Echo and Weber canyons on snowshoes. "The drifts," Blickensderfer reported, "were over the tops of the telegraph poles."

James Evans and the bridge crews crossed to Dale Creek with portable sawmills and began to derrick green timber into position for the spiderweb bridge. "It went up in three weeks," Grenville Dodge would brag. The Federal inspectors accepted it as "temporary" but ordered that it must be rebuilt in iron "within a year."

The train crews had worked overtime out of Omaha all winter. Every mile of new track, Sam Reed and Herbert Hoxie had discovered, required 40 carloads of supplies. Oliver Ames and Thomas Durant, in agreement for once, were sputtering for "400 miles of construction or better during '68." The Casements' new contract was written accordingly, stipulating "$800 a mile for anything less than two miles a day; for over two miles a day, $1,200 a mile. For delays consequent upon an unfinished grade, $3,000 a day." The work train rode the iron men back up Evans Pass and laid the line to Sherman Summit over frozen ground. Alongside the portable warehouse in Cheyenne, car builders finished the water-tank cars and additional bunk cars to be added to the train before the assault on the Red Desert.

Skunk cabbage pushed green sworls up through the skim ice on the creek banks. Workmen cussed the first buzzing of blackflies and sniffed suspiciously at the north wind. Then on the night of March 24 the winds keyed from tenor to basso. Snow hissed down from the Big Horn and fell in a blinding white curtain for forty-eight hours. Union Pacific trains stalled all along the Platte. Livestock froze to death in the corrals. Stagecoaches slithered down Cheyenne Pass a week late, their drivers' frostbitten legs green with gangrene. Sam Reed ordered grading crews back to the Summit to help the work train dig out the line. It took a week to clear enough ground to start hauling rail again.

Spring was a season of rain and floods again when a band of Sioux Dog Soldiers screamed over the tracks at Elm Creek, Nebraska, looted the station, and killed five section hands. The same day another Sioux war party looted Sidney, 202 miles west. Tom Cahoon, a freight conductor, fishing in Lodge Pole Creek, had his scalp ripped off. Cahoon, like Thompson, recovered but didn't find his scalp. (Transferred to Ogden, Cahoon spent another 20 years as a conductor on the Wasatch Division. He wore his hat tilted far back on his head to cover the bald spot. Cahoon Street, Ogden, is named for him.) The Sioux raids threw Platte Valley traffic into another snarl. Trains were held at stations until troops showed up to guard the trips between Grand Island and Cheyenne. The rumor of all-out Indian War echoed again. Sam Reed doubled freight-train schedules to make up the delay.

On the far side of Nevada, spring was a white witch too. Snows blocked 16 miles of Sierra trackage, plus the miles still to be laid on the Summit–Truckee slope. Engine plows sent out from Cisco growled and bucked until drift tops hissed down their smokestacks. In mid-March, Crocker ordered the coolies out of the tunnels, lumber camps, and snowsheds to clear the 23 miles with shovels, mattocks and blasting powder. Sunshine set off avalanches. But the Chinese hammered through. By late April their shovels were down to the yellow earth. Crocker and Strobridge rode over the hump and deployed 3,000 graders along the unrailed 7-mile gap. Powder gangs moved ahead, shattering the frozen earth with half-keg blasts. Shovel crews followed and smashed the clods into a surface smooth enough to bed the ties.

Crocker and Montague cantered through Truckee Canyon out into the green Nevada meadows. It was May 4. The East Slope rails ended at a cluster of shacks on the south bank of the Truckee River, across from the trading post and ranch of M. C. Lake. Comstock miners had named the place Lake's Crossing. The name wouldn't do, Crocker ruled; the land was now Central Pacific property by virtue of the Federal land grants and would become the junction for freight traffic to Virginia City, Carson City, and all the mines of the Comstock Lode. The new name should be patriotic and American.

One of Montague's assistants was a Mexican War veteran who had served with Jesse Lee Reno, a general later killed in the Civil War battle of South Mountain. Why not name the new town for General Reno? Crocker grinned and nodded. On May 9, the Associates' realty department held a public auction of Reno's lots. The first one brought $600, and two hundred more sold before sundown.

Crocker's white mare cantered across the desert to the grading camps being built at the foot of Pyramid Lake. The survey bosses rode in for conferences. Preliminary surveys were under way all across Nevada and Utah; location stakes would be pegged to the edge of the Salt Lake's western bluffs by midsummer. Union Pacific's crews were working out there, too, running parallel lines, the surveyors reported. "What was the decision about Salt Lake City?" Montague asked; it would certainly be cheaper to run the right of way north around the head of the lake. Crocker shook his head. This was politics. He'd urge Stanford to go to Salt Lake City, size up Brigham Young and the Mormons, and make the decision. It would be smart anyway to give some of the grading subcontracts to the Mormons.

On May 10, the day after the Reno lot auction, Hell on Wheels began its swarm over the Black Hills from Cheyenne to Laramie. Sam Reed and the Casements were ready. Troops from Fort Sanders patroled the railhead. The prefab saloons and cribhouses were ordered out beyond the town plots. Reed groaned and the telegraph operator cursed again when a message clattered in that Thomas Durant and Silas Seymour were through Omaha and due at Laramie about May 15.

Next night more gossip clicked in from Cheyenne. Durant was ordering all work stopped on the Cheyenne shops and roundhouse. He had decided to move them over the hill to Laramie. Mayor Murrin had already wired protests to New York and Washington. And it seemed that Seymour had another trick up his silk sleeve. He was gunning for Evans and Dodge again. The grade west of Cooper Lake was to be abandoned too. Instead, the line would run up the valleys of Rock Creek and Medicine Bow River; Durant agreed with

Seymour that the change would "reduce grading and save money."

Jack Casement snorted. Seymour's route was twenty miles longer than the one Evans and Dodge had plotted to Carbon Summit. Sam Reed paced the room for a moment, then strode back to the telegraph desk. "Grenville Dodge, U. S. House of Representatives, Washington, D.C.," he dictated. "Urgent you be Laramie May 16." He paused. "Better not sign it. Too many Durant ears between here and Omaha."

CHAPTER 22

SHOWDOWN

> *Dr. Durant is still here and of all men to mix ac-*
> *counts and business he is the chief . . . No one can*
> *tell by Durant's talk what he thinks of a man, his*
> *best friends may not know what he means when talk-*
> *ing to them. . . . Samuel B. Reed in a letter to his*
> wife (1868).

Throughout the winter and spring of 1867–8 the feud between
the Ames Brothers-Dillon faction and Thomas C. Durant was
as melodramatic, and furtive, as Cheyenne's struggle toward
law-and-order. There were lawsuits and counterlawsuits,
bribes, blackmail, pay-offs to Congressmen, and the stealthy
transfer of official papers to Boston.

Most of it boiled out of the Ames-Dillon decision to remove
Durant from Crédit Mobilier's board because "there is no
pleasure, peace, safety or comfort with him unless he agrees
to abide the decision of the majority, as the rest of us do."
In retaliation Durant fought the award of the master contract
west of the 100th meridian with a series of court injunctions.
The situation became even more critical when Jim Fisk, the
infamous market gambler, began a campaign of blackmail
against Crédit Mobilier. Rumor said that Durant was Fisk's
silent partner in the effort. Fisk's power over New York poli-

283

ticians was obvious. In partnership with Jay Gould and Daniel Drew, he had recently wrested control of the Erie Railroad from Cornelius Vanderbilt via an audacious pay-off of New York's Legislature. Oakes and Oliver Ames smuggled record books and other documents that would expose details of the Union Pacific-Crédit Mobilier agreements across the Hudson river to New Jersey, then obtained permission from the Department of the Interior to transfer them to Massachusetts—beyond the jurisdiction of Fisk's cronies.

The Fisk threat frightened them into new overtures to Durant. During September, agreement was reached to award Union Pacific's master contract for construction 667 miles west of the 100th meridian to Oakes Ames, but with the stipulation that Ames assign it to a board of seven trustees representing Crédit Mobilier. The seven were: Oliver Ames, Thomas C. Durant, Sidney Dillon, Cornelius Bushnell, John B. Alley, Henry S. McComb, and Benjamin F. Bates. Ames, Dillon and Alley were allied against Durant. Bushnell and McComb had been Union Pacific and Crédit Mobilier directors since 1863 and were acknowledged Durant allies. Bates, a neutral, held the balance of power.

The Union Pacific directors approved the contract on October 1. That day the Casements' work train was 228 miles west of the 100th meridian. Statistics were available to prove that construction costs west from Omaha had averaged $27,-500 a mile, including erection of stations, water tanks, side tracks, woodyards and roundhouses. Still, the Ames contract specified payments by Union Pacific of $43,500 a mile for the trackage between the 100th meridian and Cheyenne. Obviously it assured Crédit Mobilier of a clear profit of $16,000 a mile for the 228 miles already constructed—a total of $3,658,-000. Neither Government directors nor the press questioned the fact that this contract was being awarded to the brother of Union Pacific's president, who was also a Member of Congress—hence, by oath of office, a guardian representative of the

Federal Government and of its loans and land grants to Union Pacific.

During the second day of the meeting Oliver Ames entertained a motion that Durant be dropped from Union Pacific's board of directors. The motion failed by a narrow margin. Any effort to remove Durant as vice-president and general manager would have gone the same way. The gesture merely assured furtive and sadistic plots by both the pro-Ames and pro-Durant groups.

Grenville Dodge had received a block of Crédit Mobilier stock when he became chief engineer. This plus the Crédit Mobilier Scandal of 1873-4 and Union Pacific's bankruptcy in 1893 certainly influenced the speeches and writings he prepared between 1900 and 1912. Yet he was honest in emphasizing the poverty and desperate financial struggles of Union Pacific. By the time the Ames contract was approved a total of 475 miles of trackage had been built; all of it had been constructed on the flatland rate of $12,000 worth of Federal bonds a mile. The railroad's total cash income accruing from the Federal loans, then, was $5,700,000, plus the alternate sections of the land grants. But construction of 475 miles of track at an average cost of $27,500 a mile totals $13,062,000, plus overhead. Overall, Union Pacific's accumulated costs totaled in the neighborhood of $20,000,000 by the time the Ames contract was signed. And the $5,700,000 worth of government bonds were, after all, a 30-year loan, compounding 6 per cent interest, while the land grants were for virgin land long reputed to be "useless desert" and worth not more than $1.50 an acre before development. Hence, the Federal loan plus the value of the land grants totaled a third—certainly not more than half—of the actual construction costs on that initial 475 miles.

Consequently the Ames-Dillon group was forced to pursue the same dire policies that Durant originated when he tricked the Union Pacific Railroad & Telegraph Company into existence in 1863-4, invented Crédit Mobilier of America, and persuaded Herbert Hoxie to be the stooge for the 247-mile Hoxie contract. Routinely through 1867 and 1868, the railroad's first-mortgage bonds were sold or pledged at 15- and 20-per-cent discounts; a series of future-income bonds was sold at 40- and 50-per-cent discounts (an average of $700 in cash accepted and $1,000 to $1,400 pledged in repayment); and a third bond series on the land grants was sold at an average 40- to 45-per-cent discount. Just as consistently, Union Pacific's common stock refused to budge above 30 per cent of its face value.

Yet these were the only methods by which cash could be raised to build the line. Between 1867 and 1872, Union Pacific paid $13,755,000 in interest on its loans. The railroad's net earnings for the same five years totaled $13,736,000 —$19,000 less than the debt interest. But the Ames-Dillon faction, while indignantly questioning the behavior and greed of Durant, grubbed the $3,658,000 "bonus" for Crédit Mobilier by rigging a 37-per-cent increase on charges for the completed trackage between the 100th meridian and Cheyenne; and then rigged future dividends via the same technique.

Back in Washington after October 15, Oakes Ames dived into other treacherous waters by offering Crédit Mobilier bonds to Congressmen without margin payments. Since these "sales" led to his formal censure before an open session of the House in 1873 and are held responsible for his fatal heart attack a few weeks later, the humane term for his behavior is "sale without margins" rather than "bribery." The Fisk raid and Durant's suspected role in it convinced the Ames brothers and Dillon that Durant and Fisk might move into Washington and force a Congressional investigation of Crédit Mobilier's activities. "We want more friends in this Congress," Ames wrote H.S. McComb on February 22, "& if a man will look into the law (& it is difficult for them to do it unless they have an interest to do so), he can not help being convinced that we should not be interfered with." Testimony before two House committees during 1873 revealed that Congressmen who accepted Ames's offer of stock without margin payment included: Schuyler Colfax, Speaker of the House; James A. Garfield of Ohio (20th President of the United States); William D. Kelley of Pennsylvania; William B. Allison of Iowa; and James Brooks of New York. Another score of Representatives and Senators, including General John Logan of Illinois and James G. Blaine of Maine, developed fears about the political hazards involved and either decided against acceptance of the stock or changed their minds and returned it with requests that their names be removed from Ames's list.

Oakes Ames's dealings with Congressman James Brooks of New York were most flagrant violations of ethics and law. Brooks was one of the government-appointed directors of Union Pacific, hence was specifically forbidden by the Railway Acts to hold stock in the enterprise. Sometime during 1865, Brooks had told Durant that he wanted to "get" $15,000 or $20,000 of Crédit Mobilier stock. Durant put him off. In December, 1867, Brooks again demanded—or Ames offered—200 shares of Crédit Mobilier. Finally 150 shares were delivered to Charles H. Neilson, Brooks's son-in-law. The 1873 testimony indicated that Brooks paid $10,000 for 100 of the shares, but soon received a "dividend" of $5,000 worth of Union Pacific common, plus the other 50 Crédit Mobilier shares.

The majority of these Congressional "sales" took place between mid-October and January with Ames fully aware of the fact that his contract included the $3,658,000 overcharge on completed trackage. Consequently he knew that Crédit Mobilier was about to "cut the melon." On December 12, Crédit Mobilier declared its first dividend of $2,244,000 (face value) in first-mortgage bonds and $2,244,000 in Union Pacific common, or a total worth of 80 per cent of the face value of Crédit Mobilier shares. Another dividend of 60 per cent was declared on June 23,1868. Thus, typically, Congressman William D. Kelley of Pennsylvania received a check for $329 plus his paid-up shares in Crédit Mobilier without having invested a penny of "margin." If Grenville Dodge took part in any of the Crédit Mobilier "sales" to the 40th Congress, he managed to hide it. Two other Iowa Congressmen were involved. Dodge must have known what was going on.

Sometime that winter, too, Collis Huntington set a trap for Federal loans to Central Pacific across all Utah Territory to Echo Canyon. His device was arrogantly simple. He ordered Montague to prepare maps and charts for a Central Pacific right of way across Nevada and Utah to Echo Canyon, then filed them with the Secretary of the Interior as a "routine projection for the next section of our line." A few weeks later Huntington brisked back to Interior with a document that stressed the financial emergency confronting Central Pacific. He requested an advance payment of $2,400,000 worth of Federal bonds on "our new line." The request was referred to the Attorney General for an opinion. The Attorney General ruled that it was legally sound, according to the 1866 Pacific Railway Act. At that point the story leaked back to Dodge or Ames. Frantic requests went from Union Pacific to both President Johnson and Secretary of the Treasury McCulloch to "personally investigate Huntington's trick."

Meanwhile Huntington, Ames and Dodge joined forces to lobby against a bill introduced on December 9, 1867, by C. C. Washburn of Wisconsin, that would empower Congress to fix the freight and passenger rates on the Pacific Railroad. They succeeded in killing the bill in committee. Allegations were made then and later that the Ames "sales" of Crédit Mobilier stock influenced the vote. Dodge and Huntington became friends during this lobbying stint. Yet throughout the winter and spring, the Ames, Dodge and Huntington discussions about the Washburn Bill and other legislation deemed unfriendly to the Pacific Railroad would end with Huntington going off to a conference to demand the $2,400,000 trans-Utah bonds for Central Pacific while Ames and Dodge hurried to another conference to argue against the scheme.

Durant had his own scouts in Washington. If he was in alliance with Jim Fisk these "pipelines" were excellent. Hence suspicions began to plague him about Grenville Dodge. Then his temper flared, as it had against Peter Dey, George Francis Train, and a score of others. Silas Seymour, meanwhile, remained the pompously affable yes-man, ever ready to propose a plausible alternate for the construction decisions reached by Dodge and the field crews. And now there were indications that his brother Horatio had an excellent chance to win the Democratic nomination for the Presidency in July. The Republicans were being forced, by the bitterness spewed up from the Johnson impeachment trial, to resort to the weary old trick of nominating a successful general. Grant was willing to run and would probably be nominated on the first ballot. If the country reacted as violently to the Johnson trial as Congress had, Horatio Seymour might beat Grant. With the President's brother as chief engineer of Union Pacific, Durant dreamed, all would be well again; the Ames-Dillon clique would surrender.

As for the decision to move division shops from Cheyenne to Laramie, Durant had twin reasons. Seymour logically pointed out that Laramie stood between the steep run over Sherman Summit and Wyoming's Red Desert; division shops there would be in a more desirable spot than they would be at Cheyenne. Secondly, real-estate sales weren't moving as briskly as they should. A shift of shops from Cheyenne to Laramie would bring hundreds of lot buyers across the Black Hills.

Defiantly, Durant and Seymour rode off to Laramie. Dodge raced after them. Again the telegraph chattered. A delegation of merchants was waiting for Dodge on the Cheyenne platform. "The shops will remain in Cheyenne," he promised, and rode on to Laramie where the station agent filled him in on developments. Sam Reed had stayed in town only long enough to talk with Durant about details of the grading contract to Brigham Young, then coached off toward Salt Lake City; The Casements had rail down almost to Cooper Lake; Seymour was upcountry bossing the regrade toward Carbon; Mr. Durant was around somewhere—likely at the Frontier House. Dodge strolled over to Hell on Wheels. A German band tootled waltzes from a platform at the center of the big tent. Cribhouse Row sported ruby-glass chandeliers in some of the front parlors. The gambling halls and saloons were flashier and noisier than Julesburg's. General Gibbons was still in command at Fort Sanders. Again, come pay night, a taste of martial law might be necessary. But first he'd have it out with Durant. And in public. He wanted the gossip to get around.

Dodge packed his saddlebags next morning, put on Army "fatigues" and an officer's slouch hat, and told the hostler at the Casements' warehouse that he'd need a horse before 10 o'clock. Durant, he had learned, was uptown talking with the Town Lots salesmen. The meeting that followed was a moderately good model for a "Gunsmoke" climax. Durant stood in front of the Town Lots tent at the end of Main Street, arguing promotion strategies. He was an executive visiting the frontier, and dressed for the role in a slouchy suit of black corduroy with a heavy gold watch chain looped in a "Flying W" across its vest, a dapper string tie, a white shirt and straw sailor hat—effective foils for his VanDyke beard and curly pompadour.

Dodge strode up the dusty street, arms swinging. The real-estate salesmen muttered to Durant and sidled away. Durant turned, scowled, and walked slowly out into the street too. But neither "reached." Durant coldly detailed his decision to change the Cooper Lake–Carbon Summit route and transfer the division shops from Cheyenne to Laramie. In view of developments, he probably gritted a threat to demand Dodge's dismissal at the next meeting of Union Pacific's board.

Dodge roared his reply loudly enough for every gawker on the street to hear—and repeat. "You are now going to learn," he quoted himself as shouting, "that the men working for the Union Pacific will take orders from me and not from you. If you interfere there will be trouble—trouble from the Government, from the Army, and from the men themselves."

The result was precisely what Dodge wanted and far more effective than a shooting match would have been. The telegraphers gossiped. New York and Washington had the news within a day or two. Sidney Dillon went to Washington to join Oakes Ames in a conference with General Sherman. West through Carbon, Fort Steele and the Red Desert, the grade gangs and bridge crews greeted Dodge with grins and a spontaneous "Hurrah for you, General."

Union Pacific's first tunnel was being blasted out of the brown sandstone at Mary's Creek near the section Durant and Seymour were rerouting. The brown stone showed a tendency to crack and flake; the entire tunnel would have to be timbered. The Casements were building a temporary switchback over the hill to by-pass it. Temporary pile trestles, 200 to 600 feet long, were hammering up for the crossings of the Laramie River, Rock Creek, Medicine Bow River, the North Fork of the Platte, and Bitter Creek. Bitter Creek looped like a sidewinder; the route stakes called for twenty crossings, a total of 2,450 feet of spans. Truss bridges were on order from Boomer in Chicago, but only a few had reached the Laramie warehouse. Anyway, the desert haul was too impossible a task via wagons; after the Casements laid track the trusses could be hauled out by rail and placed.

At new Fort Fred Steele on the North Platte crossing, Dodge heard the latest gossip about Central Pacific. Early in June the first engine had crept down that final seven miles of 116-foot grade into Truckee Canyon. Behind it had creaked a work train that was a carbon copy of the Casements', even to water cars, a blacksmith shop on wheels, bunk cars, and a segregated diner for Irish ironmen. All down the Sierra slope the coolie gangs waved their spades and cheered. Central Pacific was in business from Sacramento to a base camp 40 miles beyond Reno. Crocker was keeping his promise of "a mile a day in '68."

Back east the feud went into full gear again. Ames and Dillon stormed into the New York office soon after Durant's return. Washington was gossiping, they claimed, that Seymour's line shift into Carbon Summit had been a deliberate trick to obtain more Federal bonds and land grants; Congress was fretting about the mutters of "corruption" coming from the Secretary of the Interior and the White House. Durant's decision to move workshops out of Cheyenne was almost as bad politically. A bill for creation of Wyoming Territory was in committee and due for passage within the month; Cheyenne would be named the capital. Where could Union Pacific hope to stand with Territory officials after it ordered repair shops, hundreds of jobs, and millions of dollars worth of local trade out of the capital city?

Durant held his ground: Seymour was a better engineer than Dodge; the changes would stand. Moreover, he repeated, he intended to go before the October board meeting with a list of charges against Dodge and a request for his dismissal.

Oakes Ames nodded, glanced at Dillon, then played their ace. General Grant, he said, planned to join General Sherman and the other commissioners at the Fort Laramie treaty talks in July. It was, of course, excellent campaign strategy for the Republican candidate to take this keen interest in the Indian Question. Generals Grant and Sherman had also expressed a desire not only to inspect the Union Pacific trackage but to hear both sides of the argument about General Dodge. They would be at Fort Sanders late in July. Durant and Seymour were expected there too.

Jacob Blickensderfer's location stakes spread over the Green River plateau to a junction with the Overland Mail road at

Church Butte, veered north of Fort Bridger to the valley of the Bear, then beelined alongside Castle Rock toward the gloom of Echo Canyon. Dodge found Blickensderfer and his crewmen cursing Nature's handiwork. Echo Canyon was crumbly shale and clay; a 772-foot tunnel would have to be blasted through one of the ridges. The job couldn't possibly be finished before the Casements arrived. The entire bore must be timbered, and the approaches cleared back 50 feet or more to diminish the danger of rock slides. The chain crews were staking a tortuous right of way eight miles long for a temporary by-pass track.

Down Weber Canyon the surveys called for two more rock bores, less than a mile apart. Tunnel Number 3 was to be 508 feet long through a cliff of black limestone and blue quartzite. Tunnel 4—and strangely enough it would have a four-degree curve—would bore 297 feet through the same tough rock. The bridge problem wasn't too bad. The survey hopscotched Weber River a half-dozen times. All jumps could be made via wood trestles until the permanent Boomer trusses arrived from Chicago.

Jogging out to these locations, the division chief gave Dodge a report on his spring surveys across Utah and Nevada. The level of Great Salt Lake was rising. One assistant engineer had almost drowned trying to take soundings. The only sensible route was north of the lake over that 7,500-foot-high desert range the Mormons called Promontory Ridge. Blickensderfer didn't see how Montague and the Central Pacific crews could reach any other decision.

Dodge groaned. Brigham Young had his grading and timber contracts. But there would be oratory when he learned that Salt Lake City, like Denver, was to be by-passed. Best to go over there and break the news as soon as they'd reached decisions on these tunnel jobs. Or could he? Dodge puzzled again over the mysterious message from Ames telling him to be ready for an emergency trip back to Laramie. Did this mean that Sherman and his retinue were planning an inspection of Union Pacific on their way home from the Fort Laramie treaty talks? Had Durant hoodwinked Ames into accepting Seymour as Chief Engineer?

They were taking sights along one of Echo's bluffs on July 23 when an orderly rode in from Fort Bridger. The telegram he delivered was from Dillon at Fort Sanders. Generals Grant, Sherman and Sheridan and the Peace commissioners were due back at Fort Sanders on the 26th. Durant and Seymour were already there. Grant and Sherman wanted to hear both sides of the argument between Durant and Dodge.

The Casements' railhead was east of Rawlins Springs. That meant, for Dodge, a 275-mile gallop in two days, then a 200-mile engine ride east through the maze of construction trains. The orderly saluted and grinned. An ambulance was on its way from Bridger to base camp, he explained, "courtesy of the Army." The General could sleep all the way across Wyoming if he wished.

At Fort Bridger, Dodge caught up on desert gossip. Red Cloud had won the three-year battle against Forts Phil Kearny and Reno and the bullyboy traffic up the Bozeman Trail. The Treaty Council at Fort Laramie brought in the most impressive array of Army brass ever seen in the West—Grant, Sherman, Sheridan, Harney, Kautz, Potter, Dent, Hunt and Slemmer. Red Cloud led in hundreds of lodges of Oglalla, Northern Cheyennes, Arapaho and Sioux. The calumet made its grave round; the chiefs spoke; the commissioners replied. Finally the generals nodded agreement. Red Cloud's hands trembled as he put his "X" on the treaty that closed the Bozeman Trail, pulled all troops out of Phil Kearny and Reno, and re-established the Big Horn country north of Wind River as land inviolate to the white man. The Wyoming Desert was as peaceful as an Ohio farm.

Jack Casement rode his black stallion out from the Latham junction, looped the lead over the ambulance tail gate, and clambered in for more gossip. He had heard that Durant actually intended to make a case for Dodge's dismissal during the talks with Grant. In a way it was a devilishly shrewd move. On July 9, the Democrats had nominated Horatio Seymour as their Presidential candidate. Durant would, it seemed, urge brother Silas's promotion from consulting to chief engineer. If Grant so much as winked an eyebrow in defense of Dodge, the Democratic National Committee could howl "favoritism" and make a pretty campaign issue out of it. Ames, Casement growled on, hadn't even had the guts to countermand Durant's order on those twenty extra miles into Carbon Summit, and it looked now as though he'd compromise on the Cheyenne-Laramie squabble, too, by approving division shops and a roundhouse for each town. Anyway, if Durant won, there just might be a strike at railhead and all along the line; payrolls were six weeks late again. Personally General Jack fancied a long fishing trip. His contract called for $3,000 a day during "unaccountable delays," didn't it? It was an enlightening chat on an auspicious day; that same afternoon Congress created the Territory of Wyoming.

The powwow that convened in the big log bungalow of the Fort Sanders Officers Club on the afternoon of July 26 was as impressive as the council with Red Cloud. Grant, Sherman and Sheridan were in "civies." General Harney wore his black cape and silk topper. The rest of the generals wore field dress splendid with gilt buttons and braid. Durant, again in the black corduroy, sat beside Silas Seymour on one side of the circle. Dodge sat across from them, with Dillon and Jesse L. Williams, the Government commissioner. If Grant, Sherman, Sheridan and Dodge found time for a private conference, no hint of it was ever made by the press or in memoirs.

Grant put the questions. One of the major reasons for giving in to Red Cloud, he pointed out, had been to calm the north country tribes and enable Union Pacific to build through to Salt Lake Valley without fighting war parties all across the high plain. Under the circumstances the Army hoped for a comparable peace among the executives of the railroad.

There was too much at stake. If Mr. Durant had charges, let him state them.

Durant unfolded a piece of paper and began reading. General Dodge, he charged, had selected "impossible routes," had held up construction while "tinkering" over tunnel and bridge projects, and had failed to locate the line into Salt Lake City.

Grant chewed his cigar and nodded toward Dodge. Dodge summarized his annual report, recounted the changes made by Seymour and Durant while he was in Washington, and detailed the work under way between Rawlins Spring and Great Salt Lake and the reasons for by-passing Salt Lake City.

The group tensed. Grant's hands slipped down to his knees. He leaned forward, staring at Durant and Seymour. "The Government," he rasped, as though the November election was assured, "expects the railroad company to meet its obligations . . . And the Government expects General Dodge to remain with the road as its chief engineer until it is completed."

General Harney's cape rustled as he turned to stare at Durant. Sherman, Sheridan and the full circle turned with him. Silas Seymour licked his lips and managed a weak smile. Durant's fingers dabbed at the black cravat; the watch chain slithered like a gold snake as he rose. "I withdraw my objections," he mumbled. "We all want Dodge to stay with the road." He walked across the room toward Dodge, right hand extended.

General Harney whipped his cape back across his belly, turned to Sheridan, and winked.

CHAPTER **23**

THE SONS OF DESERET

> *But for the pioneership of the Mormons, discovering the pathway, and feeding those who came out upon it, all this central region of our great West would now be many years behind its present development, and the railroad instead of being finished, would hardly be begun. . . .* Samuel Bowles, *The Pacific Railroad— Open. How to Go; What to See* (1869).

The Ames contract assumed responsibility for construction of Union Pacific "667 miles west of the 100th meridian." Testifying before a Congressional committee six years later, Oakes Ames claimed that the trans-Rockies route had not been determined when the contract was approved by the railroad's directors in October, 1867. But Union Pacific's timetable maps for 1870–1871 show a trackage, excepting the extra 20 miles of the Seymour loop to Carbon Summit, of exactly 667 miles between the 100th meridian and the Wyoming-Utah border.

Was the Ames contract of September, 1867, deliberately written to end on the threshold of Utah Territory and the Latter-day Saints' "empire"? Did Congressman Oakes Ames, for political and perhaps even ethical reasons, insist that the construction contract bearing his name end at the Wyoming-Utah border because Crédit Mobilier was already developing

297

plans to hoodwink Brigham Young and the Latter-day Saints in a sequential trans-Utah contract? The financial crises created in Utah by Crédit Mobilier during 1868 and 1869 make both questions logical.

A contract to use Mormons to perform $1,000,000 worth of grading and bridge construction across Utah was signed during the last week of May, 1868. The *Deseret News* of May 27th stated in its lead editorial that "a contract for the grading of the road from the head of Echo Canyon to this city has been closed between S. B. Reed, Esq., acting in behalf of the company, and President Young." Young, in turn, subcontracted with Latter-day Saints church members, "capable and responsible," who would organize crews among their families and friends to build a mile or two of grade, blast out the tunnel approaches, or prepare the masonry for bridge abutments and piers.

The prices to be paid the subcontractors by Young ranged from 27¢ for a cubic yard of earth excavation and $3.60 a cubic yard for granite removal, to $13.50 for a cubic yard of "masonry in bridge abutments and piers, laid in lime mortar or cement, beds and joints dressed, drafts on corners, laid in courses." The Reed-Young agreement stated, and the *Deseret News* stressed the fact, that "Eighty per cent of the above prices will be paid monthly as the work progresses, the remaining 20 per cent will be paid when the entire job is finished and accepted."

Negotiation of such a contract emphasizes the involved financing of Union Pacific—a legal nightmare in contrast to the brash monopoly of Central Pacific's Associates—and again poses the question of a deliberately rigged scheme by Durant, the Ames Brothers and their Crédit Mobilier allies to use Latter-day Saints Church credits to finance the right of way through the Wasatch canyons. Sam Reed signed the contract as superintendent of construction. But the Ames Contract ended at the Wyoming-Utah line. The sequential master contract for Union Pacific's construction from the Wyoming-Utah line to "junction with the Central Pacific" was not approved by Union Pacific's board—and reassigned to Crédit Mobilier—until October, 1868. This was more than four months after the Mormon gangs went to work in the canyon.

The Utah economy that spring was in dire need of new sources of revenue. The Latter-day Saints' experiments in cotton farming, sericulture, wine grapes and even sugar-beet processing, had proved expensive failures. And other agricultural production had not kept pace. Utah needed more wool, flax and grain and far larger beef and dairy herds to feed, clothe and provide employment for the thousands of converts migrating into the Promised Land.

"Just think how many things could be raised and manufactured here that would fetch very remunerative prices," General Daniel H. Wells, the Utah War hero, complained in a sermon he delivered at the New Tabernacle. "Butter that at the present time is selling for a dollar and a quarter a pound, in a country like this should not bring more than twenty-five cents. Cheese the same. These two articles are imported twelve to fifteen hundred miles, and then the Territory is not near supplied . . . Wheat is selling today at four dollars the bushel, when it should not be more than half that price. It is so with every other article of our own consumption."

The *Deseret News'* editorials about the contract with Union Pacific could "see great cause for thankfulness," because "Now, no man need go East, or in any other direction, in search of employment. There is enough for all at our very doors and in the completion of a project in which we are all interested. Coming as it does when there is such a scarcity of money and a consequent slackness of labor, it is most advantageous . . . Those who owe may pay their debts, and have the necessary funds to send for machinery and establish mercantile houses in the various settlements."

In joyous anticipation, storekeepers opened their stocks for credit buying by the subcontractors Young approved. Sam Reed had promised that the railroad would deliver "all the necessary supplies . . . to the terminus of the Railroad, which those who take contracts can make arrangements for obtaining in any necessary quantity." But railhead was still 300 miles east of Echo. Wagon trains had to be organized to bring the stuff in. Meanwhile the subcontractors ran up local bills for provisions and other supplies needed at the canyon camps.

The Latter-day Saints' response was so speedy and their organization so prompt that some of the camps were forced to wait a month or longer for Blickensderfer and his surveyors to drive location survey stakes and tell the crew bosses where and how to grade their sections. Most of the tent and shack colonies had been built before Grenville Dodge rode into Echo during early July. On the day of the Durant-Dodge showdown at Fort Sanders, Edward Sloan rode to the head of Echo to establish what the *Deseret News* called the "Railroad in the Canons Bureau." The reports he sent back to Salt Lake City during the next eight months provide the best panorama extant of the Great Iron Trail's gargantuan routine. On July 31 he wrote:

> The line runs along the mountain on the east of the little *cañon* and the side rolls with dips and spurs which make a succession of heavy fills and cuts. Bishop Sheets has about three quarters of a mile which commences with a high embankment where it joins Bishop Young's 2800 fill ... There is a cut and fill along the side of the mountain in this contract, 350 feet long, where the ground is so precipitious that it has to be terraced to hold the earth thrown down, or there would be danger of the whole sliding away when melting snows and Spring loosen the earth. Then follows a cut 300 feet long, which is thirty-seven feet deep on the upper side and 13.5 on the lower side, most of it through decomposing rock. A small fill of 100 feet and a cut of 250 feet and about ten feet deep, is followed by a fill of some 1,550 feet, of which Bishop Sheets does 150 feet, J. W. Young doing the other 1,400. There is a culvert under this 110 feet; and another 120 feet will come in the heavy fill further down. The Bishop has sixty-five men and eighteen teams at work and wants more help.

He visited Tunnel No. 1 and found "about 150 men at work . . . who work in shifts, and thus keep at it night and day. The contractors expect to get through it by the first of March; and the intention is to cut through with machinery, driving the drills by steam."

The "absence of profanity, disorder or quarrels was highly gratifying," he continued. "In but one camp of less than one hundred men, out of between two and three thousand working in the two *cañons*, did I hear profanity; and it is not likely to be tolerated there long . . . Order governs, harmony reigns and the best of feelings exist. After the day's work was done, the animals turned out to herd and the supper over, a nice blending of voices in sweet singing proved that the materials exist among the men for a capital choir, and there is some talk of organizing one. Soon after the call for prayers was heard, when the men assembled and reverentially bowed before the Author of all blessings."

Three thousand men digging and blasting through the gloomy red gorges of Echo Creek and Weber River proclaimed that Utah would become the battleground for the final handouts of Federal bonds and grant-land deeds to the Pacific Railroad builders. Leland Stanford arrived from Central Pacific's railhead sometime during June, 1868, engaged a suite at Hotel Newhouse, and bustled up to the Lion House. His letters to Mark Hopkins indicate that he was in Salt Lake City most of the time until December and was soon on a first-name basis with Young.

Grenville Dodge, Mrs. Dodge and Sidney Dillon reached Salt Lake City on August 12. J. R. Perkins alleges, in the official Dodge biography, *Trails, Rails and Wars,* that Dodge and Dillon immediately made an appointment with Samuel Montague to seek an agreement on a Central Pacific-Union Pacific meeting point west of Salt Lake. "The chief engineer of the Central Pacific shook his head," Perkins wrote. "He did not possess the authority in dealing with his road that Dodge assumed in constructing the Union Pacific. But he did convey the pleasing information that the Central Pacific had also decided to build north of Salt Lake." Dillon was in Salt Lake City with Dodge, thus Dodge could not have "assumed authority" in suggesting a junction point agreement to Montague. Dillon and Dodge spoke with the approval of the Ames Brothers and the Crédit Mobilier majority. Furthermore, Leland Stanford was in the same hotel and would have been consulted, just as Huntington could have been queried by telegraph or through a conference with Oakes Ames in Washington. What seems more probable is that Dillon, Stanford, Dodge and Montague met several times during mid-August to argue about the trans-Utah "route plan" that Huntington had filed with the Department of the Interior. It was also logical to consult on the route around Salt Lake, then determine who would break the news of Salt Lake City's by-pass to Brigham Young.

Either Dodge or Dillon decided to make the first announcement of the northern route to Young, or Stanford passed along the insinuation that Central Pacific we being forced to build north of the lake, too, because of Union Pacific's decision to by-pass the City of the Saints. Dodge, at eighty, recalled a fiery sermon in the Tabernacle during which Young denounced him for "influencing the Union Pacific Company to build north of the lake."

But there were deeper reasons for Young's outburst. Three months had passed since Reed and Young had signed the grading contract. The Echo Canyon subcontractors had finished the thirty miles of tortuous embankment between Wasatch and Echo City and were putting the finishing touches on bridges and working double shifts on the tunnels. But Union Pacific was just getting around to the master contract for James Davis. Not a nickel of the "80 per cent a month" payments had been seen in Salt Lake City. The Canyon workers were complaining; their families were complaining; the Eastern jobbers were harrying the storekeepers who harried the subcontractors, who in turn rode into Temple Square and harried Young. Any thundering Brigham Young did about the Salt Lake City by-pass had the heady steam-up of Union Pacific's no-pay tactics to push it into a Sunday morning sermon.

Leland Stanford either heard the sermon—with silent glee —or picked up its Monday-morning reverberations. He wired Huntington. Huntington pressured both the White House and Secretary of the Interior Browning for the two-thirds "advance payment" on the bonds for Central Pacific's trans-Utah route. Secretary Browning veered to Huntington's views and began urging the Treasury Department to hand over the bonds.

Coincidentally, Charles Crocker was experiencing a series of segregation threats about "that damned coolie labor." On December 1, 1867, a mob of 150 white miners at French Corral, Nevada, had assembled on the claim of Scharden & Bell, driven off all the Chinese employed there, and burned their shacks. Warrants were issued for 88 of the mob. On the day of the hearing the 88 marched through Nevada City to the courthouse with a hired band and a color guard. The judge fined David Norrie, the alleged ringleader, $100 but postponed the trial of the other 87 "indefinitely." When Crocker's 12,000 Chinese deployed across the Truckee Meadows three months later, threats to "burn 'm out" began to burgeon down from Virginia City saloons. The Chinese grade camps would extend 200 miles beyond railhead. One mob of half-drunk Vigilantes from a mining camp could trigger a race war that would cripple construction for months and forfeit all of Utah to Union Pacific. Crocker and Trowbridge appealed to the Army. From May on, United States Cavalry patrolled the work camps.

Stanford feared a spread of the Anti-Coolie Labor Association's propaganda into Utah. Forthright editorials in the *Deseret News* against the "exploitations of Chinese labor" revealed the Latter-day Saints' attitude. Huntington reported excellent progress in his efforts for trans-Utah bonds. And Union Pacific was in disgrace on Temple Square because of the delinquencies on the Reed-Young contract. Early in September, Stanford closed with Young on a Mormon grading contract for Central Pacific to build right of way between Weber Canyon and the Nevada Line. He guaranteed $3 to $6 a day for manual and skilled labor and $10 a day for wagonmen. And he gave a cash down payment.

News of the contract traveled to New York. Early in October, Grenville Dodge returned to Salt Lake City with Thomas Durant. They appeared, in public, to be on amiable terms. The suite they engaged at Hotel Newhouse was near Stanford's. Presumably this was a first meeting for the two ex-Albanians. But there is no evidence that either was in the mood to reminisce. Durant paid off part of the $500,000 overdue on the Sam Reed contract, then began negotiations for a second grading contract with Young. He was of course consistent in his double dealings. And he seems not to have shared Stanford's scruples about using "coolie labor" for the Union Pacific embankment that was to parallel Central Pacific's across Utah. On October 10 Durant sent a telegram to Ted Judah's co-founder of Central Pacific, D. W. Strong, at Dutch Flat, California. It authorized Dr. Strong to "contract with Ah Him or Ah Coon or any responsible party" for 2,000 Chinese laborers to be delivered to Union Pacific's agent at Central Pacific's Nevada railhead. Durant offered wages of $40 in gold for a month of 26 working days, free transportation of tents and cooking utensils, and "soldier protection." Strong did not answer the telegram or its sequels. Grudgingly, Durant signed a second contract with Young for Mormon grading.

The three contracts meant a total of $3,000,000 worth of construction labor for the Mormons. The largest problem, Young now knew, would be to collect the money. Beyond that it was a battle between giants. The land they would blast and gouge was largely desert. Again the call went out for subcontractors on the Pacific Railroad. Durant wanted a mile or two of bank thrown up near the Nevada line in order to substantiate Union Pacific's claim to land grants and loans across

Utah. Stanford feinted back by ordering a few miles of Central Pacific grade up Weber Canyon toward the bleak cliffs of Devil's Gate.

But the earnest race developed that fall across the wastelands north of the lake. There for 200 miles Mormon friends and neighbors built rival base camps 100 feet apart and began work on two embankments that had been deliberately surveyed to crisscross each other. Stanford complained to Mark Hopkins that Blickensderfer's surveyors were running so many lines, "some crossing us and some running within a few feet of us, and no work on any, that I cannot tell you exactly how the two lines will be." Later he grumbled that, "The U.P. have changed their line so as to cross us five times with unequal grades between Bear River and Promontory. They have done this purposely as there was no necessity for so doing . . . We shall serve notices. . . ."

The Mormon crews entered into this fox play with zest. A gang of Union Pacific graders "borrowed" dirt from a Central Pacific embankment to fill their own; the Central Pacific gang stole out before evening prayers and shoveled it back into their line. The sport became dangerous when gangs began to work on parallel rock cuts. "The two companies' blasters work very near each other," the *Deseret News* reported, "and when Sharp & Young's men first began work the C. P. would give them no warning when they fired their fuse. Jim Livingston, Sharp's able foreman, said nothing but went to work and loaded a point of rock with nitro-glycerine, and without saying anything to the C.P., 'let her rip.' The explosion was terrific . . . and the foreman of the C. P. came down to confer with Mr. Livingston about the necessity of each party notifying the other when ready for a blast." (Thirty years later, Grenville Dodge recalled that "the laborers upon the Central Pacific were Chinamen, while ours were Irishmen, and there was much ill feeling between them. Our Irishmen were in the habit of firing their blasts in the cuts without giving warning to the Chinamen on the Central Pacific working right above them. From this cause, several Chinamen were severely hurt. Complaint was made to me by the Central Pacific people, and I endeavored to have the contractors bring hostilities to a close but, for some reason or other, they failed to do so. One day the Chinamen, appreciating the situation, put in what is called a 'grave' on their work, and when the Irishmen right under them were all at work let go their blast and buried several of our men. This brought about a truce at once. From that time on the Irish laborers showed due respect for the Chinamen, and there was no further trouble." The General Dodge story, like many Old West legends, appears to be apocryphal. Neither "Anon" nor any of the reporters gathering for Pacific Railroad's finale published anecdotes about an Irish-Chinese blasting feud. The Dodge story appears to have had its origin in the *Deseret News* episode about the Mormon grading gangs.)

Stories about "the rowdies, the gamblers, the patrons of drinking saloons" pacing Union Pacific's railhead in from the states created fear in all the communities of northern Utah. Hell on Wheels and its bloody sequel of "necktie parties" and Vigilantes proclaimed the wave of the future for Ogden, Logan, Farmington and perhaps even Salt Lake City and Provo. "Such people," warned the *Deseret News* as early as June 8, 1868, "think the world owes them a living. They hatch mischief and breed trouble wherever they go. Vice and vicious indulgences are congenial to them. We have no room for such characters, much less sympathy."

"It is a capital idea for our citizens," Editor George Cannon later advised his readers, "to have loaded firearms in their dwellings in all localities where there is the least reason to suspect or anticipate the visits of such characters. A gentleman of this city has written us a letter containing a good suggestion on this subject. He advocates the idea of a shrill whistle, something like those used by policemen in the East, being on hand in every house in localities infested by this lawless element, so that in case of alarm the blowing of the whistle, never to be had recourse to except in such cases, would speedily call assistance."

The approach of the East's "rowdies" was the more ominous because of the 5,000 husbands and sons working on railroad contracts, 50 to 200 miles from home. Mormon wives were used to frontier hardships. Most of them were as skilled as their husbands in operating homesteads; some were deft herdswomen. But, as the *News* deplored with unconscious male superiority, guns were "not of much avail in the hands of women, from the fact that many of them have not nerve and pluck enough to use them."

That winter, too, the prices of farmstuffs soared. Both Central Pacific and Union Pacific were working in desert wilderness. It was cheaper to haul hay, grain and foodstuffs out of Utah than it was to interrupt the flow of construction materials along the single tracks out of Omaha and Sacramento. The railroaders' bids sent hay to $100 a ton, potatoes to $7 a bushel, oats to $10 a bushel. But, in the American tradition, most of the profits went to jobbers and middlemen. And they were forced to "put it on the books." Crédit Mobilier was reneging again on payments for the grade contracts, as well as the provisions. Thus the realization of the Pacific Railroad, urged by leaders of the Latter-day Saints for a generation, was heralded by inflation, family hardships and widespread dread of the Era of the Rowdies.

The week before Christmas, 1868, the word came. Edward Sloan was writing another series of work-camp reports for the *Deseret News*. He wrote from Echo City on the 20th:

> The stubborn facts are before us. But thirty days since, one stone dwelling-store . . . an inn, with an outhouse, one tippling shanty, Wells Fargo & Co.'s rude quarters, a telegraphic operation, and a half-occupied log cabin or two . . . were the "teeth and toe nail" of Echo City. Today I have counted . . . exclusive of the U. P. R.R. buildings, some fifty structures, most of them true enough, mere duck tenements . . . Under this vigorous spread of cotton luxuriate wholesale and retail groceries, dry goods,

general merchandise, clothing, hardware . . . bakeries, black-smith and wagon shops, cheap Johns, carpenter shops . . . saloons, doggeries, whiskey-holes, dram-barrels, gambling-hells . . . restaurants, eating places, lunch covers, pie and gin resorts, corrals, hotels under shingles and dimity, "private dwellings," whence feminity stalks out with brazen publicity . . . expressly denominated here as *nymphs du grade* . . . This is but the be-ginning. Since it has become so certain that the locomotive will reach the mouth of Echo, the whole paraphernalia of Terminitish-Babylon has disgorged itself towards this fated spot. They are coming, coming, coming.

That same day Central Pacific's coolies were finishing the warehouses of a new base camp at Carlin, Nevada, while rail-head clanged toward the mining-boom town of Elko, 90 miles from the Nevada-Utah border. The day of the Railroad was at hand for the Promised Land, and all the "gluttonies of the flesh" that paced it.

CHAPTER **24**

KIDNAP

The rocks were worn in various forms—grand old towers, castles and cathedrals. We passed an emigrant encampment. The cattle were tethered nearby, and the long, low wagons stood out in bold relief against the clear grey sky. There was something very picturesque in their bright costumes and in their roughly constructed tents. Great fires had just been lighted for the night. The sun had gone down, and only a rich crimson glow was left in the west that lighted up the party, and made a picture of exquisite beauty. The engine thundered by, and we soon left them far behind. . . . Reverend F. W. Damon, Editor of *The Friend,* Honolulu, written on one of the first through trains of the Pacific Railroad (May 13, 1869).

The socio-economic changes that paced Union Pacific's tracks across Nebraska and Wyoming and into Utah changed the nation's concept of the West. The Whitney-Benton dream of a throughway to India had persisted with politicians and promoters since the 1830's. During 1867 and 1868 it was replaced by the potentials of a New West that was not a desert, but could be cropped, timbered, mined and urbanized almost as thoroughly—and devastatingly—as the Ohio Valley or the Mississippi Basin. The mirage of a Great Iron Trail for the goods of Europe and the wealth of Asia resolved into the Promised Land of Mormon and camp-meeting prophecy.

The hope of an American monopoly on the Europe-Asia traffic was dead. In June, 1868, Henry M. Stanley was in Egypt. A day or two later he began filing a series of articles from Port Said to the New York *Herald* about the "canal through Suez." More than 20,000 Arabs and Europeans were at work on the vast ditch, and engineers agreed that it would be open to deep-water traffic between the Mediterranean and the Red Sea by October, 1869. The channel depth was 26 feet; the width would vary from 180 to 300 feet. It could handle the largest freighters and passenger ships. Bombay would be 7,000 miles from London instead of the 11,000 miles via Capetown or the 20,000 around Cape Horn. The Pacific Railroad, Stanley made clear, was being built ten years too late to profit from the Europe-Far East trade. His prediction was seconded by General Charles W. Darling, Engineer in Chief for the State of New York, and others who inspected "the great Suez works" that year.

These opinions may have influenced the planning of Union Pacific and Central Pacific. At least, two distinct methods of financing became obvious about this time. Central Pacific's Associates determined to gamble their profits on the development of a railway and steamship empire that would bring them a virtual monopoly on West Coast traffic, from Oregon to Mexico and east to Utah and Louisiana. But most of Union Pacific's directors swung around to Durant's cynical conviction that the only profits they could expect would come via the deceits of the Crédit Mobilier construction contracts and the sale of land grants. The decisions veered Central Pacific's owners toward creation of the gigantic Southern Pacific Company and lured Union Pacific toward a national scandal and eventual bankruptcy.

Central Pacific's expansion program on the Pacific Coast began in 1867 when its Contract & Finance Company took over the tottering Western Pacific Railroad and completed its

trackage between Sacramento and San Jose. In 1868, negotiations began for the San Francisco & San Jose Railroad. In
September, 1868, the Associates organized the San Francisco
Bay Railroad, assigned the construction contract to their Contract & Finance Company, and hired another 2,000 Chinese
to build a line 26½ miles from Oakland to a Western Pacific
junction. Coincidentally, they opened ferry lines into San
Francisco from Oakland and Alameda. By the time the race
with Union Pacific ended the Big Four owned all of the railroad routes into San Francisco, operated ferryboat and steamship lines through the bay, and were in a position to launch
railroads south and southeast from San Jose and north to
Oregon.

During the same years Union Pacific's directors merely
wrangled and grubbed dividends for Crédit Mobilier. In the
fall of 1868, rumor spread through Echo and Weber Canyons
that Union Pacific would start its grade toward the Snake River
and Oregon "within a few weeks"; the *Deseret News* deemed
the story valid enough to print. But the order never came;
Union Pacific construction from Granger, Wyoming, to a junction with the Oregon Short Line did not begin until 1880.
Another opportunity was lost by the Ames-Durant failure to
beat the Kansas Pacific into Denver via the obvious water-
level route up the South Platte from Julesburg. (The Colorado
Central built this trackage before 1875.) Similarly, no effort
was made to win Arizona and Southern California traffic via
Brigham Young's proposed route southwest from Ogden
through Salt Lake City and St. George.

Union Pacific's tracks virtually created Nebraska and Wyoming and could have dominated Colorado, Utah, Idaho, Oregon, Arizona and Southern California as well. The reason for
the Ames-Durant failure to do this traces back to Crédit Mobilier and Thomas Durant's gambler's urge to "grab a wad
from the construction fees—and get out." A comparison of
statistics supports this conclusion. Crédit Mobilier's charges to
Union Pacific Railroad and Telegraph Company for the 1,100

miles of track between Omaha and Promontory totaled $93,-546,287 in cash and bonds—a contemporary gold value of more than $77,000,000. Thus construction costs were billed at an average of $70,000-plus per mile. Central Pacific's involved accounts' juggling of the Associates, the Crocker Construction Company and the Contract & Finance Company indicates construction costs averaging $64,000 a mile between Sacramento and Promontory.

But the construction charges paid to subcontractors and provisioners by Crédit Mobilier totaled only $50,720,000, or little more than $45,000 per mile—$19,000 a mile *less* than the cost estimates finally pried out of the Big Four by Federal investigators during the 1880's. The $27,000,000 difference between Crédit Mobilier's charges to Union Pacific and its payments to subcontractors could, at $45,000 per mile, have financed construction of a Pacific Coast outlet for Union Pacific to either Portland or Los Angeles.

Reports on freight and passenger revenues during the construction years are just as revealing. Both lines operated freight, mail and passenger services between terminals and railhead. Central Pacific's revenue between 1864 and the end of 1869 totaled $10,799,849. Costs of $4,561,922 were charged against this. The road conceded a net income of $6,237,927 on transportation services.

Union Pacific did not open public transportation services out of Omaha until 1867. During the next three years (1867–70 inclusive) it listed revenues of $20,888,669—almost twice as much as Central Pacific admitted for the 1864–69 period. But Union Pacific billed $15,416,288 of this to "operational costs" and conceded a net income of only $5,472,381—$765,-546 *less* than Central Pacific's conceded net on approximately one half as much business.

Consistent with this policy, Crédit Mobilier declared five more dividends between January 3 and December 29, 1868, with a face value of $14,786,022 and a contemporary cash value of $9,003,214. During the same months Union Pacific was running into debt and frantically making loans, at 15- to 20-per-cent annual interest, to meet operating and equipment costs plus the payments to Crédit Mobilier. By the summer of 1869 Union Pacific's current debts exceeded $6,000,000.

This was the economic chaos dominating New York head-quarters while Sam Reed and the Casements cajoled the gangs into new records across the most brutal terrain of the line. Somehow they bluffed around the paymasters' persistent fail-ure to show up, outtalked—or strong-armed—the crews who threatened to strike, then as winter neared stepped the work week to seven days with promises of double pay for Sundays—when the paymaster did roll in from Omaha.

In late July the Casements poised at the new town of Ben-ton. Just why Benton was located on the desert six miles from the oasis of General Rawlins' Spring remains a mystery. It was Union Pacific's only tribute to Senator Benton and a scurvy one. "The streets were eight inches deep in white dust as I en-tered the city of canvas tents and polehouses," wrote J. H. Beadle in *Underdeveloped West*. "The suburbs appear as banks of dirty white lime, and a new arrival with black clothes looks like nothing so much as a cockroach struggling through a flour barrel. The great institution of Benton was 'The Big Tent' . . . a nice frame building 100 feet long and 40 feet wide, covered with canvas and conveniently floored for dancing, to which and gambling it was entirely devoted . . . Twice every day immense trains arrived and departed, and stages left for Utah, Montana and Idaho. All goods formerly hauled across the plains came here by rail and were reshipped . . . The streets were filled with Indians, gamblers, 'cappers,' saloonkeepers, merchants, miners, and mulewhackers."

Benton's life span was too brief for Vigilantes to organize. By August 11 it was Wyoming's first ghost town. The Case-ments were averaging more than two miles of track a day. Ironmen and graders learned the value of the Mexican som-brero that summer; sunstroke built a trail of graves through

Bitter Creek, Point of Rocks and Salt Wells. Crew bosses sent out youngsters with six-shooters to clear rattlesnakes off a section before the shovelmen and dump carts moved in. Mule deer, elk, moose and antelope fed in the blue-gray shadows of the buttes. With sage hens and now and then a few piquant, porklike prairie dogs, they provided the most varied protein diet yet. But the Irish, Cornish and Scandanavians still favored a feast of beef from the Casement's railhead herd.

The Army's concessions to the Indians in the Fort Laramie and Fort Bridger treaties ensured peace along the railroad. A Sioux war party led by Roman Nose jumped Major George "Sandy" Forsyth and 28 cavalrymen at a fork of the Republican River south of Julesburg that summer. (Frederic Remington would immortalize the battle in a painting.) Another Sioux party derailed a Union Pacific train near Oglalla, Nebraska, but fled when the passengers began slamming lead into them from the coaches. In Wyoming the most dangerous assignments of the summer for North's Pawnee Scouts were to hunt down mules and horses spooked out of the grade camps by young Shoshone and Arapaho and to order away the squaws operating cut-rate "cribs" in the brush.

The Hell on Wheels' blacklegs and the Vigilantes were the actual Western savages of the Wyoming crossing. The "masked-rider" mode spread east to Sidney, Nebraska, where 100 hooded Vigilantes surrounded a jail, called out two prisoners accused of gun murders, hung them and rode off. Laramie's first mayor and city officials resigned the week after the Dodge-Durant harangue on Main Street; neither Durant nor the Town Lots Company invited the Army in for a spell of martial law. Gamblers, pimps and gunmen ruled the town until August when a Vigilante Committee of 20 lynched a tough known as "the Kid." Thereafter the Vigilantes began active recruiting, and by October had 500 members. Most of them gathered for an assault on the gambling casinos and Cribhouse Row on the night of October 29. Five men were killed and 15 wounded in gun fights. Before dawn four more

"Hell-towners" dangled from telegraph poles along the Union Pacific tracks. Vigilantes patrolled the streets on Election Day; the second city government stayed put.

The routine persisted at Bryan, Bear River City and Wasatch. At Wasatch, in 1869, travelers were told, "Out of 24 graves here, but one holds the remains of a person who died a natural death—and she was a prostitute who poisoned herself." Bryan, thirteen miles west of Green River, was another of the division points. Masons built machine shops and a 12-stall roundhouse. A stage line began semiweekly runs to South Pass and the Sweetwater mines. Hell on Wheels paused for a few weeks; the usual brawls followed; a Vigilante Committee formed.

At Bear River City, within shouting distance of the Utah line, Legh Freeman and the *Frontier Index* finally met their comeuppance in the same freebooter way. The Freemans unloaded their press at the townsite sometime during October, and, typically, began to boom the location as "the Queen City of Western Wyoming." The Town Lots Company, meanwhile, decided on another townsite two miles away, and named it Evanston for Silas Seymour's favorite victim, Engineer John Evans. Both communities became trade and amusement centers, not only for the grading and bridge gangs, but for hundreds of tie hacks working in Bear Valley forests. The Freemans claimed 15,000 circulation for *Frontier Index;* the issues averaged fifteen columns of display advertising by Chicago, Salt Lake City, Laramie, and Bear River City merchants.

Again gunmen moved in with saloons and cribwomen. Drunks were robbed and garroted; holdups became a nightly commonplace. On November 10 a Vigilante Committee formed at Bear River City, picked up a gunman called "Little Jack O'Neil" and two companions, and hung them. The rumor spread that Legh Freeman was "Chief of the Vigilantes." Freeman pungently denied it in the *Frontier Index,* issue of November 13, but added, "We are in favor of hanging several more who are in our midst . . . There are plenty of men who rather delight in doing the dirty work of hanging without us, as was evidenced Tuesday night, and as will be witnessed again if the ring leaders are found in town by midnight of this Friday, November 13."

The standard recital of the riot that followed claimed that friends of the hanged men incited tie hacks and grade gangs against Freeman, and led them in an assault on the Index office. But the real reason for the mob may have stemmed instead from the lead editorial in that same November 13th issue. Legh Freeman was in a foul mood; General Grant's election over Horatio Seymour had just been conceded. Freeman poured Secesh bitterness into his editorial:

WHAT WE EXPECT—PREPARE FOR THE WORST

Grant, the whiskey bloated, squaw ravishing adulterer, monkey ridden, nigger worshipping mogul is rejoicing over his election to the Presidency. On the fourth of March next, the hellborn satrap will (if he be alive) assume the honors (?) and robe of a DICTATOR . . . The road to the White House which Grant has traveled over during our last campaign is paved with the skeletons of many thousand soldiers whom he slaughtered uselessly during his western and southern military career. A blindly infatuated people seem to have rejoiced over the actual murder of their friends and kindred—Eastern mothers must tremble for the safety of their daughters' virtue, knowing that the gaudy military uniform of their President and *ruler* covers the filthy, lecherous carcass of a libertine, seducer and polygamic squaw keeper. . . . Time only will tell how this "elevation of one of the mob" will end, and in the meantime we advise our friends to be prepared for the worst. Booth still lives. *Sic semper tyrannis.*

Thousands of Union Pacific's builders were Union Veterans; both Grenville Dodge and Jack Casement had served under Grant as generals; Grant was still the Army's Commanding General. The facts have never been clarified about the march on Bear City that shaped up after the November 13th issue reached the graders and tie-hack camps. Legh Freeman later claimed that he was "done in" by "General Williamson, the Crédit Mobilier Town Lot agent at Fort Bridger." The Salt

Lake City *Daily Telegraph* of November 20 shrilled that "The telegraph informs us that a terrible state of affairs exists at the magic city of Bear River. Some 200 rioters have possession of the city; they have burnt down the offices of the *Frontier Index* and fears are entertained that the whole city will be destroyed. The muss arose from the action taken by the Vigilante Committee in hanging three men on the 11th instant, and it is stated that the citizens have fired upon the rioters, killing 25 and wounding 60."

Indications are that Legh Freeman signed the *Frontier Index* death warrant when he published that editorial. Union veterans roared in, told the Freemans to "git," smashed the press and burned the office. Legh and Ada Freeman went back to Bryan and announced plans for publication of the *Frontier Phoenix*. Legh covered the Golden Spike ceremony at Promontory the following May as editor of the new newspaper. In 1875, when the couple founded the Ogden *Freeman,* Legh was as vindictive as ever. His masthead slogan then read: ANTI-MORMON—ANTI-CHINESE—ANTI-INDIAN. That paper also failed.

The birth struggles of the new towns across Wyoming were of little interest to the Ames Brothers, Dillon and Durant. They nagged the Casements and Dodge for more speed. The Casements' contract demanded speed too. They badgered the ironmen to a new challenge. Central Pacific's Chinese were only 400 miles west. The Casements began posting daily "lay-down" by each road. The muttering trailed up the line: "No bunch of Chinamen's going to show us up!" Union Pacific's pace stepped up to three . . . four . . . five miles of new track a day. Slamming out of the Bitter Creek barrens toward Green River one September dawn, the gangs laid six miles before dusk and gasped in to dinner with the boast, "That'll show 'em!" But it didn't. A few days later Central Pacific laid seven miles in a 14-hour day.

Edward Creighton and a party of Iowans toured to rail-head in mid-October. In 1861 Creighton had built the first transcontinental telegraph along the Pony Express route. The Casements planned a record-breaking lay-down for his visit. The crews tumbled out at 4 A.M. and had the first half mile of rail down by sunrise. By sunset Union Pacific was seven and a half miles closer to Great Salt Lake.

A day or two later Crocker sent a wire to the Casements: THE CENTRAL PROMISES TEN MILES IN ONE WORKING DAY. The message was relayed in to Durant in New York. "Ten thousand dollars," Durant challenged, "that you can't do it before witnesses." Crocker replied, "We'll notify you," then told Strobridge to select a flat stretch somewhere along the head of Salt Lake. The potential of racism bothered him, though. He decided it would be best to use only Irish ironmen that day; no sense in asking for a race riot.

The aspen shivered naked in November fogs when the Casement gangs reached the 7,540-foot crest of the Bear River Divide. Fifty miles ahead the graders were making first contacts with the Mormons on the Echo and Weber Canyon digs. The zealous "Anon" recorded their arrival at Tunnelville, 12 miles below the mouth of Echo:

> At this stage of the work come along the company's swarms of "ould Ireland's" sons, direct from the scene of hostilities at Bear River . . . [They] at once supplanted the industrious "shifts" of Bishop Sharp. This Sunday morning the Bishop drew off his men to other work, giving the Celts full possession. Not fully aware of such change, this evening as I passed down, everything tunnelward seemed unaccountably metamorphosed. Not one familiar face, . . . When we crossed the river into Tunnelville, then I understood the cause. It is claimed by the newcomers that they "can put her through" (that is, the tunnel, of course) within six weeks, which if accomplished, will be doing more in that space of time than has been done during the past summer and fall. . . . Our estimable Bishop Sharp evinces no perceptible dullness under these cutting approximations. His new neighbors and he are upon very affable terms.

Trackage groped across the Utah line in snowstorms during December, and on Christmas Day was 966 miles out of Omaha at Wasatch. The year's build was 425 miles of main line and 100 miles of siding, plus machine shops and roundhouses at Laramie and Bryan and the spawn of a dozen towns. That week Central Pacific was operating trains 300 miles west of the California border. Its railhead probed toward Elko, the new treasure town for the White Pine mines.

Christmas in the Wasatch gloom was a respite of drugged sleep, with the snow piled above the train windows. Durant was there, in conference with the Casements and the division engineers. Sam Reed established division headquarters at Echo City and wrote his family in Joliet, Illinois, to "come out for the finish." Anon wrote of the warehouse where, "tools and supplies are issued to contractors, incredible as it may appear, to the enormous amount of $350,000 per month." On the morning of the 26th Durant sledged on to Tunnelville. Work must go on, he ordered; promise double wages if necessary.

During the next three months Union Pacific fought the white hell that the coolies had experienced around Summit Tunnel and on the Sierra's east slope. Both Dodge and Reed had erred by failing to provide snowshed protection for the Black Hills and Wyoming Basin. Central Pacific's 37 miles of snowsheds were finished; publicity releases out of Sacramento smugly announced that "no Central Pacific train is running more than two hours late." But from February on, Eastern papers carried successive features about Union Pacific trains stalled in Evans Pass . . . at Rawlins . . . on the Red Desert. At Echo the stockpiles of iron ran low. The Irish failed to "put'r through" at Tunnelville. Grade gangs sledged back into Echo to dig out snowdrifts 20 feet high so that track could be laid, without ballast, on the frozen earth. Anon wrote from there on March 24:

The track from Echo to this point is sadly in need of ballasting. . . . The ties were, for the most part, laid upon snow, with a chunk of ice, snow, or frozen clod crammed hastily underneath to "bring 'em up to the straight edge." Now that these arctic proppings have slid from under, the ties, instead of supporting the rails, hang dangling in the air, suspended from the rail by the spikeheads. In other places, the ties have "squashed" nearly out of sight in the slush of a winter finished grade. In other instances, below here, the entire grade has slid off into the river, or to the bottom, cars and all . . . Last night while Mr. Maltoy's train was dragging its slow length along over the 3,000 feet of trestle work around the tunnel point a box car, filled with humans, was thrown off the track and came frightfully close being precipitated into the river bed . . . This morning another one was thrown off of the same work. It is a ten degree curve and so sharp that it is grating business for any sized engine to drag a train through.

The curving trestle Anon described was around Tunnel No. 3, 508 feet long, in Weber Canyon. Tunnel No. 2, at the head of Echo, wasn't blasted through until January and didn't open for transit until mid-May, a week after the Golden Spike ceremony. To circumvent it, the Casements had laid track on river-bed trestles and up cliff faces in an awesome roller coaster 8 miles long.

Nitroglycerin was the standard explosive used on all the Wasatch tunnels. Again, Anon provides the best detail about its use:

> No blast in rock or rifled gun bears any comparison, in effective force, with glycerine. I saw a single drop . . . it was like a drop of olive oil . . . exploded by concussion with a hammer on a rock. It sounded like a musket. A few drops thus exploded go off with musket force. Even the empty glycerine cans are dangerous commodities . . . As they accumulate in camp, they are now put in some secure place and exploded by fire; and I am informed that, by the trifling smearings remaining in the cans, the tin is literally torn into fragments . . . With powder, the average progress in tunneling here was less than two feet per day of 24 hours. With glycerine, an average daily progress is made of about six feet, with but about one-third of the expense.

Anon also reported the existence of a glycerin house near the west end of Tunnel No. 3. It caught fire one morning in

March but was saved when "the glycerin man dashed in regardless of consequences, with two pails of water, by a judicious application of which he succeeded in quenching the flames." Presumaby this was only a storehouse, and the tins were freighted in from the manufacturing shack somewhere in the Black Hills or perhaps deep in the Wasatch. No historian has yet succeeded in running down a report about Union Pacific's nitroglycerin manufacturing shacks or the chemists who did the blending.

It was March when the ironmen swung through Devil's Gate, the lowering defile that tumbles Weber River out on the east slope of Salt Lake Valley. The bridge there, Mormon Elder John Taylor wrote to the *Deseret News*, ". . . has in it, I am informed, 180,000 feet of timber and was put up in one week . . . The mountain sides have fallen, the valleys have been exalted, the pathway has been made through the mountain fastnesses and the railroad is now *un fait accompli*."

A brass band led the parade through Ogden to meet the spikers at the head of Main Street. The street banners read HAIL TO THE HIGHWAY OF NATIONS! UTAH BIDS YOU WELCOME. Grenville Dodge, Sam Reed and the Casements rode down to share in the cheers; then they pleaded an "emergency" and asked to be excused from the afternoon's festivities.

Another message was in from Durant; Collis Huntington had won his campaign. The last official meeting of President Johnson's Cabinet on March 3 ordered the Treasury Department to turn the $2,400,000 worth of Federal bonds over to Central Pacific for the route across Utah. Secretary of the Interior Browning coupled it with a peremptory order to Union Pacific to "Halt all work west of Ogden." But on March 6, at his first Cabinet meeting, President Grant annulled the Johnson order, ruled that no bonds were to be issued to either Central Pacific or Union Pacific until a commission investigated "the Utah situation," and advised on a junction point for the completion of the Pacific Railroad. Dodge was to come to Washington at once.

"Stay with it," the four ruled that afternoon. "Trackage heads west at dawn. We should be able to win half of Utah, at least."

Over the 150 miles now separating the railheads, chaos began to thunder. Crocker and Strobridge ordered Chinese out to the Salt Lake ridges to supplement the Mormons. After March 1, hundreds of Union Pacific's veterans moved out too. The *Deseret News* stepped up its coverage of the race and on March 5th reported:

> Five miles west of Brigham City is situated the new town of Corinne, built of canvas and board shanties. The place is fast becoming civilized, several men having been killed there already. The last one was found in the river with four bullet holes through him and his head badly mangled. Work is being vigorously prosecuted on the U.P.R.R. and C.P.R.R., both lines running near each other and occasionally crossing . . . From Corinne west thirty miles, the grading camps present the appearance of a mighty army. As far as the eye can reach are to be seen almost a continuous line of tents, wagons and men.
>
> Junction City, 21 miles west of Corinne, is the largest and most lively of any of the new towns in this vicinity. Built in the valley near where the lines begin the ascent to the Promontory, it is nearly surrounded by grading camps . . . The heaviest work on the Promontory is within a few miles of headquarters. Sharp & Young's blasters are jarring the earth every few minutes with their glycerine and powder, lifting whole ledges of limestone rock from their long resting places, hurling them hundreds of feet in the air and scattering them around for a half mile in every direction.
>
> At Carlisle's works a few days ago four men were preparing a blast by filling a large crevice in a ledge with powder. After pouring in the powder they undertook to work it down with iron bars. The bars striking the rock caused an explosion; one of the men was blown two or three hundred feet in the air, breaking every bone in his body, the other three were terribly burnt and wounded with flying stones.

President Grant's Commission of Federal Investigators, headed by Major General G. K. Warren, rode into the desert, decided the situation was hopeless, and became a cheering gallery. On April 7 the Casement work train reached Corinne; Central Pacific's railhead was only 50 miles west.

Side by side, across a deep gorge on the east slope of Promontory Ridge, rival construction crews built crossings. Central Pacific decided on a durable fill, 170 feet high and 500 feet long; 500 coolies worked there, with 250 wagons, through February, March and early April. Silas Seymour ambled back in as Union Pacific's acting chief engineer when Dodge went to Washington. Seymour ordered a trestle, 400 feet long and 85 feet high, built across the gorge. A reporter for San Francisco's *Daily Morning Call* saw it nearing completion and wrote, "It will shake the nerves of the stoutest hearts of railroad travelers when they see that a few feet of round timbers and seven inch spikes are expected to uphold a train in motion."

One evening during the first week in April, President Grant summoned Dodge to a conference at the White House. The discussion lasted three hours. Grant threatened that unless Central Pacific and Union Pacific decided on a junction point within a week the Government would move in, stop all construction, and launch a full investigation of the finances of both companies. There are reasons for believing that Grant knew some of the details about the operation of Crédit Mobilier as well as those of the Associates. And he was intimately familiar with the Ames, Durant and Dodge enmities.

Huntington, Durant and Dodge went into conference on the morning of April 9. Dodge reported the White House interview. Huntington grumped but gave in. By dinnertime a contract had been drawn to join the two lines at Promontory Summit. Both companies would accept Federal bonds to an official terminal "within 8 miles west of Ogden." Central Pacific would buy Union Pacific's trackage between this legal terminal point and Promontory. On April 11, Congress approved the agreement by joint resolution. Orders went out to stop all grading except on a main line to Promontory Summit.

Quiet crept back over the desert. Idle crews gathered in Corinne's Hell on Wheels to brood about back pay and the prospects of layoff. Crocker sent telegrams to Stanford and Durant announcing that Central Pacific's "display" of 10 miles of tracklaying in one day would take place on Promontory's west approach beginning at dawn on April 29. Casements' ironmen sneered; there wouldn't be enough mileage left on Union Pacific's line to answer the challenge.

But Crocker promised a pageantlike race as a prelude to the Golden Spike ceremonies scheduled for the first week in May. And Durant had put up the $10,000 bet. A Palace car carried Durant, John Duff and a dozen other Union Pacific executives and their wives toward Utah sometime during the week of April 25th.

Writing from Sam Reed's Echo headquarters on April 27, Anon reported other details that have been puzzling historians ever since:

> The Hon. Sidney Dillon supersedes Dr. Durant in the general management of the U.P.R.R. This gentleman, together with Supt. S. B. Reed, Col. Seymour, Mark Seymour, H. M. Hoxie and two engineers passed down to the end of track on Friday evening last [April 23] to institute a final survey and measurement of the road, from Ogden to the Promontory Summit, prior to sale and transfer to the Central." [In other dispatches that week, Anon indicated that Dillon was using the Lincoln car, and stated that "a man was killed coupling it at Wasatch."]
>
> Through Weber Canyon the track is yet very wavy . . . Tunnel No. 3 fired its last glycerine blast yesterday. After a strike of two weeks for their wages, the workmen finally resumed three or four days ago. Tomorrow evening the first car will probably pass through this 508 feet of tunnel work. Four of the eight Howe Truss bridges to be put in below Lost Creek are already up . . . The longest bridges in the canyon are 300 feet span. The bridges are made in Chicago. Every piece of timber, every bolt, rod, plate and fastener of the bridge, exactly fitted, is laid down at the point

desired, from the cars. They are put together without any interruption of the trains.

The Palace car hooked onto the overnight train out of Cheyenne must have been creaking up the Bear River Divide during midmorning April 27 or 28. One of the car windows shattered; a bullet cracked into the woodwork; the engine slammed to a halt. Several of the party were thrown to the floor. A woman screamed. Durant, stooping to the level of the window ledges, scuttled to the vestibule and peered out. A gang of white men were crouched on the bank, guns trained on the car. Two of them started walking toward the car; one of them carried an uncoupling hammer.

Durant cowered for an instant, then stepped out to the platform and barked, "What's the meaning of this?" The men laughed and swung their guns toward him. The one hammering at the coupling pin stopped, spat, and straightened up. "Jes' a leetul layover, Dr. Durant," he drawled. "You're stayin' right here until we get our back pay. Anytime you wanta talk about it, we'll be here waitin'."

CHAPTER **25**

UNION

> *. . . that Peace may flow unto them as a gentle*
> *stream, and that this mighty enterprise may be unto*
> *us as the Atlantic of Thy strength and the Pacific of*
> *Thy love. . . .* Conclusion of Dedication Prayer, Rev-
> erend John Todd of Boston at Promontory Point
> (May 10, 1869).

James Strobridge and Bull Crocker clumped through camp by
starlight on April 28. They had hand picked 848 men and 41
teams of horses for the effort at the tracklaying record. Promontory Point was only 14 miles east; this was the last chance.
But if they fell short, Union Pacific could only try for a draw;
its ironmen were already within 9½ miles of Promontory.
Strobridge still wore a patch over the eye blinded by the glycerin blast at Summit. Crocker strode like a conqueror king
reviewing his troops. This would be his last day at railhead.
He was to ride back to Sacramento that night with Stanford to
represent the Associates at the May 8th celebration being organized in Sacramento for Golden Spike Day.

The crews moved out at dawn, Chinese tielayers and loaded
wagons in advance, trailed to trackhead by eight Irish ironmen.
The roadbed wound around the south flanks of the North
Promontory range, then over the Rozell Flats toward Promon-
326

tory Summit. The display was superb ballet. Sam Reed, the Casements, and a cluster of Union Pacific bosses watching it from a hilltop could only curse in admiration. Any criticism and envy they expressed, they realized, would be directed at themselves, because the coolies and Irishmen were demonstrating the time-and-motion studies and assembly-line formula that the Casements had pioneered by the invention of the work train in 1866, and both lines had perfected through experimentation and open spying on each other.

The Chinese, trotting in quickstep, literally danced the ties from wagons to roadbed on a bobbing belt of denim and coolie hats. The eight Irishmen paced behind them—heaving 120 feet of rail a minute from the cart, racing it to the ties—and stepping smartly aside so the spikers and fishplate men could move in. All without one misstep. The hammers clanged against the spikeheads in chorus; the wrenches flashed four times in full arc above the fishplates. The track aligners chorused crowbars forward until the foreman's arm dropped in the signal for "Hooold it!!" The line of Chinese ballasters flashed shovels and legs in the ludicrous tamping waddle of "the gandy dance." There were no steam-driven tools; no gadgets. This was Man, in primitive unity, demonstrating the ancient efficiency of his skill-of-the-hands, while on each horizon the symbol of a machine future fumed from locomotive stacks. The machine would have its day when the cowcatchers touched at Promontory. This was Glory Day for the men who had built the Great Iron Trail with bare hands and coordinated skills.

When Strobridge yelled "Lunch break!" at 1:30 P.M., the new high iron shimmered six miles across the flats. The Casements and Sam Reed cantered back to the Central Pacific's work train for lunch with Stanford, Crocker, Strobridge and Montague. Congratulations blended with jocular arguments about technique. Crocker finally snorted the guess that "Dr. Durant never had meant to show up." The comment was answered with such studied nonchalance that Stanford passed the word along to Central Pacific's Salt Lake City office that night to "do some investigating." (The Durant Kidnapping story broke in the San Francisco *Bulletin* on May 10.)

Strobridge had reserve crews waiting to step into any spot in the race, but the starters were lined up on the mark at 2:30. The ballet-precise march continued, stagelit by the blue shadows on the slopes. The "Lay off!" shout came after 7 P.M.— exactly 10 miles and 200 feet from the dawn starting line. During the 12 hours and 45 minutes of the work day Central Pacific's champions had placed 25,800 ties and 3,520 lengths of rail, driven more than 55,000 spikes, and screwed on 7,040 fishplates. The eight ironmen had carried more than 2,000,000 pounds of rail.

The Casements and Sam Reed rode back to their railhead. If they had only "talked"—then or years later—one of the most mysterious kidnappings in all the West's gun-spry history would have been clarified. Books and articles written about the Pacific Railroad's finale have consistently varied the date of the Durant-Duff kidnapping from May 5 through May 13. But all of these dates are contradicted by a May 2nd letter from Grenville to Anne Dodge, the on-the-scene dispatches filed by Anon, and the diary of Colonel Leonard H. Eicholtz, Union Pacific's bridge engineer.

Dodge, writing his wife from Devil's Gate on May 2, said:— "I am returning tonight from Promontory Point, writing in a car as I get a chance at the stopping places. *Dillon is at Echo; Duff and Durant are at Salt Lake.*" (Italics are the author's.) Both Anon's reports to the *Deseret News* and the Eicholtz diary assert that Dillon, *Durant* and *Duff* were all at Devil's Gate when spring floods wrecked the Weber River Bridge there between May 5 and May 8. Finally, Chicago and Salt Lake City newspaper reports indicate that Durant made a normal two-day journey east from Ogden to Omaha between May 13 and May 15. Via deductions, then, the indication is that the Durant-Duff kidnapping occurred on April 26 or 27 while

Durant was en route to Central Pacific's tracklaying on April 28.

Writing from Echo City on May 5, Anon gave *Deseret News* readers a hint of the anger seething against Union Pacific officials. "The U. P. seems rather disposed to retrenchment," he wrote. "Their pertinacity in clinging to funds is not a very sweet *morceau* to squads of contractors, some of the enterprising mercantile gents of Echo being also rather crusty over it." But the *Deseret News* failed to publish an account of the kidnapping—and for good reason. Suspicion points to the involvement of Mormons in the affair. Coincidentally, Union Pacific was more than $1,000,000 in arrears again on those "80-per-cent monthly" contracts with Brigham Young and the Latter-day Saints.

The first published report of the 36- to 48-hour "layover" by the Durant-Duff Palace car on the Bear River Divide alleged that the ransom figure demanded by the graders and tie hacks was "$12,000 due them in back wages." On May 13 the Reverend Charles Damon interrupted his transcontinental train journey for a day at Cheyenne and spent part of that evening composing a report on "Dr. Durant's Holdup" for *The Friend*, the Honolulu, Sandwich Islands, church magazine he edited. Reverend Damon fixed the kidnapping date only as "the week before the Golden Spike ceremony," of May 10, but stepped the ransom demand up to $253,000. J. R. Perkins, in *Trails, Rails And War,* stated that, "the contractors . . . wired the Union Pacific offices at Boston and said that the vice-president of the road would be held until the company paid its bills. President Ames, frantic lest Durant should meet with violence, wired Dodge at Salt Lake and told him to go and release the officials at all hazards. Dodge hurried a message to Fort Bridger and requested that a company of soldiers be sent to the scene of the trouble. But the soldiers never got there, for the telegraph operator at Piedmont, in sympathy with the workmen, took the dispatch off the wires. The contractors sent another message to Dodge warning him that the trouble would spread to a general tie-up unless the company met its obligations within twenty-four hours. Dodge telegraphed Oliver Ames for $1,000,000 to pay off hundreds of employees, including trainmen, who had received no money for months, and the president of the Union Pacific, alive to the situation, wired the full amount; the men were paid and the wheels began to move."

The New York *Sun* and the Damon accounts expanded on this by alleging that "if a military force had been sent to rescue Durant and his companions, teams were ready harnessed to have 'spirited' them away to the recesses of the mountains, where they would have been kept hostages until the money was paid."

The holdup must have been carefully planned, with fellow conspirators all along Union Pacific's route. The telegraph demand for ransom money to Oliver Ames in Boston simultaneously tapped its implications to every stationmaster and Army telegrapher along the 2,500 miles between Piedmont, Wyoming Territory and Boston. Army troops were stationed at Fort Bridger, less than 20 miles from the kidnap scene; other rescue expeditions could have been sent out from Echo City, Fort Steele or Fort Sanders.

The Army's failure to enter this showdown between Durant and the railroad workmen could have traced back to the opinions of Durant held by Army officers—especially after Durant's other showdown with Grant and Dodge at Fort Sanders in 1868. But equally puzzling are: the *Deseret News'* failure to report details and the date of the kidnapping; the coincidence of the $1,000,000 in back pay overdue to Brigham Young and the Latter-day Saints; and the missions tour of April 25–May 12 that "prevented" Brigham Young's presence at the Golden Spike ceremony on May 10.

The grand finale of the Pacific Railway was one of the greatest triumphs in Brigham Young's amazing lifetime. He and the elders had fought and pleaded for the Pacific Railway since 1852. Young was the first Far West subscriber to Union Pacific's initial stock issue in 1863. He had volunteered the services of Mormon grading crews, surveyors, blasters and tie hacks during the 1863–64 conference with Sam Reed. And, as Sam Bowles alleged—and Dodge also conceded—Union Pacific could not have won the race into Ogden without the heroic services of the Mormons. Still, between April 25 and May 12, 1869, Brigham Young took a tour of southern Utah.

There is not one shred of evidence to directly involve Brigham Young in the Durant-Duff kidnapping. But there is the unquestionable fact that he was the shrewdest politician and sagest judge of human instinct in the West. Three questions chuckle out a century later: Did Brigham Young suspect, or know, that "some of the boys" could not resist this golden opportunity to collect back-wages? Did he plan the April-May mission trip south so that he would not be involved if anything did happen? Did he stay away from Promontory Point on May 10 because, in St. George or elsewhere, the Deseret telegraph tapped the story of the kidnap to him, and he realized that Durant would still be "madder'n a dunked tom-cat" on Golden Spike Day?

Whatever happened, the Durant-Duff kidnapping did not . . . as the New York *Sun* and other correspondents assumed . . . cause the postponement of the Golden Spike ceremony from May 8 until May 10. Vanity was solely responsible. Again, Nature . . . or was it Manifest Destiny? . . . adjusted the time-table of the Pacific Railroad and mystically dictated its completion as an anniversary memorium to Theodore and Anna Judah.

Central Pacific built its trackage to Promontory Summit on May 1. Union Pacific installed its side track there on the same day, although glycerin crews were still blasting the route through Carmichael's Cut, four miles east, and carpenters hammered up the last golliwog span of the Big Trestle. Tracks were laid across it on May 5. A trainload of rails eased out on it. The structure squealed, swayed—and held. A few hours later the last blast banged in Carmichael's Cut. On the afternoon of May 7, Casements' ironmen finished the lay-down to the Promontory Summit side track. Sunset colored the storybook ending as Union Pacific's Engine No. 60, with Jack Casement aboard, hissed into the side track. Central Pacific's No. 66 Whirlwind was parked near its own railhead 100 feet away. Both engines "let go" with a raucous salute. This moment—6 years, 3 months and 29 days after Central Pacific's groundbreaking ceremony—was the meeting of the rails for the Pacific Railroad.

Meanwhile the layoff of grading gangs increased the crime in northern Utah. A series of gang rapes terrorized Ogden and Brigham. The *Deseret News* reported one such instance:

> Some days since, late in the evening, two men who had been working on the railroad obtained access to the home of Mr. G. Wolverton at North Ogden under pretext of wanting a night's lodging. Both were in liquor. Mr. Wolverton was away from home at the time, and the fiends taking advantage of his absence, ravished his wife and daughter. The latter is said to be about 13 or 14 years old. News of the affair having reached the police, they succeeded in capturing one of the men, named St. Clair. . . . When the news of this outrage reached the ears of Mr. Wolverton, he determined to rid the world of the monsters who had brought ruin upon his family. The police had confined St. Clair in the county jail at Ogden and Mr. W. watching his opportunity, as the prisoner was passing into his cell, emerged from the place in which he had concealed himself unknown to anyone, and shot St. Clair twice. Both bullets took effect, but did not kill the prisoner at once. Before his death, he acknowledged that both he and his companion forced the girl and her mother, and added that he felt free after having made the confession. He died the night before last.

Another ex-grader, "convicted of rape and sentenced to fifteen years imprisonment," was shot and killed by "the husband of the injured woman" while the penitentiary's warden was bringing the prisoner across the Weber River. "The husband," said the *News,* "was indicted by the grand jury for murder, and was tried yesterday. He was acquitted by the petit jury, who brought in a verdict of 'justifiable homicide.' "

On May 14, the Omaha *Herald* published an account of the experiences of a Henry Wolfe in Corinne on or about May 5.

> Mr. Wolfe says that on alighting from Wells, Fargo's coach at the end of U. P. track, about half a mile from [Corinne], on the 5th inst., he was seized and thrown into a wagon . . . The ruffians drove back to the city and conducted him into a small room, when producing a rope, they threatened to hang him unless he gave them everything valuable he possessed . . . he gave them $65 in gold, $7 in greenbacks, his valise, which with its contents he valued at $200, and a U. P. R. R. ticket from Junction City to Omaha. When Mr. Wolfe reached Brigham City, he obtained a warrant, and was directed to the U.S. Marshal in Corinne; he found the deputy Marshal, but he refused to serve the warrant unless he and his aide were paid $100 in cash. Having been robbed of all his means, he was unable to pay the money, and was compelled to go East without obtaining any assistance or redress, carrying his warrant along with him.

In Central Pacific's Camp Victory on May 6, two Chinese began a wrangle about a $15 debt. Sides formed, fist fights began, and by midafternoon a rampant free-for-all was in progress. "Both parties sailed in with every conceivable weapon," a correspondent of the San Francisco *Chronicle* wrote. "Spades were handled, and crowbars, spikes, picks and infernal machines were hurled between the ranks of contestants." Yung Wo, one of the initial arguers, was killed. Strobridge refused to comment on the total number of wounded.

> Colonel C. R. Savage, a Salt Lake City photographer, had been hired by Union Pacific. His diary tells us of a visit to the Casement camp on May 7: "In sight of their camp was the beautiful city of Deadfall and Last Chance. I was creditably informed that 24 men had been killed in the several camps in the last 25 days. Certainly, a harder set of men were never before congregated together. The company do the country a

service in sending such men back to Omaha . . . At Blue River the returning 'Democrats,' so-called, were being piled upon the cars in every stage of drunkenness. Every ranch or tent has whiskey for sale. Verily, men earn their money like horses and spend it like asses."

At Echo City, Anon was writing these details:

> The bridges in Weber Canyon are on the rampage. The past few days, sun has sent the liquidizing snows in torrents through their rugged course. First went under the wagon crossings . . . next . . . the . . . railroad crossings. The bridge at Devil's Gate commenced giving way last night. The 300 feet of trestle work at Strawberry Ford next evinced signs of "caving." The first bridge below the Narrows, or Slate Point, next succumbed.
>
> In consequence of these disasters, no train passed through the canyon yesterday and today. "All hands and the cook" have been summoned to the rescue. Car loads of lumber have rolled from the construction yard as on wings of lightning to the point of fracture, and every requisition has been made that could in any degree facilitate the work of reparation. *Vice Presidents Durant and Dillon and the Commissioners were also at the front to observe the situation and direct the repairs.* [Italics are author's.]

The diary of Colonel Eicholtz confirms Anon's report in detail, including the presence of "Durant, Dillon, Duff, Reed and Seymour" at the washed-out bridge. Eicholtz supervised construction of a 50-foot "strainbeam truss" for the broken span.

Dillon and Reed had been in Echo, negotiating settlement of a strike at Tunnel 3 and calming other back-pay demands. Durant and Duff, as confirmed by Dodge's letter of May 2, had gone on to Salt Lake City, quite possibly to arrange for distribution of some of the $1,000,000 to the Latter-day Saints and their contractors. They planned to meet Dillon at Ogden, then ride in state out to the Golden Spike ceremony.

But the Devil's Gate washout left Dillon's Lincoln car—and probably the Durant-Duff Palace car—stranded on the east bank of the gorge. Stanford and his "nabobs" from California, Nevada and Arizona were riding into Promontory in a luxuriously outfitted private train. Neither Durant nor Dillon wanted to face the jibes from Central Pacific and the nation's press if they arrived in a boxcar, or even in one of the Casements' sleeping cars. Vanity held them at Devil's Gate from May 5 until the late afternoon of May 9.

California's wave of enthusiasm that week was a stark contrast. From San Francisco to the Nevada mining camps, old bitternesses against the Associates were laid aside. Central Pacific concentrated all its publicity skills on the two-state celebration. Stanford and Hopkins suggested to David Hewes, one of Central Pacific's largest supplies contractors, that a solid-gold spike would be an appropriate object to highlight the dedication ceremony at Promontory. Hewes paid $350 for it and had it engraved with the names of all of Central Pacific's executives. The San Francisco *News Letter,* alert to a good promotion gimmick, presented a second gold spike. West Evans, the contractor supplying most of Central Pacific's ties, ordered a "last tie" in laurel wood, hand polished and waxed. Pacific Union Express Company rushed through a silver-plated sledge to be used for the "last blows." Nevadans cast a silver spike and sent it down from Virginia City. A. P. K. Safford, the new governor of Arizona, arrived from Tucson with a fourth spike, symbolically smelted from his Territory's iron, silver and gold. The outburst fired David Hewes' enthusiasm. He gave his jeweler a rush order for a number of "Last Spike" gold rings jeweled with moss agates, and for several inch-long gold spikes that could be used as watch fobs. (One of the fobs was purchased by an Air Corps pilot in Panama in 1941. He said he had bought it from a Polish flyer who alleged he bought it in Ethiopia from a French Army officer.)

The Stanford Special shrilled out of the Sacramento Station on the morning of May 6, the gold-and-silver implements on display in satin-lined cases in the drawing-room car. The guests aboard included General Sherman's brother William, Chief Justice S. W. Sanderson of California and Governor Safford

of Arizona. The train barely escaped a catastrophe next morning near the California-Nevada line. Chinese lumbermen were
cutting trestle timbers above the entrance to Tunnel No. 14.
A 50-foot log jumped the skid and fell into the right of way, its
3½-foot butt against a rail, just as the Stanford Special
rounded the tunnel approach curve. The log crippled the engine and ripped the steps off one side of Stanford's private car.
The tie-up delayed arrival at Reno until late morning. There,
presumably, Stanford first learned about the likelihood of postponement for the Golden Spike ceremony until the 9th or 10th,
due to the bridge washouts.

But it was too late to change the plans in Sacramento. More
than 25 special trains were bringing crowds into town on the
8th; some had already left. The Sacramento *Union* reported:

> The first delegation arrived as early as five A.M. It was a spe-
> cial train from Reno, bringing the Virginia and Golden Hill fire-
> men . . . Next came the trains from Colfax and Lincoln, bringing
> a vast delegation of military and citizens from Placer, Nevada,
> Yuba, Sutter, Butte and Colusa counties. Sixty-five extra cars
> were brought into requisition to accommodate these . . . By nine
> o'clock the city was crowded in all the principal streets with
> the largest, most orderly, and eager number of people ever col-
> lected here at one time . . . The signal which announced to all
> the laying down of the last rail and the driving of the last spike
> at Promontory Point was given by a shot from the Union Boy
> and simultaneous blasts from twenty-three locomotives on the
> levee and the ringing of all the bells in the town. This deafening
> clamor lasted for 15 minutes.

The May 8 signal of "the last blow" came from Charles
Crocker rather than from a telegrapher. It set off a mile-long
parade, a speech by Governor H. H. Haight, a "delicious col-
lation" of punch and free lunch, and an evening banquet at
which Crocker—after six years and four months of slander—
was cheered and recheered. His brief, proud speech was the
only one of the day that recognized the role of the Chinese.
"In the midst of our rejoicing," he reminded the thousand
guests, "I wish to call to mind that the early completion of this

railroad we have built has been in a great measure due to that poor, destitute class of laborers called the Chinese—to the fidelity and industry they have shown—and the great amount of laborers of this land that have been employed upon the work."

San Francisco took the cue from Sacramento and set off a three-day celebration by ringing the fire bell in City Hall Tower while the Army fired a 220-gun salute from Fort Point.

Back at Promontory, the Casements inherited the chore of acting as official hosts for the Union Pacific. (Grenville Dodge left no hint of his whereabouts on the 8th and 9th. Presumably he was among the official kibitzers at Devil's Gate.) The Stanford Special wheezed up to Promontory Summit in a drizzle that soon pattered into a downpour and alternated with fog and high winds for thirty-six hours. The Casements ordered a banquet dinner with champagne in their diner and sent over a procession of curtained carriages to bring the Stanford party aboard. During the evening General Jack announced an excursion trip next day to Taylor's Mill, Corinne, Ogden and Weber Canyon.

Again, there is no record that the May 9th train excursion got as far as Devil's Gate or that Durant, Dillon and Duff drove down to greet it. Through the lashing rains, meanwhile, the Casements' ironmen laid the last 2,500 feet of track to the Summit, then set out the two final rails, under tarpaulin, that would be used for the Golden Spike ceremony.

May 10th's sky was flawless; the mountain winds promised frost. Two trains shuddered across the Big Trestle in the midmorning. The first trailed the Lincoln and Palace cars; the second carried excursionists plus three companies of the 21st Regiment.

The Golden Spike ceremony itself was somewhat petty. Not more than 600 gathered around the 30-foot gap when the two engineers climbed into their separate cabs. Thomas Durant had a raging headache. Dodge and Dillon argued with Stanford and Strobridge about details. Several of the ironmen were drunk. "The crowd pushed upon the workmen so closely," complained J. H. Beadle, "that less than twenty persons saw the affair entirely, while none of the reporters were able to hear all that was said."

Two bands had boarded one of the Union Pacific trains at Ogden. They struck up a march at noon. Major Milton Cogswell, with crusty General Patrick Conner in review, led his battalion out to a double-file line on the west side of the tracks. A line of grinning Chinese picked up one rail; Casement ironmen lifted the other. Strobridge and Reed walked between them, carrying the polished laurel tie. They laid it in position, stepped back, and gave the signal. The last rails clanged into place.

The Reverend John Todd of Pittsfield, Massachusetts, official correspondent for Boston's *Congregationalist* and New York's *Evangelist* magazines, had been drafted that morning to offer a dedicatory prayer. Then someone remembered that John Sharp, the Latter-day Saint "railroad bishop," was there as Brigham Young's representative; he was asked to pray too. At 12:40 P.M. the telegraph operator, W. N. Shilling, impatiently tapped: WE HAVE GOT DONE PRAYING. THE SPIKE IS ABOUT TO BE PRESENTED. From Salt Lake City to Boston, New York, and Washington, his message sent bell ringers to their posts and swept silence across waiting crowds.

The final ritual seemed pompously endless. Leland Stanford gave a five-minute speech. The California, Nevada, and Arizona spikes were ceremoniously dropped into bored holes in the laurel tie. Finally an ordinary iron spike was inserted into the holes, and one of the Casements' sledges was handed to Stanford for the first of the symbolic last blows. Stanford swung and missed, grunted, and handed the sledge to Durant. Durant, grimacing against his headache, swung and also missed. The process was too wearying for telegrapher Shilling. He tapped the three dots that set off the national celebration, while Strobridge and Reed divided the task of actually driving the spike home.

Whistles shrilled in every city and roundhouse across the continent. San Francisco and Sacramento repeated the May 8th bedlam. Shilling's three dots triggered a magnetic ball hoisted above the dome of the United States Capitol and set off an afternoon of parades and an evening of banquets. The Liberty Bell echoed across Independence and Washington Squares. The choir of Trinity Church at the head of Wall Street chanted a *"Te Deum"* while the battery at Castle Garden crashed a 100-gun salute. Chicago cymballed off a four-mile parade followed by a banquet address by Vice-President Colfax.

In New York City, Collis Huntington put down his pen as the gun salute began and Trinity's chimes clanged into the glory of "Old Hundredth." His eyes were misty; he snorted and turned back to the accounts books. Now the real test was coming. Would the books show that the thing could be made to pay?

In Washington's suburbs spry Asa Whitney ordered up his mare, as usual, and went for an afternoon jog around his estate, Locust Hill. Since 1852 nobody had bothered to consult him about ideas for the Pacific Railway. He saw no reason to remind the world that it now ran just about where he had said, in 1844, that it should run.

At Des Moines, State Railway Commissioner Peter Dey wired his congratulations to Dodge, sighed, and turned back to his work.

In San Francisco, the new editor of *Overland Monthly* hunched over his desk. A strange elation had seized him as the gun salutes echoed on May 8 and again today. Bret Harte began scribbling the poem that was to lead off his next editorial page:

What was it the engines said,
Pilots touching, head to head,
Facing on a single track,
Half a world behind each back?

A woman rocked in the parlor of a white house at Greenfield, Massachusetts. For some reason, when the news came that the Golden Spike would be driven on May 8, she had smiled disbelief. But today, since breakfast time, she had been serenely aware of the hour and moment that the whistles would begin blowing at the Boston & Maine roundhouse. Her eyes were fixed on the spire of St. James Church and the glimmering greensward of the cemetery beyond. The whistles shrieked. Anna Judah's hands trembled as she put on her hat and shawl and began the walk to her husband's grave. She did not need to look at the clock. Twenty-two years before, at 3 P.M. on May 10, she and Ted Judah had been married. "It seemed," she wrote years later of that afternoon, "as though the spirit of my brave husband descended on me, and together we were there. . . ."

CHAPTER **26**

HORIZONS

> *Today the people of Chicago enmasse, without distinction of age, sex, business, party, race, nationality or condition, will unite in celebrating the most auspicious and important event which has yet marked the history of our city—the completion of the first Pacific Railroad. Other railroads to the Pacific will follow this, and of one of them—the Northern Pacific—Chicago will also be practically the eastern terminus. But there can never be, in the history of railroad enterprise on this continent, another occasion so full of cause for triumph and mutual congratulation as that we celebrate today. The completion of the present Pacific Railroad is the climax of the railroad enterprises, not only of the past but of the future. . . . Like the printing press, the steam engine and the telegraph, it opens up a new era. . . .* Lead editorial, Chicago *Tribune* (May 10, 1869).

In 1836, when New West destiny poised railroad historymakers at the Hudson-Mohawk junction, the village of Chicago had 3,820 residents. In 1852, when Farnam and Durant's Michigan Southern won the railroad race into Chicago, the city's population was only 30,000. But on Golden Spike Day, 1869, there were 300,000 Chicagoans. And during the next twenty years the population trebled, to pass the 1,000,000 mark in 1890.

This spectacular surge to "Queen City of the West" and second largest city in the United States was a direct product of the railroads. By 1870, San Francisco newspapers were conceding that "Chicago has captured the manufacturing trade of the West."

Chicago's growth and initiative in the 1860–1890 period is also symbolic of the Pacific Railway's social and economic influences on the West. As the Chicago *Tribune* had correctly prophesied in its lead editorial of May 10, 1869 [quoted in part at the head of this chapter], completion of the Great Iron Trail opened a new era for all of the United States.

Economically, Golden Spike Day heralded four massive campaigns:

1. *Technologic conquest* of all the trans-Missouri West. In 1870, Northern Pacific Railroad began construction of its Duluth–St. Paul–Oregon trackage. The Atchison, Topeka & Santa Fe took new heart in its drive to cross the Rockies via Raton Pass. In 1871, Pennsylvania financiers began construction of the Texas & Pacific Railroad, with Grenville Dodge as chief engineer, along the route that Jefferson Davis and James Gadsden had visualized and plotted about.

2. *Exploitation* of the West's huge stores of gold, silver, copper, coal, zinc, wood, and petroleum. By 1870, Nevada's new Battle Mountain Mining District had 32 mines and 2 smelters in operation, and was blasting out its first shipments of copper ore for smelters in Wales. Montana copper, first mined at Butte in 1880, became that Territory's most profitable industry before 1885.

3. *Development* of cattle and sheep ranches, wheat farms, fruit and citrus orchards, and other agricultural crops that became the foundation of foreign trade after 1880. European capital, especially British, began to seek investment in Wyoming rangelands and livestock herds in 1869. By 1886, Wyoming had 8,000,000 cattle and 500,000 sheep on range.

4. *Transportation* of the machinery and materials that enabled transformation of the Great Desert via reservoirs, irrigation systems, and eventually electric powerlines and transcontinental highways. The United States' first coast-to-coast road—the Lincoln Highway, U. S. 30—ploddingly paralleled Union Pacific's

right of way into Salt Lake City, then veered southwest via the Pony Express Trail into San Francisco.

Sociologically, the Pacific Railway triggered at least five basic changes—or innovations—in the American Way:

1. *Five-day transportation between the Atlantic and the Pacific* was inaugurated with the through trains which operated as "hotel trains" from Omaha to Sacramento in 1869. These included Pullman's Palace sleeping cars and commissary cars.

2. *The Hobo* was a product of the Union Pacific's ironmen, blasters and graders. These rugged characters followed the technologic frontier across the West and built the Northern Pacific, Denver & Rio Grande, Santa Fe, Burlington and Southern Pacific. Coincidentally, the Hobo adapted to such seasonal jobs as the Kansas wheat harvests, Pacific slope fruit harvests, circuses and construction work. Chicago's Skid Row and New York's Bowery became their most famous wintertime headquarters. (The term roots from the greeting "Ho, beau!" "Hi, Dandy!")

3. *The "butcher boy,"* peddling candy, sandwiches, pillows, soap, towels, cigars, magazines through the hotel-trains and shoddy immigrant-trains was born in 1869, too. He popularized "the ham san'wich," the dime-novel and "genuine Indian souvenir." Through him developed the national folkway of terminal-shops at railway stations, bus depots and airports.

4. *The Cowboy* evolved in the ranching country adjacent to Union Pacific. (Texas claims the credit, but Wyoming, Colorado and Montana did the job.) Owen Wister, Emerson Hough, Frederic Remington, Charles M. Russell, Theodore Roosevelt, Prentiss Ingraham, Ned Buntline and other creators of the Wild West Saga used the Union Pacific's countryside as locale for their books and paintings. Actually, the Cowboy was a kind of rural Hobo.

5. *Chinese labor* contributed much to the unrest of industrial employees during the 1870's, and became a basic factor in the organizational birth of trade unions and the American Labor Movement. The use of $1-a-day "coolies" by Central Pacific intrigued Eastern manufacturers and Southern cottongrowers. Between 1870 and 1880, Southerners made a series of unsuccessful efforts to supplant Negro labor with Chinese on Louisiana, Alabama and Georgia plantations. The first Chinese

laborers reached Chicago in 1869–70. Owners of shoe factories in Massachusetts first used Chinese successfully as strikebreakers in 1873. The Chinatowns of New York, Boston, Chicago and San Francisco are direct products of the Central Pacific's coolies.

Thus the Great Iron Trail changed both economic and social routines for the entire United States through its realization of Northwest Passage. But so drastic were these changes that their process of envelopment all but obliterated a public awareness of the Pacific Railway as the real conqueror of the New West and as a hero figure in the Old West Saga.

A community of symbolic folk figures developed during the settlement and economic exploitation of the high plains and the Rockies in the final quarter of the nineteenth century. Writers, artists and balladeers of the era followed the formula for all national sagas and shaped their characters of the West into idealizations of Good and Bad. The Scout, the Cowboy, the Sheriff, the Cavalryman and the Settler were given virtues of fearlessness, piety and superman wisdom by Prentiss Ingraham, Ned Buntline and the other score of writers who produced our dime novels. Buffalo Bill's Great Wild West Show —with Major North's Pawnee Scouts as a featured act—enhanced this dime-novel pattern and helped fix these five Good heroes and their virtues into the saga. Cessily Adams' painting of "Custer's Last Stand"—a barroom favorite—ushered in the hundreds of "Nature's Noblemen" paintings and drawings by Remington, Russell, Currier and Ives, and the staff artists of *Leslie's Weekly* and *Harper's*. The popularization of cowboy songs and Western fiddle tunes—many of them borrowed from the South's camp-meeting "sings"—gave this new symbolism of the Good heroes another stature puff.

But black emphasizes white. (For decades the moving-picture industry's Westerns drove home this contrast by dressing the hero in a white Stetson and the villain in a black one.) One nucleus of the Bad was ready made. Like any other environment, the West had its juvenile delinquents—the Billy the Kid type. Also the West provided scope for youngsters suffering from war shock—the James Boys, the Youngers, et al. From this small group the dime-novelists, artists and balladeers perfected the Bad Man. The Western Bad Man was, after all, a poor creature and a victim of circumstances. A Superbad was essential to round out the folklore. And this, between 1869 and 1890, was the need that moved the Railroad out of the Hero class of the Old West. Thanks to Crédit Mobilier, Jim Fisk, Thomas Durant, the Big Four and sundry successors who were neither more nor less than supine Organization Men, the Railroad became the West's first prototype of Superbad.

A Crédit Mobilier scandal flared after a series of exposé articles in the New York *Sun* during September, 1872. Its obvious purpose was to defeat U. S. Grant for a second term and further the Liberal Republican and Democratic nominations of Horace Greeley. Thus, as a "rigged deal," both the organization and research techniques of the Poland committee created by Congress that fall must be viewed with bias. It found Oakes Ames and James Brooks guilty of malfeasance and recommended their expulsion from the House. But the House, in a roll-call vote on February 18, 1873, rejected the Poland committee's recommendation by adopting a resolution of censure against Ames and Brooks. Ames died during a heart attack less than a month later.

Concurrent with the Crédit Mobilier scandal, the Granger movement swept the farming areas of the nation. On April 7, 1871, the Grangers achieved their first legislative victory by pushing a Railroad act through the Illinois Legislature; it empowered the State to create a "Railroad and Warehouse commission" to establish maximum freight and passenger rates and "prohibit discrimination." The railroads became the favorite "Big Trust" bogeyman for the Grangers and other grass-roots' movements.

The monopolies achieved by the Big Four in their Southern Pacific Company . . . the raffish feuds of Jim Fisk, Jay Gould, Jay Cooke, J. P. Morgan, Cornelius Vanderbilt, Jim Hill, Ben Holladay, Henry Villard and the other "railroad kings" . . . the highhandedness of the railroad police and land agents . . . the exaggerations of the artists and copywriters employed to "dazzle up" the 1870–1900 promotions of railroads' grant-land sales all gave plausible logic for a national image of the Railroad as the Superbad Man in the West's saga. Symbols of the New West achieved their folklore pedestals. Buffalo Bill, Tom Mix, Bat Masterson, Wyatt Earp and Billy the Kid became household familiars. As the Railroad itself became the Superbad character, railroad men like Judah, Dodge, the Casements, Reed, Montague, Dey—and even the ironmen and the coolies—ebbed toward the shadows.

Here the saga-makers distorted history. The Superbad figure in the saga of the American West was undoubtedly a composite of Federal office holders. Officials in the Pierce, Buchanan, Lincoln and Johnson Administrations were responsible for the bumbling, unrealistic mandates of the Pacific Railroad surveys during the 1850's and the Railway Acts of 1862, 1864 and 1866. The inability of the 1862–70 Federal loans to finance more than one-third of the construction costs for the Pacific Railway was obvious to bankers and engineers; why wasn't it obvious to Federal officials? Even during the Civil War the Federal government borrowed money at 5 to 7 per cent; why did it charge 6 per cent interest on its too meager 30-year loans to Union Pacific and Central Pacific?

Similarly, the clumsy procedure dictated for the creation of Union Pacific begged for the type of trickery that Thomas Durant used in 1863–64 to launch the organization and to invent Crédit Mobilier. And the perpetuation of Crédit Mobilier . . . the Ames-Durant, Dodge-Durant, Dodge-Seymour and other power feuds . . . the lusts of Hell on Wheels . . . the yellow-slavery conditions in Central Pacific's camps . . . Collis Huntington's scheme to obtain Federal bonds for the trans-Utah right of way . . . Crédit Mobilier's delinquencies in the Brigham Young-Latter-day Saints contracts . . . Oakes Ames's gifts of Crédit Mobilier stock to fellow Congressmen could not have been maneuvered without the passive approval and administrative inefficiencies of Congress, the Department of the Interior and numerous Cabinet members. Historically, the bumbling Politician and Office Holder must wear the black Stetson.

The full truth may never be revealed. The railroad's dreamers and builders were not status seekers—or even skilled publicists. No memoirs or diaries were published by Durant, the Ames Brothers, Dillon, Judah, Asa Whitney or the Big Four. The best source of material extant is in the series of interviews conducted by H. H. Bancroft during the 1880's on Huntington, Crocker, Stanford and Hopkins. The letters of Judah, the Casements and Reed are unfound, scattered or unresearched. Grenville Dodge's memoirs and official biography were, for various reasons, too little and too late.

The records indicate that Thomas C. Durant was voted out as Union Pacific's Vice-President and general manager at a board meeting during late May, 1869. He voluntarily came to Washington in 1872 to testify before the Poland Committee. But there, as always, he answered questions sparsely and made no effort to expound on the maze of circumstance that had caused him to be such a lone wolf in his twenty years as a railroad promoter. He lost most of his fortune during the "Black Friday" stock-market crash of 1873, and spent the last decade of his life trying to promote an Albany–Canada railroad. His grave in a Brooklyn cemetery should be a shrine of the American West's saga, because—irrespective of his motives or techniques—Thomas Durant did wrest Union Pacific from the political shilly-shallying of the 1862 Pacific Railway Act; did launch the technologic pioneering of the Casements' work train, Sam Reed's relays and Grenville Dodge's engineering genius; and did badger and cajole the Union's Pacific Railway out across the Chicago–Platte Valley's "Central Route."

The continuing financial crises of Union Pacific forced the Ames Brothers out of office in 1871. Thomas A. Scott, president of the Pennsylvania Railroad, succeeded Oliver Ames as

Union Pacific president. He brought George M. Pullman and Pullman's not-so-silent partner Andrew Carnegie into the board. (In 1873, Carnegie's J. Edgar Thomson Works rolled the first steel rail for Union Pacific.)

Sidney Dillon succeeded to the presidency of Crédit Mobilier, became a partner of Jay Gould, neatly sidestepped the Crédit Mobilier scandal, and served two terms (1874–1884, 1890–1892) as Union Pacific's president. His memory still echoes along New York City's Park Avenue; one of his firms designed and built the Park Avenue tunnels into Grand Central Station.

Grenville Dodge developed alliances with Jay Gould and Thomas A. Scott. In 1872, with the backing of Scott and J. Edgar Thomson, he became chief engineer for the Texas & Pacific Railroad. (The panic of 1873 closed it down, despite its use of chain-gang labor.)

General Jack and Dan Casement sold their pioneer beef herd to the Colorado cattle king, John Iliff, took their work train back to Cheyenne, and built the Cheyenne–Denver branch of Union Pacific. The work train was auctioned off at Denver in 1873–4. The Casements spent the rest of their lives on construction jobs for the Erie & Titusville, the Canada Southern, the Nickel Plate, and a score of short lines. In 1897, at the age of sixty-eight, General Jack contracted to build his second Pacific Railroad—a line from San José, Costa Rica, over the Sierra to the Pacific Coast. He finished it in 1903, then spent the last six years of his life developing natural-gas wells in Ohio, the Diamond-C cattle ranch in Western Colorado, and wheat farms in Kansas.

Sam Reed accepted a bid to Canada and became one of the principal engineers in the construction of the Canadian Pacific. So, like General Jack Casement, he built two Pacific Railroads.

Samuel Montague and J. H. Strobridge devoted the rest of their careers to the development of the Southern Pacific's lines.

So the saga of the Great Iron Trail's construction ended. As this book is written, the American West is slowly awakening to its heritage. Scholarship succeeds the "bang-bang" novels and movies. The National Cowboy Hall of Fame & Western Heritage Center at Oklahoma City, the National Agricultural Hall of Fame at Kansas City, the Beehive House in Salt Lake City, the splendid State Museums at Lincoln, Denver and Cheyenne, are indicative of eventual causal awareness about the real winners of the West.

In time, too, the New West may have its Parthenon—a massive shrine and enrichment center to those men who visualized, fought for, and built the Union's Pacific Railway. Rearing high above the eternal bleakness of Promontory Point, it would symbolize the realization of Northwest Passage, the end of the Great Desert myth and the birth of the Union and Pacific's United States as a world power.

CHRONOLOGY OF THE
PACIFIC RAILWAY

1818   Thomas Hart Benton, editor of the St. Louis *Enquirer,* wrote series of editorials urging construction of a Northwest Passage canal and road system to connect Missouri and Columbia rivers.

1819   Robert Mills, architect for Bunker Hill and Washington Monuments, urged Congress to consider construction of a railway between Mississippi and Columbia valleys.

1821   Construction of the world's first passenger railway, The Stockton & Darlington, was authorized by Great Britain's Parliament.

1826   March 4   Theodore Dehone Judah born in Bridgeport, Conn.

      October 7   The U.S.A.'s first railway, The Quincy Tramway, opened its three miles of track between Quincy, Mass., granite quarries and the Neponset River's tidewater.

1831   January 15   The first American-built locomotive, *Best Friend,* opened passenger service on South Carolina R.R., Charleston to Hamburg.

      April 12   Grenville Mellen Dodge born at Danvers, Mass.

1832   *The Emigrant* of Ann Arbor, Mich., editorially proposed New York to Oregon railway.

351

1836   Theodore Dehone Judah, Leland Stanford, Charles Crocker, Thomas C. Durant, Sidney Dillon, Bret Harte, Collis P. Huntington, Samuel Montague, Philip H. Sheridan and Willian Tecumsah Sherman all lived at, or visited, pioneer railway junction of Albany and Troy, N. Y.

Texas won War of Independence and became a Republic.

Rev. Marcus Whitman and party crossed Oregon Trail to site of Walla Walla, Wash.

Chicago began Illinois & Michigan Canal.

1838   Congress ruled that railroads could be used as U. S. Postal routes.

Rev. Samuel Parker, who had explored the West with Rev. Marcus Whitman, pronounced the feasibility of a Pacific Railway via the South Pass–Snake River route of The Oregon Trail.

1841   Bartleson-Bidwell wagon train pioneered trans-Utah route that the Pacific Railway would follow 28 years later.

1845   Congress first heard Asa Whitney's petition for a land-grant 60 miles wide and extending from Mississippi to Columbia valleys along which the Pacific Railway would be built. Whitney estimated construction costs at $65,000,000.

That fall, at Commercial Convention in Memphis, Tenn., James Gadsden of Charleston, S. C. urged a South & Pacific Railway, via the all-slavery route through El Paso. Sam Houston, John C. Calhoun and Jefferson Davis supported the Gadsden plan.

1847   May 10   Theodore Judah and Anna Ferona Pierce married at St. James Episcopal Church, Greenfield, Mass.

1849   Thomas Hart Benton introduced bill for Federal financing of Buffalo Trail highway and railroad from St. Louis to San Francisco.

1852   February 20   First passenger train from East reached Chicago via Michigan Southern & Northern Indiana R.R.

1853   May 27   Peter Dey and Grenville Dodge began survey for Mississippi & Missouri R.R., Rock Island, Ill. to Council Bluffs, Iowa.

Summer. Jefferson Davis, U. S. Secretary of War, organized Army engineering parties to explore five likeliest railway routes between Mississippi Valley and the Pacific.

November 22 Dey-Dodge survey completed to bank of Missouri River.

December 30 James Gadsden signed treaty with Mexico for purchase of 45,535 square miles of territory from Gila River south (i.e., The Gadsden Purchase) to provide route for South & Pacific R.R.

1854 Mid-May Theodore and Anna Judah reached Sacramento to begin surveys for California's first railway, the Sacramento Valley.

May 28 Grenville Dodge and Anne Brown married in Danvers, Mass., then honeymooned west to homestead on Elkhorn Creek, 25 miles west of the village of Omaha.

1855 Spring Jefferson Davis began organization of U. S. Army Camel Corps as patrol force in Southwest deserts, along proposed route of South & Pacific R.R.

Fall Davis announced that reports from the Army survey teams along the five proposed Pacific Railway routes indicated that South & Pacific's route would be cheapest and most expedient.

1856 Fall Theodore Judah reached Washington for futile, winter-long lobby to obtain $200,000 Federal grant for detailed survey of the Sacramento-Salt Lake-Platte Valley route.

1859 February 13 Hannibal & St. Joseph R.R. completed trans-Missouri trackage and became first railroad to reach bank of upper Missouri river.

Spring Samuel R. Curtis of Iowa introduced Union-and-Pacific Railway bill in Congress.

August 19 Abraham Lincoln and Grenville Dodge, in hotel-porch conference at Council Bluffs, discussed Platte Valley route for Pacific Railway.

October 11 California Convention on the Pacific Railway appointed Theodore Judah its agent to carry petition for Federal aid to Pacific Railway to Congress.

1860 April 13 Pony Express completed first 10-day run with mails between San Francisco and St Joseph, Mo.

1861   April 30   Theodore Judah completed organization of Central Pacific Railroad Co. of California, with Leland Stanford as president, Collis P. Huntington as vice-president and Mark Hopkins as treasurer.

1862   Spring   Theodore Judah appointed secretary of both House and Senate committees on Pacific Railway Act.

July 1   President Lincoln signed Pacific Railway Act.

September 2   Commissioners from 20 States and Territories met in Bryan Hall, Chicago to create Union Pacific Railroad & Telegraph Co., with William B. Ogden as president, Thomas W. Alcott as treasurer and Henry V. Poor as secretary.

December 27   Charles Crocker & Co. awarded contract for first 18 miles of Central Pacific roadbed.

1863   January 8   Ground-breaking ceremony for Central Pacific at Sacramento.

Summer   Power struggles between Theodore Judah, Charles Crocker and Collis P. Huntington reached crisis.

October 30   Illegal stock purchases by Thomas C. Durant enabled transfer of Union Pacific Railroad & Telegraph Co. to private management, with John A. Dix as president, Thomas C. Durant as vice-president and general manager.

November 1   Theodore Judah died in Metropolitan Hotel, New York City, a few blocks from office where Union Pacific's new officers were meeting.

December 2   Ground-breaking ceremony for Union Pacific on Missouri River bluffs, two miles north of Omaha.

1864   Spring   Thomas Durant, George Francis Train and associates created Crédit Mobilier of America from Pennsylvania Fiscal Agency.

Summer   Contract for construction of 247 miles of Union Pacific to 100th meridian assigned to Herbert Hoxie, Iowa politician, who promptly re-assigned it to Crédit Mobilier.

1865   January   Peter Dey resigned as Chief Engineer of Union Pacific.

Spring   Charles Crocker began hiring Chinese "coolies" for Central Pacific's work-gangs.

August   Colfax-Bowles party toured Central Pacific's 50 miles of track up Sierra's west face.

September 22   Major General Grenville Dodge and patrol, besieged by Crow war-party, discovered Lone Pine Pass across Black Hills.

November   General William T. Sherman, perched on nailkeg, rode Union Pacific's first "Grand Excursion" from Omaha 15 miles to end-of-track.

1866   February 8   J. S. and D. T. Casement contracted to build first construction-train and undertake tracklaying for Union Pacific.

Spring   Samuel B. Reed and Hoxie organized Chicago-St Joseph-Omaha relay route for delivery of Union Pacific's supplies.

April   Casement's construction-train began laying track at record-breaking pace of one mile a day.

July   Central Pacific's tracks entered Dutch Flat, 67 miles from Sacramento.

August   Union Pacific gangs fought off first Indian attack near Plum Creek, 200 miles west of Omaha.

October 15   Special train left New York City with guests for Durant's Grand Excursion to the 100th meridian.

November 22   Casement construction-train wintered in at junction of North and South Platte rivers, thus founding North Platte (i.e., the first Hell-on-Wheels).

November 23   Oliver Ames elected president of Union Pacific Railroad & Telegraph Co.

November 25   Central Pacific gangs began gargantuan task of hauling locomotives, rails, supplies up wagonroad from Cisco 15 miles across Sierra summit.

1867   Early Spring   First nitroglycerin factory presumably built near Donner Lake by Central Pacific.

March 6   Anti-Coolie Labor Association founded in San Francisco.

April   Heavy floods and snowslides wrecked trackage along both railroads. Crocker and Montague reached decision to build snowsheds through Sierra.

July 4   Generals Rawlins and Dodge christen new city of Cheyenne.

July 23   Percy Browne, chief of Union Pacific survey crew, fatally wounded during siege by 300 Sioux in Wyoming's Great Basin.

August   Henry M. Stanley, reporter for the Missouri *Democrat,* pronounced Julesburg, Neb. "The wickedest city in America."

August 6   Cheyenne raiders, led by Chief Turkey Foot, achieved first derailment and looting of Union Pacific train (i.e., near Plum Creek, Neb.).

August 30   Rawlins-Dodge conferred with Brigham Young about L.D.S. contract for grading through Wasatch.

October 1   With trackage completed 250 miles west of 100th meridian, Union Pacific's directors finally awarded contract for construction 667 miles west of 100th meridian to Oakes Ames.

November 13   Union Pacific tracks entered Cheyenne.

December   Central Pacific completed Summit Tunnel.

1868   April   Casement work-train laid track down west slope of Black Hills and founded Laramie.

May 4   Central Pacific trackage reached Lake's Crossing, Nev., and village name changed to Reno.

May 26   Samuel Reed and Brigham Young signed contract for grading by L.D.S. crews down Echo and Weber canyons.

July 26   The "show down" conference on the Durant-Dodge feud held at Fort Sanders, Wyo., with General U. S. Grant presiding.

Christmas Week   Union Pacific trackage entered Echo canyon, Utah; Central Pacific entered Elko, Nev.

1869   January   First Union Pacific engines steamed past 1,000 Mile Post in Weber Canyon.

February   Mormon work-crews blasted parallel Union Pacific and Central Pacific grades across desert north of Salt Lake.

March 3   Union Pacific entered Ogden, Utah.

April 9   Huntington, Durant, Dodge agreed on Promontory Point as meeting place for Union Pacific and Central Pacific tracks.

April 27 or 28   Thomas Durant and guests kidnapped by Union Pacific work-gangs near Bear River, Wyo. and held for ransom of "$1,000,000 in back wages."

April 29   Crocker's work-gangs gave record-breaking display of laying 10 miles of track.

May 10   Golden Spike ceremony at Promontory Point on 22nd Wedding Anniversary of Theodore and Anna Judah.

ACKNOWLEDGMENTS AND
BIBLIOGRAPHY

The genesis and construction of the United States' first transcontinental railroad was literally an all-American operation. Brilliant leaders of the North and South argued and plotted about its route and financing for a generation before the outbreak of the Civil War. Its engineers and builders were preponderantly New Englanders and New Yorkers, with an extraordinary number of the principals migrating from the Albany-Troy area. The bulk of the construction materials and equipment was manufactured in the Northeast. Supply routes to railhead extended from the Canadian Border to the Straits of Magellan.

Thus, obviously, data on the genesis and construction years of Pacific Railroad are tucked away in libraries, private collections, and newspaper files all across the continent. My principal sources for final assembly of the facts incorporated in *The Great Iron Trail* were: The Bancroft Library, Berkeley Campus, University of California; the Newberry Library, the University of Chicago's W. R. Harper Memorial Library, and the Chicago Historical Society, Chicago; the Union Pacific Museum, Omaha; the St. Joseph Museum, St. Joseph, Missouri; and the Utah State Historical Society, Salt Lake City.

But thanks are also due scores of institutions and individuals who graciously undertook research in a variety of areas in order that I might have a clearer overview of "American Destiny" between 1836 and 1870. They are listed geographically below:—

New York: Edward A. Chapman, Librarian, Rensselaer Polytechnic Institute, Troy; Dr. Albert B. Corey, New York State Historian, Albany; Clayton Hoagland, the Biddle Co., New York; Merrick Jackson, American Iron and Steel Institute, New York; Marc Jaffe, Editorial Director, Bantam Books, New York; Warren Ranney, Grange League Federation, Ithaca; T. Lefoy Richman, American Social Health Association, New York; Malcolm Reiss and Paul R. Reynolds, Paul R. Reynolds and Son, New York.

Delaware: Public Relations Dept., E. I. duPont de Nemours & Co., Wilmington; Norman B. Wilkinson and associates, Eleutherian Mills-Hagley Foundation, Wilmington.

District of Columbia: Robert H. Land, the Library of Congress; Charles O. Morgret and associates, Association of American Railroads; Lt. Col. Roderick A. Stamey, Jr., Historical Services Division, Dept. of the Army; Alfred Stefferud, historian and Editor of the *USDA Yearbook.*

Massachusetts: Paul Deland and other editorial devotees of "serendipity" at the *Christian Science Monitor,* Boston; Mrs. Anna Taylor Howard, School of Nursing, Boston University; Dr. William P. Murphy, Boston.

Ohio: Mrs. Harold A. Furlong, Chardon.

Illinois: Dr. Paul Angle and his competently gracious librarians, Chicago Historical Society; Mrs. Lorraine Brown and Mrs. Gwen Olmsted, Skokie; Mrs. Pierce Butler and Dr. Stanley Pargellis, Newberry Library, Chicago; Dr. Mark Krug and Dr. Robert McCaul, University of Chicago; Franklin R. Meine, historian and editor, Chicago; Mrs. Billie Paige, Chicago.

Missouri: Mr. and Mrs. Roy E. Coy, St. Joseph Museum; Mr. Don Ornduff, Editor, the *Hereford Journal,* Kansas City; Don L. Reynolds, St. Joseph Museum.

Nebraska: Edwin C. Schafer and associates, Union Pacific R.R. Co., Omaha; the staff of the Union Pacific Museum, Omaha; Miss Mildred Goosman, Joslyn Art Museum, Omaha; Mr. and Mrs. Walter G. Zimmermann, Omaha.

Colorado: That ever-refreshing spring of Western Americana, Mrs. Agnes Wright Spring, formerly State Historian of Wyoming and now State Historian of Colorado; Mr. Jack Casement, Padroni.

Wyoming: Mrs. Lola Homsher, State Archivist, Cheyenne.

Utah: Theodore Cannon, Information Chief, Church of Jesus Christ of the Latter-day Saints; David W. Evans, David W. Evans Associates, Salt Lake City; Dr. A. R. Mortensen, John James, Jr., and other "staffers" of the Utah State Historical Society during 1960–61; Frank C. Robertson, another dependable spring of New West fact, Springville; ebullient Sam and Lila Weller, Zion Book Store, Salt Lake City.

California: Paul Bailey, historian and Editor of Westernlore Press, Los Angeles; Richard H. Dillon, historian and librarian, the Sutro Library, San Francisco; Dr. George P. Hammond, Dr. John Barr Tompkins and Dr. Dale L. Morgan, the Bancroft Library, Berkeley; John Kan, proprietor of Kan's Restaurant, San Francisco; Charles Leong, Chinese-American historian, San Francisco; Louis B. Londborg and Willard W. Williams, Bank of America, San Francisco; Wally Raymond, Levi Strauss and Co., San Francisco; J. G. Shea and associates, Southern Pacific Company.

New Mexico: Dr. S. Omar Barker, historian, poet and lovable guy, Las Vegas; Dr. Robert M. Utley, Historian, National Park Service, U. S. Dept. of the Interior, Santa Fe.

North Carolina: William S. Powell, author and librarian, University of North Carolina, Chapel Hill.

Quite apart from my biases, my wife Elizabeth Zimmermann Howard deserves exclusive . . . and exalted . . . Thanks. During the sixteen months of this book's preparation, Mrs. Howard coupled teaching at the University of Chicago's School of Education with the exhaustive detail of her Ph.D. dissertation. Yet, in the miraculous ways of The Woman, she found time to discuss my research problems, critique correspondence and manuscript, "neaten up" the stacks of letters, xeroxes, photostats, carbons and reference-books, prowl the University of Chicago libraries for books long out of print and, beyond all, to provide me the spiritual-nourishment that is vital to any author during those drowning-hours of mass preparation. This book could not have been written without her Faith, Love and Wisdom.

Books

Alter, J. Cecil. *Early Utah Journalism*. Salt Lake City: Utah State Historical Society, 1938.

Anderson, Nels. *The Hobo*. Chicago: University of Chicago Press, 1923.

Angle, Paul M. *The Chicago Historical Society, 1856–1956*. Chicago: Rand McNally & Co., 1956.

Ashton, Wendell J. *Voice in the West*. New York: Duell, Sloan & Pearce, Inc., 1950.

Bancroft, Hubert Howe. *History of Utah*. San Francisco: The History Co., 1890.

———. *Some Reflections of an Early California Governor*. An 1883 interview with Frederick F. Low, edited by Robert H. Becker. Sacramento, Cal.: Sacramento Book Collectors Club, 1959.

Berkeley, Grantley F. *The English Sportsman in the Western Prairies*. London: Hurst and Blackett, 1861.

Bowles, Samuel. *Across the Continent*. Springfield, Mass.: Samuel Bowles and Co., 1866.

———. *Our New West*. Hartford, Conn.: Hartford Publishing Co., 1869.

Browne, J. Ross. *Resources of the Pacific Slope*. New York: D. Appleton and Co., 1869.

Chisholm, James. *South Pass, 1868*. Edited by Lola M. Homsher. Lincoln, Neb.: University of Nebraska Press, 1960.

Crawford, J. B. *The Crédit Mobilier of America*. Boston, Mass.: C. W. Calkins and Co., 1880.

Dodge, Grenville M. *How We Built the Union Pacific*. Vol. 59, Senate Documents. Sixty-first Congress, Second Session. Washington, D.C.: Government Printing Office, 1910.

Emory, W. H. *Lieutenant Emory Reports*. Albuquerque: University of New Mexico Press, 1951.

Fogel, Robert William. *The Union Pacific Railroad—A Case in Premature Enterprise*. Baltimore, Md.: The Johns Hopkins Press, 1960.

Galloway, John D. *The First Transcontinental Railroad*. New York City: Simmons-Boardman, 1950.

Goddard, Fred B. *Union Pacific; Where to Emigrate and Why*. New York City: Union Pacific Railroad Co., 1869.

Golding, Harry. *The Wonder Book of Railways*. London: Ward, Lock & Co., Ltd., 1930.

Hebard, Grace Raymond. *Washakie*. Cleveland: The Arthur H. Clark Co., 1930.

Horan, James D. *The Great American West*. New York: Crown Publishers, Inc., 1959.

Kaempffert, Waldemar. *A Popular History of American Invention*. New York: Charles Scribner's Sons, 1924.

Kull, Irving S. and Nell M. *A Short Chronology of American History, 1942–1950*. New Brunswick, N. J.: Rutgers University Press, 1952.

Leland, Charles Godfrey. *The Union Pacific Railway, Eastern Division or Three Thousand Miles in a Railway Car*. Philadelphia: Ringwalt and Brown, 1867.

Lewis, Oscar. *The Big Four*. New York City: Alfred A. Knopf, Inc., 1938.

Loofbourow, Leon F. *In Search of God's Gold*. San Francisco: The Historical Society of the California-Nevada Annual Conference of the Methodist Church, 1950.

Martin, Edgar W. *The Standard of Living in 1860*. Chicago: University of Chicago Press, 1942.

Nevada Writers' Project. *Nevada—A Guide to the Silver State*. Portland, Ore.: Binfords and Mort, 1940.

Perkins, J. R. *Trails, Rails and War—The Life of General G. M. Dodge*. Indianapolis, Ind.: The Bobbs-Merrill Co., 1929.

Rae, W. F. *Westward by Rail: The New Route to the East*. New York City: D. Appleton and Co., 1871.

Rand McNally & Co. *Rand McNally's Pioneer Atlas of the American West.* Historical text by Dr. Dale L. Morgan. Chicago: Rand McNally & Co., 1956.

Russell, A. J. *The Great West—Photo Views Across the Continent Taken Along the Lines of the Union Pacific Railroad.* New York City: Union Pacific Railroad Co., 1869.

Sabin, Edwin L. *Building the Pacific Railway.* Philadelphia: J. B. Lippincott Co., 1919.

Seymour, Silas. *Incidents of a Trip Through the Great Platte Valley to the Rocky Mountains and Laramie Plains in the Fall of 1866.* New York City: D. Van Nostrand Co., Inc., 1867.

Stanley, Henry M. *My Early Travels and Adventures in America and Asia.* New York: Charles Scribner's Sons, 1895.

———. *The Autobiography of Sir Henry Morton Stanley.* Boston and New York: Houghton Mifflin Co., 1909.

Van Gelder, Arthur P. and Schlotter, Hugo. *History of the Explosives Industry in America.* New York: Columbia University Press, 1927.

Writers' Program of New York. *New York—A Guide to the Empire State.* New York: Oxford University Press, 1940.

Wyoming Writers' Project. *Wyoming—A Guide to its History, Highways and People.* Edited by Agnes Wright Spring. New York: Oxford University Press, 1941.

Periodicals and Manuscripts

Associated Medical Members of the Sanitary Commission. *Venereal Diseases with Specific Reference to Practice in the Army and Navy.* New York: John F. Trow, 50 Green St., 1862.

Bancroft, Hubert Howe. "The California Chinese, 1860–92." An unpublished bibliography in Bancroft Library, Berkeley Campus, University of California.

Casement, John (Jack) Stephen. Biographical feature article. Painesville, Ohio, *Telegraph,* July 5, 1939. Lake County Historical Society, Mentor, Ohio.

The Chicago *Tribune,* 1861–70.

The *Deseret News,* Salt Lake City, Utah, 1865–69.

The *Friend,* Honolulu, Sandwich Islands, 1861–1870. Complete file at Newberry Library, Chicago, Ill.

The *Frontier Index,* 1867–68. The most complete file extant is at Bancroft Library, University of California, Berkeley. The Union Pacific Museum, Omaha, has one copy.

George, Henry. "The Chinese in California," New York *Tribune,* May 1, 1869.

Judah, Anna F. *The Theodore Dehone Judah Papers.* Unpublished correspondence with David R. Sessions and Amos P. Catlin of the H. H. Bancroft staff, 1889. Berkeley, Cal.: The Bancroft Library.

Larson, A. Karl. "Pioneer Agriculture," *Utah Historical Quarterly,* July, 1961.

Leonard, L. O. "Builders of the Union Pacific," *Union Pacific Magazine,* 1922–23.

Miller, David E. "The First Wagon Train to Cross Utah, 1841," *Utah Historical Quarterly,* Winter, 1962.

Moss, J. B. "St. Joseph and Denver City Railroad," St. Joseph, Mo. *Union Observer,* Aug. 27, 1937.

Rigdon, Paul. An unpublished collection of data on early history of Union Pacific Railroad from the files of Union Pacific Railroad Historical Museum, Omaha, Nebraska.

Rodman Gibbons and Co. *Eleutherian Mills-Hagley Foundation.* Unpublished correspondence from the San Francisco agent of E. I. du Pont de Nemours & Co., 1866–68. Wilmington, Del.

St. Joseph, Mo. *Herald,* 1867–68.

U. S. Dept. of the Interior. *Reports Upon the Pacific Wagon Roads.* Senate Executive Document No. 36, 35th Congress, Second Session, 1859.

Utah *Weekly Reporter,* Corinne, Utah, 1869–70.

Utley, Robert M. "The Dash to Promontory," *Utah Historical Quarterly,* April, 1961. Salt Lake City: Utah State Historical Society.

INDEX